Theo-
logy
&
Life

Story Theology

by

Terrence W. Tilley

Preface by

Robert McAfee Brown

A Michael Glazier Book
THE LITURGICAL PRESS
Collegeville, Minnesota

ABOUT THE AUTHOR

Terrence W. Tilley received his Ph.D from Graduate Theological Union at Berkeley. He taught at Georgetown University from 1976 to 1979. Presently Tilley is assistant professor at St. Michael's College. He has been published in the *Journal of the American Academy of Religion, Theological Studies, Horizons*, and the *Anglican Theological Review.* Among his latest works is *Talking of God: An Introduction to Philosophical Analysis of Religious Language.*

A Michael Glazier Book

published by

THE LITURGICAL PRESS

2	3	4	5	6	7	8	9

Library of Congress Cataloging-in-Publication Data

Tilley, Terrence W.
    Story theology / by Terrence W. Tilley ; preface by Robert McAfee Brown.
        p.   cm.
    Reprint. Originally published: Wilmington, Del. : M. Glazier, 1985. (Theology and life series ; v. 12).
    "A Michael Glazier book."
    Includes bibliographical references and index.
    ISBN 0-8146-5464-9
    1. Storytelling—Religious aspects—Christianity. I. Title.
  II. Series: Theology and Life series ; v. 12.
    BT83.78.T54   1990   90-47809
                                                      CIP

For Maureen,
Elena and Christine,
with love,
and thanks for their patient care.

CONTENTS

ACKNOWLEDGMENTS

Many people have helped me over the years in which I have been writing this book. I owe them all many thanks. In particular, I am grateful to my colleagues in the department of religious studies at St. Michael's College, Joseph Kroger, Richard Berube, S.S.E., Paul Couture, S.S.E., David Bryan, S.S.E., and Joseph McLaughlin, S.S.E., for their criticisms of an early version of the material now in chapters five through seven during a departmental colloquium. I appreciate the comments written on various parts of the manuscript by Stanley Hauerwas, Diane Yeager, Michael Goldberg, Peter Tumulty, Philip Foubert and James W. McClendon, Jr. I found helpful the comments on an earlier version of chapter nine from the participants in a Roundtable Discussion during the 1983 Annual Meeting of the American Academy of Religion and on an earlier version of chapter one from participants in the colloquium on "Narrative, Character, Community, and Ethics" in the University of Dayton, November, 1984. Students in graduate and undergraduate courses at St. Michael's have heard some of these ideas in various forms over the years and have forced me to be as clear as I could be. Where I have failed in substance or presentation of these ideas, it is probably because I have not heard these kind and generous voices well enough.

St. Michael's College has supported this work in various ways. Dean Ronald Provost granted a reduction in my teaching load from four courses to three for the Spring semester, 1983, to work on this book and another project. Ellen Nash, Judith Vigneau, Caroline Tanguay, Matthew Valerio, and Mary Murphy are students who provided secretarial help to our department and have worked on this book as part of their duties. Ms. Tanguay, Jody Megnia, and Christine Paré helped compile the index.

Professor David Baker generously read the proofs, caught numerous blunders, and made helpful suggestions.

Professor Robert McAfee Brown graciously provided a preface for the book. I am very grateful for his generous comments.

The editorial staff at Michael Glazier, Inc., made many suggestions to improve the structure and style of this book. Their thoughtful criticisms have made it far better and have helped me to express my ideas more clearly.

There are surely others whom I should thank formally, including the many people with whom I have discussed these ideas and from whom I have learned much. To any whom I have inadvertently omitted, my apologies.

The deepest acknowledgment is to Maureen Tilley. She has read numerous versions of this work, been unsparing with her time, generous with her guidance and criticism, and been a partner in everything.

PREFACE

Once upon a time, not many years ago, a professor of theology who bears my name was morally outraged by the immensity of the United States' military presence in Vietnam, and frustrated at how difficult it was to engender outrage in others. More than that, I was also embodying Protestantism's favorite indoor sport: feeling guilty. Dan and Phil Berrigan, Bill Coffin, Joan Baez and many others were putting a great deal more on the line in the name of protest than I was. Why were they so far ahead of me in terms of commitment and risk-taking? What was the matter with me? Why was I so timid and ineffective?

In the midst of this unsatisfying state of mind and heart, I found myself sharing a motel room with Rabbi Abraham Joshua Heschel, one of the few Jewish leaders who was in the front ranks of Vietnam protest, and one of the few human beings I truly revere, a man with the face and beard and manner of a prophet from the Hebrew Scriptures. (I used to say, in the more *macho* era from which I trust I have been delivered, that if it turned out that God was anthropomorphic, then God would look like Heschel. Having since learned a healthy suspicion of masculine images of deity, I don't say that anymore, but I let the remark stand to indicate that anything Heschel says to me will possess a high degree of authority.)

We had been participating in a demonstration together, and I seized upon the fortuitous occasion of our joint room assignment to share my concern with him, asking him how to handle a sense of inadequacy, a feeling that I should be doing more than I was doing, a conviction that compared to the others in the movement I was something of a slacker. I'm morally certain in retrospect that what I craved were a few precise pointers, a few easily remembered suggestions.

Heschel surprised me. There were no pointers, no suggestions. Instead, he put his hands on my shoulders and said, "My friend, let me tell you a story..."

And he told me a story I had never heard before, although (because of the doors it opened up) it is a story I have heard many times since — one of the great Hasidic tales.

"When the great Rebbe Zushya," Heschel continued, "was on his deathbed, he lamented to his friends how little he had accomplished in his lifetime. And so someone asked him, 'Rebbe, are you afraid of the judgment soon to come?' And the rebbe almost said 'Yes,' but he paused before doing so, and then he said, "No. For when I appear before the Almighty — may the Divine Name be forever blessed — I will not be asked, 'Why were you not Moses?' I will only be asked, 'Why were you not Zushya?'"

Heschel stopped. That was it.

And I am left to testify that that story told me more —and over the years has continued to tell me more — than I could possibly have learned from any series of four observations on how to cope with psychic insecurity, or three steps to neutralize feelings of inadequacy. For Heschel simply reminded me that the question I had been asking was the wrong question. The issue would never be, "Why were you not Dan Berrigan or Bill Coffin?" but only, "Why were you not Bob Brown?" He took my conversational lob, threw the ball right back to me with authority, and demanded that I run with it.

And to whatever degree I have been able to do so since then, in at least a little less frenetic fashion than before, is all due to...the power of a story.

It is the power of stories that Terrence Tilley is celebrating in these pages. Jewish stories, Christian stories, "secular" stories, Bible stories. Particularly Bible stories and Biblical images, which are the stuff of all good stories.

They will be wrong who approach this book and say, "Oh, nothing but another example of the latest fad, narrative theology." True, there is a lot of narrative theology making the rounds these days, though most of it isn't as good as the pages that follow. But the important point the author drives home is that "story theology" isn't some new "fad," it's as old as the faith itself. The way the faith got launched, in both its Jewish and Christian versions, was when somebody had a question and somebody else said, "My friend, let me tell you a story..."

It happened around campfires, as people tried to explain the stars; it happened in Egyptian slave quarters, as people dreamed of being free; it happened through a forty year trek across the desert, as people tried to define themselves; it happened during periods of exile, when the dreams of freedom had to be reborn. And it happens in our own time when people, no longer attracted to elaborate theological systems, seek to go behind the propositions to discover once again a lost vitality that begins to emerge when the magic words have been spoken, "Once upon a time..."

All kinds of stories are treated in these pages — stories that build up worlds, and stories that tear them down, along with stories that invite us to do some of the building up and tearing down ourselves; stories that invite us to ask "Why?" breathlessly rather than ask "What?" matter-of-factly; stories that remind us, to our great joy, that we are not as alone as we feared — since once we have a story, a *good* one, we have to share it, and community is born.

The minute we enter into the process with the author, we will forget all about the "fad" business, for we will discover that we are back to basics, to bed rock, to what counts most, since the password for getting there is very clear: "My friend, let me tell you a story... Once upon a time..."

Robert McAfee Brown

INTRODUCTION

Many Christian believers and thinkers have considered stories to be decorations for the Sunday Sermon or mere illustrations of the heart of faith. The point of the present book is to show that Christian stories provide the central and distinctive structure and content of Christian faith. The assumption which underlies this work is that without the stories of Christianity, there could be no Christianity. Stories do not merely decorate or illustrate, but provide the substance of faith. The better one understands the Christian stories, the better one understands the Christian faith.

The present book is not the only attempt to construct a narrative theology. Biblical scholars, constructive theologians and theological ethicists, both Protestant and Roman Catholic, have published numerous works centering on narratives. Yet two different types of flaws and omissions have marred these attempts to present a story theology.

Some have attempted to write a theology that has no narrative structure even though they write of stories or claim to do a narrative theology. These continue the unhappy tradition of taking stories as decorating or illustrating the 'real message'. While stories surely can be used in this way, this approach makes no novel contribution beyond those made by traditional approaches. A true narrative theology must contribute a new way to explore, transform and proclaim Christian faith. The present book, by making stories primary and doctrines derivative, provides a truly fresh approach to Christian theologizing.

Others have paid attention to the ways narratives structure faith, but have focused their work too narrowly to provide a complete narrative theology. Some have neglected to notice the different *genres* of story, either taking all stories as if all were of one *genre*, or using the term "story" so vaguely as to evacuate it of all significance. Some intentionally concentrate on one *genre* of story, e.g., myth or parable. They intentionally eschew the attempt to write a full Christian narrative theology. Some have taken the biblical stories as the sufficient stories for Christianity and neglected the narratives that have shaped the rest of the Christian traditions. Many have either neglected to raise or refused to answer the question of the truth of the stories which constitute the Christian traditions, retreating to a fideistic commitment which equates what they want to believe with what is true, or asserting that the True Story is The Christian Story without showing how an outsider might come to recognize the truth. My debts to all of them will be seen in the notes and the "for further reading" sections of the following chapters. The present book seeks to use their insights while avoiding their narrowness.

To construct a full, fundamental narrative theology for Christianity requires a variety of investigations. Chapter one shows how stories give definite, although not absolute, meaning to the key doctrines and ideas of Christianity. This opens up the possibility of retelling traditional stories as a primary way to do theology. Chapter two shows the context in which narrative theologies have emerged and chapter three argues that it is crucial to attend to the varied functions and various forms of narratives. With this ground cleared, chapter four presents an extended exercise in narrative theology by examining stories of the future and showing how non-narrative eschatology can create problems for Christian faith. Having argued for and illustrated the importance of stories, chapters five through seven provide the heart of a Christian narrative theology. Following the analysis from the third chapter, the parables, actions, and myths of Jesus are explored. But those Biblical stories are not the whole story! Christians carry on Jesus' story by accepting his stories and adapting them to their own context by forming a community of disciples, the body of Christ. Chapter eight shows how critical and constructive hagiography contributes to a narrative theology for Christianity. Chapter nine shows by what standards one can call a story true. This is especially important if one advocates participation in the ongoing story of Christ, for how can one advocate participation in what one cannot say is true? An epilogue meditates briefly on the live options for our stories today.

Story Theology provides a way to solve three major problems for contemporary Christian thought. First, a Christian needs to see what difference it makes to be a Christian. By comparing and contrasting the stories that shape the lives of Christians with those that shape the lives of others in our culture, that distinctiveness can be shown. Second, a Christian needs a way to be true to Jesus of Nazareth that neither evacuates his life and teaching of its decisive significance (as some liberal theologies do) nor idolizes him into the exclusive possession of a chosen few (as some conservative theologies do). By construing the stories of Jesus as primary, rather than the doctrines about him, both of those unhappy roads can be avoided. Third, a Christian needs to evaluate not only the stories which constitute the Christian past, but also the stories which offer possibilities for restructuring one's own life in the present. By attending to life-stories and considering standards of truth for stories, the ways to come to know the Truth and thus to be free (Jn 8:32) can be seen.

Welcome to the work!

1

THE DANCE OF METAPHOR

I heard the beat of centaur's hoofs over the hard turf
As his dry and passionate talk devoured the afternoon.
"He is a charming man — But after all what did he mean?"—
"His pointed ears....He must be unbalanced,"—
"There was something he said that I might have challenged."
—from T.S. Eliot, "Mr. Apollinax"

Metaphors are locomotives of meaning. They bear the freight of insight from place to place. They roll into the settled cities of our ideas, blasting their horns to announce the new arrival, shining their headlights to dazzle the citizens. The arrival of a powerful metaphor alters the geography of our thoughts and forces us to redraw our conceptual maps.

The most powerful metaphors drive on forever. They never die — although they may be sidetracked. After a while, they get up steam again and blow through the smooth, neat streets of newly constructed suburbs, rudely awakening our comfortable concepts from their quiet slumber and jumbling our straight boulevards and cookie-cutter houses.

Other metaphors expend all their motive power on their first trip. They can then work only where they settle down. They become dead metaphors. They live on as root ideas to structure our worlds, official titles to rule our days, codewords to form our conversations, settled concepts to use without a thought, stereotypes, lingo, jargon and puns. It is not far from the truth to say that the houses of our intellects are built of the corpses of metaphors.

The ways metaphors dance have fascinated literary critics, philosophers, and theologians. In our century, analyzing what metaphors do and how they do it has become a central task for these choreographers of language. They have charted the dazzling dances of metaphor in the theaters of our mind, applauded the virtuosi whose leaps of wit have revealed the new by outstripping the old, and finally left the galleries to dance onstage, gifted amateurs in performance. And so we critics have become entertainers, lured by the beauty of the dance to execute the steps ourselves.

But is a metaphor a train? Or is it a dance? Or both? Or neither? We are left in the position of the observer of Mr. Apollinax: "What did he mean?" "There was something he said that I might have challenged." We have been dazzled by metaphors, by metaphorical descriptions of metaphors and theorists of metaphors, and are left impressed, but puzzled or unsettled. What does it mean?

This question is usually answered by translating or parsing the metaphor into a set of similes and dissimiles until one has exhausted the 'content' of the metaphor. "A metaphor is like a train in that it carries unexpected excess baggage, can be used in various conceptual schemes as a train can be used in various cities.... A metaphor is unlike a train in that it doesn't travel on tracks, it isn't made of iron..." As this exploration proceeds, various facets of metaphors' function will appear ("it can crash, it needs bridges to get from one point to another, it can bring destruction as well as construction," etc.). Some of these will be debatable, and the very process of debating the "proper" translation of the metaphor and its "correct" meaning will reveal endless dimensions of a metaphor.

Now there is nothing wrong with the process of parsing a metaphor. Yet, it often exhausts the patience of the analysts long before it plumbs the depth of the metaphor. It also —necessarily — robs metaphor of its power to evoke new insight, just as a whispering critic who dissects every move can destroy one's appreciation of a performance. It also tends to obscure one key function of religious metaphor: how using metaphors provides the bridge over which faith moves from the tradition of the community into the life of the individual.

There is, however, another way to show what a metaphor means. One can place it in a story. This does not merely illustrate a metaphor, but also explores it, in a definite context, in order to show what it means.

Key Christian ideas are metaphors which have been contextualized by inclusion in prototypical narratives. These metaphors thereby become canonical and "bear the content of faith."[1] The key concepts of Christian faith — creation, fall, incarnation, atonement, church, eternal life, trinity — are all metaphors at rest, metaphors which have become Christian doctrines. For example, consider the Pauline metaphor, "the church is the body of Christ." This metaphor powerfully expresses an insight into the nature of the church. It can be paraphrased into similes and dissimiles as successfully as any metaphor can: "The Church is like Christ's body in that it is the way Christ is in the world, is composed of Christ's members, is ruled by a head, etc." "The Church is not like Christ's body in that it is not a single organism, will not die on a cross, etc." Such an analysis can deliver propositions to express the meanings of the Church as Christ's body. Debates about its real significance can occur. Dogmas may be proclaimed to fix its meaning. This process of exploring canonical metaphors is propositional theology, i.e., the analysis, exploration, transformation, systematization, and proclamation of the canonical metaphors, the concepts of Christianity.

[1] James Wm. McClendon, Jr., *Biography as Theology: How Life-Stories Can Remake Today's Theology* (Nashville: Abingdon, 1974), p. 97.

Now there is nothing wrong with doing propositional theology. However, it can lose the oak of metaphor in a forest of paraphrase. It can rob central Christian concepts of their power to evoke new insight. But, most importantly, propositional theology has difficulty showing how the faith enters into the lives of believers. Only after the tasks of propositional theology are completed can pastoral or practical theology begin its struggle to say how the systematized structure of doctrine enters into the life and practice of Christians. At this point we are as far from "You are the body of Christ and members thereof" (1 Cor 12:27) and its provocative power as we are from any metaphor at the end of the paraphrase.

Yet the key ideas of Christianity are actually carried into the lives of believers in two much more direct ways. The first way is through the rituals in which they participate. For example, the metaphor of the body of Christ is key not only for the Church, but also for the Eucharist. Consider the following:

> What happens in that ritual meal? Is it not this: that in connection with the meal bread is said to be, bread is seen as, bread is taken as, the body of the Church's Lord? And wine is taken as his blood poured out for us? Some of course will say, not "taken as" but *becomes* the body; whereupon others will be quick to reply not "becomes" but *represents* that body. With these old disputes I have at the moment no concern — I wish rather to call attention to the disputants' common ground, that in the rite *this* is (in some sense) *that* — *hoc est corpus meum*, this is my body.[2]

The very sacrament central to the Christian life is an enacted metaphor. By participating in this sacrament Christians reaffirm and reinforce their own participation in the body of Christ which is the Church. Examples could be multiplied, but the point is that participating in enacted metaphors is

[2]*Ibid.*, pp. 98-99.

one way in which the key concepts of Christianity enter into the lives of Christians. And by such participation people enter into the life of Christianity. Ritual provides a bridge between individual and community.

A second way in which a metaphor enters into the life of a Christian is through the stories in which it is incorporated. John Shea has claimed that "whenever our biographies are deeply probed, a root metaphor appears."[3] When a person probes her or his life to see what makes it meaningful, s/he discovers a metaphor which structures that life: "I am a Christian"; "I am a selfless humanist"; "I am a seeker of wholistic selfhood"; etc. A person may have to try out a host of images or metaphors before finding one at the root of life. The very discovering of a metaphor that fits will bring one to see one's life in a new way.

But the metaphors which might fit our lives are given to us in the stories which form the traditions in which we live, be they humanist, Christian, therapeutic, etc. So to say what that root metaphor means for us is to tell or retell, to adopt or adapt, the story carrying that metaphor from the tradition into one's own life. Thus, the metaphor a story carries can be used to express the meaning of a life. The process of story-telling — especially that of autobiography — provides the bridge for canonical images and metaphors from the community or tradition to the individual.

To be a Christian is to use Christian canonical metaphors, to adapt or adopt the stories which carry them to one's own life, and thus to provide meaning and unity for one's life. This use of stories provides another way to answer the question of what metaphors, concepts or doctrines mean. By telling and exploring the stories which contextualize key Christian ideas, a person can show what they mean. That process of discovering, creatively transforming, and proclaiming the stories which carry the key ideas of Christianity is the distinctive work of a Christian narrative theology.

---

[3]John Shea, *Stories of God: An Unauthorized Biography* (Chicago: Thomas More Press, 1978), p. 56. I do not assume that these are *live* metaphors.

Two preliminary claims must be defended to show the need for a Christian narrative theology. First, it must be shown that understanding a story is a way to understand the metaphor or concept it contextualizes. Two examples will make that point. A fictional story shows the meaning of "selfless humanist." A biographical sketch contextualizes "seeker of a wholistic self." Second, it must be shown that a narrative theology differs significantly from a propositional theology in its handling of stories in theory as well as practice. Comparing and contrasting them explicitly will make that point.

"A Selfless Humanist"

Everyone knows what a selfless humanist is in contemporary American culture. He is a man who was one of the heroes of the sixties in the U.S.A. He thought the right — liberal — thoughts. He fought the good fight. He put his body on the line even at the cost of danger to himself. He was kind to the underprivileged and led the fight against unjust discriminations. Our man is concerned in theory and in practice for *humanity.*

This brief portrait of a selfless humanist is drawn from many narratives. It has been compressed into a stereotype. So now "concerned humanist" is a codeword, a dead metaphor. However, consider a story of a concerned humanist, the story of Sheppard, a prototypical concerned humanist. Flannery O'Connor tells a story that gives a definite meaning to this metaphor.

In "The Lame Shall Enter First," Sheppard is portrayed as a widower with a ten-year-old son whose life has been dulled by his mother's death. Sheppard worries over his son, Norton, but can find no way to rekindle a light in those eyes. Sheppard believes his son is wallowing in his selfish grief. He thinks Norton will never really amount to much in spite of his other advantages because Norton is so selfish. Sheppard believes that Norton will never be able to become a good and selfless, concerned man like himself.

Sheppard is employed as a recreation director by the city in which he lives. On Saturdays, he volunteers his time as a counselor at the local reformatory. In the course of his work there, he met a young man named Rufus Johnson, a fourteen-year-old, street-wise, fast-talking, Holy Bible-spouting, club-footed delinquent. In spite of Rufus' disdain for Sheppard and his taunting of Norton, Sheppard takes Rufus into his home.

Sheppard seeks to save Rufus. He buys both boys a telescope, arranges for a new shoe to be made for Rufus' foot, and defends Rufus from the "persecution" of the police. In spite of Rufus' taunts, Norton perks up, especially at the thought that his mother is *on high*, for Rufus has told him that anyone who accepted Jesus and was good was not burning in hell and was in heaven. Sheppard counters this with his own belief that his wife lives on only in the good deeds that live after her.

Eventually Sheppard becomes disturbed over the abuse of his hospitality by Rufus. Not only is he feeding Norton religious nonsense, but also he is making Sheppard feel guilty for not trusting him enough. Then, at dinner one evening, Rufus avers that he has "lifted" a Bible which "tells" him that unless one repents, one goes to hell. Norton urges Rufus to repent so he won't go to hell, but Rufus refuses. Sheppard attacks the Bible as a book to hide behind and, when Rufus opposes him, Sheppard sends Rufus away from the table. Rufus leaves in triumph, for he seems to have shown that Sheppard is on the side of the devil.

Sheppard is heartsick at his failure, a failure compounded when he goes up to the attic and discovers his son Norton peering through the telescope and waving wildly at the stars — he had discovered his dead mother there!!! Sheppard dismisses him to bed, descends to the living room and is greeted by the local cop who has caught Rufus redhanded in a crime. Rufus is about to be hauled off to jail. As the gloating policeman hauls him off, Rufus adds insult to injury by (falsely) accusing Sheppard of "making suggestions."

Sheppard is distraught. But he consoles himself by contemplating how much he had done for Rufus. He did more for Rufus than he did for his own son. He did all that he could. He did more for Rufus than he did for his own son. *More than he did for his own son!*

He then comes to see the literal truth of what he said. He had sacrificed his own boy's welfare on the altar of his self-regard. He had been blind to what he had done, but now he could see. He came to his senses. He knew what he must do. He would make everything new and different and better between him and his son.

> He groaned with joy. He would make everything up to him. He would never let him suffer again. He would be mother and father. He jumped up and ran to his room, to kiss him, to tell him that he loved him, that he would never fail him again.
>
> The light was on in Norton's room but the bed was empty. He turned and dashed up the attic stairs and at the top reeled back like a man on the edge of a pit. The tripod had fallen and the telescope lay on the floor. A few feet over it, the child hung in the jungle of shadows, just below the beam from which he had launched his flight into space.[4]

Now Sheppard is a good man. He lives with the best of intentions. He is a selfless humanist. But the point of O'Connor's story is to show that one way of living out that metaphor is to be blind to what one is doing, to be unable to recognize the true pattern of one's acts before a comedy of errors is transformed into a nauseating tragedy.

Sheppard's story tells of a life whose meaning comes from helping through kindness. But it also tells of a man whose life's meaning interfered with his seeing what truly needed doing. Now, is this story the right way to understand the metaphor of "selfless humanist," of the person who denies the transcendent and the religious? Some Christians might

[4]Flannery O'Connor, *The Complete Stories* (New York: Farrar, Straus and Giroux, 1981), pp. 481-482. The previous thirty-seven pages of the story had set me up so perfectly to expect a happy ending that the final paragraph made me ill.

say yes; others would not. However, the point is that we don't know what the codeword "selfless humanist" means until we know what story gives meaning to that metaphor; its meaning is free and indeterminate without a story, and because we merely hear the codeword doesn't mean we know the story the code encapsulates.

"A Seeker of a Wholistic Self"

Everyone knows how Americans in the seventies and eighties use the codeword "wholistic" and how the journeys into a "self" have become an American preoccupation. But what does it mean to seek a wholistic self? Christopher Lasch reports the story of the one-time political activist, Jerry Rubin, who embarked on one such search after his activist phase. Lasch writes:

> Jerry Rubin, having reached the dreadful age of thirty and having found himself face to face with his private fears and anxieties, moves from New York to San Francisco, where he shops voraciously — on an apparently inexhaustible income — in the spiritual supermarkets of the West Coast. "In five years," Rubin says, "from 1971 to 1975, I directly experienced est, gestalt therapy, bioenergetics, rolfing, massage, jogging, health foods, tai chi, Esalen, hypnotism, modern dance, meditation, Silva Mind Control, Arica, acupuncture, sex therapy, Reichian therapy, and More House — a smorgasbord course in the New Consciousness...."
>
> Rubin sees his "journey into myself" as part of the consciousness movement of the seventies. Yet this "massive self-examination" has produced few indications of self-understanding, personal or collective. Self-awareness remains mired in liberationist cliches.... As a skillful manipulator of the common coin, a self-confessed "media freak" and propagandist, he assumes that all ideas, character traits, and cultural patterns derive from

> propaganda and "conditioning"....Like many ex-
> radicals, he has succeeded only in exchanging current
> therapeutic slogans for the political slogans he used to
> mouth with equal disregard of their content.[5]

The tragedy is that Rubin's story is not exceptional, but
typical for those whose self-identification is "seeker of wholistic self."

Many people have no key metaphor or story which gives
their life meaning. They shop the therapeutic supermarkets
seeking a self. But the story that gives meaning to the
metaphor of "seeker" is the story of a solitary Narcissus who
is concerned with and loves only himself. "If I seek to
construct my self so that I am free from all others, so that my
life is my own, and my story told in no story but my own, I
will be free to be and make a whole me." But this vision of
the self, pandemic in American culture, leads the visionary
to be blind to the whole story s/he lives, ignoring that
Narcissus died for love of himself. In short, when seeking a
self replaces being a self, the seeker can never stop long
enough to tell a story coherent enough to support a life.

Perhaps the most serious symptom of our lack of coherent and lasting stories to structure each of us as a self worth
being is our approach to sexuality. Lasch beings the story
well:

> Efficient contraceptives, legalized abortion, and a "realis-
> tic" and "healthy" acceptance of the body have weakened
> the links that once tied sex to love, marriage, and pro-
> creation. Men and women now pursue sexual pleasure as
> an end in itself, unmediated even by the conventional
> trappings of romance.
>
> Sex valued purely for its own sake loses all reference to
> the future and brings no hope of permanent
> relationships.[6]

[5]Christopher Lasch, *The Culture of Narcissism: American Life in an Age of
Diminishing Expectations* (New York: Warner Books, 1979), pp. 45-46.
[6]*Ibid.*, p. 326.

What Lasch doesn't bring out clearly is that in the context of those "weakened links," we have no story which is powerful enough to make sex meaningful rather than just fun. It is not so much the truly healthy acceptance of our bodies that is bad. Rather, it is that the "sex act" has become isolated from our stories; it is something we do incidentally; the sharing that is part of the romantic view of sex never penetrates into our stories of our lives, only into relieving our tensions and enjoying each other. We come to think of sex as an "it," some*thing* which we value for its own sake. "It" can never be understood as essentially part of me, as I am not an "it" in any essential way. While people surely may, in these circumstances, simultaneously masturbate, we cannot humanly integrate. In short, if Rubin's story *is* emblematic of what it means to seek a wholistic self, then those who use that metaphor to structure their lives may be living out a story not worth living out. But one has to know the story —not merely the codeword — to discover that or to refute it.

The Tasks of Narrative Theology

The tasks of any Christian theology are to explore the traditions of, to transform (when necessary) the formulations of, and to proclaim the meaning of the Christian faith. A Christian *propositional* theology engages in exploring, transforming and proclaiming the doctrines of Christianity. A Christian *narrative* theology undertakes exploring, transforming and proclaiming the stories of Christianity. If stories give meaning to the metaphors/stereotypes/codewords /doctrines which we use, then a narrative theology is more fundamental than a propositional theology. The differences between the two approaches can be displayed by considering their different tasks.

For a Christian narrative theology, the first task is *to uncover the stories which show what the Christian keywords mean.* Like the propositional theologian, the narrative theologian must seek to understand the Christian traditions and to distinguish those traditions from ones incompatible with supporting Christian faith. But the narrative theologian does not center on the doctrines of the Christian and other traditions, but on the narratives which form those traditions. Some myths, stories which establish "the world in which we live and out of which we act,"[7] are compatible with the stories of creation, redemption and sanctification central to the Christian tradition. Others have no room for these actions, or distort them beyond recognition; these must be excluded.

Yet the great stories of Christianity are celebrated in various sacraments, narrated in many texts, and sung in different hymns. Because different Christians do not share the same ways of sacrament, text, and hymn, the different Christian traditions will differ significantly over the meaning of the key Christian metaphors, doctrines and keywords. The narrative theologian bares the diverse stories of Christianity. But the narrative theologian cannot accept or reject those diverse stories on the basis of their compatibility with some doctrinal statement, but must judge them on their compatibility with the narratives central to the tradition. In uncovering the variety of Christian narratives, the narrative theologian shows the multiple meanings of the Christian keywords.

The second task of a Christian narrative theology is *to transform creatively (when necessary) the narratives of the tradition.* Like the propositional theologian, the narrative theologian recognizes that in new contexts new ways of expressing the tradition must be discovered. But the propositional theologian seeks to *extract* true dogmas, true statements, or true articles of a Creed from the old story, and to find new ways to express those propositions in a new system, to express the old truths in a new context. The narrative theologian sees problems with the presuppositions, the status and the tactics of such a theological approach.

Propositional theology presupposes that narratives are dispensable portrayals of religious faith. Yet this is not necessarily true. In the explorations of the two stories of this chapter, it becomes clear that one did not know the

---

[7]Shea, *Stories of God*, p. 52.

meanings of the metaphors until one knew the stories in which they were embedded. One has to uncover the content and structure of the stories in order to determine the meanings of the elements in the stories. If one neglects the stories, one cannot understand the elements. For instance, Christians have claimed that Jesus is God's son. To show what this claim means, the New Testament tells a number of stories with, as we shall see below, varying content, varying form, and, thus, varying meanings for the claim. Early Christian theologians had to decide which of a number of possible ways to retell that story was most faithful to the received traditions. So, although Arius (256-336) could affirm that Jesus Christ was God's son, he and his followers were judged heretics because the story that structured their understanding of the relationship of Christ to God portrayed Christ as subordinate to God, rather than as a Son equal to the Father. Thus, if one's avowal of a doctrine or understanding of a metaphor is made in the context of and given meaning by the wrong story, such an avowal or understanding — even using the same form of sound words as is traditional — will be wrong. It will be heretical because such an understanding or avowal means differently from what it would in the standard story or set of stories. One cannot presuppose that narratives are dispensable for understanding religious faith.

Propositional theology assumes the status of the definitive statement of the faith. Yet historical theologian Maurice Wiles has pointed out the problem with this assumption:

> A "true" doctrinal statement (though the phrase is less simple than appears on the surface) can, it may be admitted, never lose its truth, but it can lose its relevance. A statement whose truth or falsity can be determined only in terms of a world-view that is dead and gone can hardly be a statement of direct relevance to subsequent ages..."[8]

[8] Maurice Wiles, *The Making of Christian Doctrine: A Study in the Principles of Early Doctrinal Development* (Cambridge: Cambridge University Press, 1975), p. 9.

The doctrinal statement, "God created the heavens and the earth" may never lose its truth. However, the affirmation of such in the Nicene Creed was performed in the context of a myth or world-view in which the creation was pictured in terms of the "three-decker universe": the dome of the heavens covered the flat earth, beneath which lay the underworld. Within that myth, Christians understood what it meant to affirm that God created the heavens and the earth. Yet *we* live in a different world. Christians with a myth or world-view which tells of the beginning of everything in a "big bang" need to understand how God could be involved with creation in the context of *our* myth. Propositional theologians presume that they need merely to update their propositions. Narrative theologians see the need for new ways to tell the story of creation. The central function of propositional theology is not the definitive statement of the faith: that is an impossible task. Rather, propositional theology is derivative from narratives as literary criticism is derivative from literature; it cannot carry the message, but is indispensable to guide and criticize those who proffer ways to tell the stories anew.

Propositional theology works to make new and better systems of doctrines. Narrative theology seeks to make a religious tradition vibrant in a new context by telling new stories. In the past, when Christian theologians viewed the revelation of God as the communicating of propositions from God to scribes who wrote them down and embellished them in stories, the task of theologians was to extract those propositions from the Bible or the Church, accept them, and then develop a system of thought based upon them.[9] Today, when this view of revelation has been supplanted by a more personalistic view, the task of theology has changed. Rather than attempting to reformulate old propositions into new systems, theologians should be telling new stories.[10] This

[9]Compare William Nicholls, *Systematic and Philosophical Theology* (Baltimore: Penguin Books, 1971), p. 22.

[10]Examples of theology primarily concerned with propositions include progressive Catholic Richard P. McBrien, *Catholicism* (Minneapolis: Winston Press, 1980), Volume One, pp. 25-26 or liberal Protestant John McQuarrie, *The Faith of the People of God: A Lay Theology* (New York: Scribner's, 1972), p. 12.

means that narrative theology suggests different tactics for both conservative and progressive theologians. A more progressive theologian will be able to convey the significance of religious experience by telling stories of living with God. A more conservative theologian will be able to convey the singificance of what God reveals in telling stories of God's mighty acts. Both conservative and progressive theologians can creatively transform the stories which provide the meaning to the central doctrines of Christianity by telling stories new and true. In sum, a Christian narrative theology sees the transformative task of theology, the continuing responsibility to represent the traditions, as done better by telling stories to keep the central metaphors alive and true than by cutting and pasting the metaphors-become-doctrines into a system.

The third task of a Christian narrative theology is *to proclaim and manifest the Good News.* The propositional theologian conceptualizes the message and instructs or suggests proper responses by the hearers of the word. The narrative theologian communicates the good news by telling a story of Christ and living it as well. But, as chapter seven shows, various metaphors have been used to express the central meaning of what Jesus did and said and who he was; as chapter eight shows, people in various eras have attempted to live out that story in startlingly different ways. This diversity delights the narrative theologian, for the great variety of canonical stories contextualizing those central metaphors shows that the metaphor of "Christ" is alive and powerful, roaring through many different areas of our tradition and altering the geography of our concepts. Christians keep trying to tell the stories, to keep alive the central images. We must come to realize that we cannot tell the finally right story until the *end* of the story — which time has not yet come, for the whole story of God and humanity is not yet told.

Both narrative and propositional theologies seek to show Christians the central and distinctive meaning of their own faith. But where propositional theologies concentrate on presenting true propositions, defending them, and reminding the faithful of them (often using stories as illustrations of these profound truths), narrative theologies tell, evaluate and re-tell the stories (always using the help propositional theology can give). In sum, the style of narrative theology differs from that of propositional theology even though the concerns are similar.

Summary

This chapter has presented the need for, tasks of, and distinctive contributions of a narrative theology. It frees up the metaphors that connect faith and life. It works to uncover, transform, and proclaim the stories which provide the form and content of Christian faith. It displays a three-fold distinctive vitality.

First, narrative theology recognizes the irreducible and provocative multiplicity in Christianity. As John Shea, a Catholic theologian, has written, "The God who bargains with Abraham and Moses will not budge with Jonah. . . . The loving Father of Jesus does not visit the death of his Son."[11] The stories of God cannot be captured in a system.

Second, faith and action, so distantly related in propositional theology are inseparable in narrative theology, for "faith is not the still point of the turning world but a force which makes the world turn faster. Our journey is not the way of adjustment in order to survive but the way of struggle in order to transform."[12] Metaphors told in story and acted in ritual must empower the imagination and action of Christians.

Third, a narrative theology shows how a Christian acts. As Stanley Hauerwas, a Methodist theologian, has suggested, no theory of propositional theology can show me how to move from the injustice of my life to a justified life or from violence to peace. However, when I contrast the story

---

[11]Shea, *Stories of God*, p. 75. For a discussion of the work of another Roman Catholic narrative theologian, John Dunne, C.S.C., see Lonnie D. Kliever, *The Shattered Spectrum* (Atlanta: John Knox Press, 1981), pp. 158-168. Dunne's approach differs markedly from Shea's.

[12]*Ibid.*

of myself with the model stories of Christianity, I can come to see those differences. And if the stories of peace and justice canonized by my community can truly be made my own story, then the distance between who I am and who I ought to be is overcome.[13]

In sum, a narrative theology must begin in the dancing of metaphor, develop through the learning of stories, and end in the living of truth.

[13]Representative of Hauerwas' works are *A Community of Character* (Notre Dame: University of Notre Dame Press, 1981) and *The Peaceable Kingdom* (Notre Dame: University of Notre Dame Press, 1983).

2

WHY STORY THEOLOGY? THE BACKGROUND STORY

God made man because he loves stories.
—Elie Wiesel[1]

In order to understand a person, a movement, a symbolic action, or a provocative metaphor, one needs to appreciate the context in which each arose. The purpose of this chapter is to sketch the religious and theological context in which narrative theologies have been developed and to show the concerns these theologies were designed to meet and the problems they hope to illumine and resolve. The real root of narrative theology and its importance, however, appears in the quotation which heads the chapter.

The Shaking of the Foundations in Theology

Although narrative theologians are certainly indebted to European theology, story theology is a thoroughly American movement. The theological context for its emergence is the situation of both Roman Catholic and Protestant theol-

[1]Elie Wiesel, *The Gates of the Forest,* trans. by Frances Frenaye (New York: Holt, Rinehart and Winston, 1966), p. xii.

ogy in the U.S.A. during the early 1960's, a time in which theological foundations were shaken.

The reforms initiated by the Second Vatican Council (1962-65) were the occasion for a new freedom in theological work that startled many American Catholics. Since the late nineteenth century, when Pope Leo XIII had urged the study of St. Thomas' works, Catholic theologians had spent much of their time and energy adapting Thomas' insights to modern needs. After the first decade of the twentieth century, when Pope Pius X had condemned a number of very progressive theologians as "modernists" and inaugurated an era of vigilance that suppressed almost all progressive theology, the only thing Catholic theologians seemed to be able to do was to write footnotes to Thomism. Yet through the work of a number of progressive Thomistic theologians that came to the fore during the Council, it became clear that terms other than St. Thomas' might be used to express the faith, and might fit the present era better than St. Thomas' terms. Catholic theologians found themselves free to explore new ways to think of and to represent the faith of the Church.

With the waning of the age of the giants of twentieth century Protestant theology — the age of Karl Barth, Rudolf Bultmann, Paul Tillich and Reinhold Niebuhr, to name a few — younger Protestant theologians in America found the decade of the 1960's a time to explore new ways to understand and proclaim their faith. The more novel were lumped together as "death of God" theologians and summarily dismissed from ongoing theological discussions. The more reactionary were scorned as romantic visitors to an imaginary past. In the search for new and true expressions of faith, a number of new theologies emerged: theologies of hope, of secularity, of freedom, etc. Each highlighted a theme that would provide a solid central focus for Christian faith — or so their proponents proclaimed. Although each has presented an insight into Christianity, none has received unqualified support from more than a handful of thinkers.

Some Christians heard the many notes sounded by these many trumpets as noisy confusion. Ecclesiastical officials bemoaned the indifference of many Christians; many Christians bemoaned the "irrelevance" of their church. A few intellectuals had been converted by the preaching of the death of God by academic interpreters of philosopher Friedrich Nietzsche. But more had been seduced from faith in the God of Abraham, Isaac, Jacob and Jesus by the allurements of the god of SUCCESS. To climb to the top, to look out for number one, to insure financial security, to succeed in business (no matter how) became the practical faith and the practiced worship of many. The stories by which Americans lived, stories broadcast into their living rooms, proclaim the religion of SUCCESS. And to live in those stories, to shape one's life to conform to them is to abandon the God whom Christians have worshipped.

Catholicism with opened windows and Protestantism with uncertain trumpets in a culture of narcissism do not suffice to produce a theological movement. This is only the general context for the movement. A number of factors provide important components within that context. Without them narrative theology would not have arisen. The following sections of this chapter will describe four very significant factors.

The Challenge from Philosophers of Language

The tale of the challenge to religious faith issued by empirical-analytical philosophers has been told often. Between the first and second world wars, in Austria and England, a group of philosophers, grouped as "logical positivists," sought to discover how the language we use could be meaningful and true. Their analyses led them to claim that those statements that pictured the way things were in the world and could be verified by a person were truly meaningful. Thus, if I were to say, "Bowser loves me," and when I entered my living room, my dog wagged his tail and licked my hand, your observation of this homely scene would verify my statement, as you could see what facts it pictured and how well it pictured them. Were Bowser to snarl at me and cower, that scene, observed by you, would be pictured in a rather different statement. The logical positivists thus claimed that meaningful statements were those which we could verify (or falsify) by seeing if they pictured facts; meaningless statements were those which could picture no facts and which could not be verified or falsified by checking them.

The *verifiability theory* showed quite clearly the meaning of statements of common sense or science. But what about moral claims? What facts do moral values picture? Can we verify the claim, "Abortions are morally evil," by seeing whether there are any abortions performed? Would the occurrence or the non-occurrence of induced abortions verify that claim? Since neither set of facts would answer that question, it seems the case that moral claims — as they picture no definite facts — are meaningless. While my moral claims may be autobiographical reports of my personal preferences or expressions of my emotional reaction to certain events, I cannot claim them to be truly meaningful since they picture no facts, and can't be verified by checking facts.

And what of religious claims? We know how to go about verifying "Bowser loves me." How can we verify "God loves me"? Religious claims refer to no specific facts or set of facts unambiguously. No set of facts seems available that would constitute a falsification of the claim, either — as Bowser's negative reaction to me *would* falsify my claim that Bowser loves me. The logical positivists' theory of language also would inter the claims of religion in the graveyard of meaninglessness. Thus, the positivist theory of language consigns religion and morality to, at best, a private, subjective sphere, leaving science and common sense the field of the meaningful and public.

Obviously, this view of religion and morality provoked numerous reactions. Some philosophers argued that the stipulation of verifiability as the criterion for meaningful language was arbitrary. They acknowledged the difference of moral and religious from scientific and common sense claims, but averred that the difference did not make morality and religion meaningless. A few even counter-stipulated that the very *lack* of verifiability shows what was *really* the most meaningful language.

Rather than hurling stipulations at each other, philosphers began to try to discover just what *use* various sorts of statements had. Scientific statements are *used* to state scientific conclusions. Common sense sayings are *used* for everyday purposes in everyday talk. What *use* could religious and moral utterances have? As the uses of scientific statements indicated their meaning, might not the uses of religious and moral statements analogously indicate their meaning(s)? As might be expected, religious claims were discovered to be used for a number of purposes. For our present purposes, philosopher of science R. B. Braithwaite offered a very interesting account in his 1955 Eddington Memorial Lecture, "An Empiricist's View of the Nature of Religious Belief."[2]

Braithwaite claimed that when a person used language religiously, he or she expressed an *intention* to live in a certain way. For a religious person to say, for instance, "God is love," is to declare an intention to live a life of love. The religious person is not thereby trying to describe the world in pseudo-scientific terms, but is *using* religious language with the meaning of declaring an intention to live within the world in a particular way.

What makes these declarations religious, Braithwaite claimed, was not their form alone, but rather the *stories* that people associated with their intentions. A true Christian, for instance, both proposed to live according to Christian moral principles and associated that intention with the Christian set of stories. The Christian does not have to believe all these stories to be literally true, but merely has to entertain them, so as to help the believer carry out professed intentions. In fact, Braithwaite noted, some of the most effective stories were known to be fictional, including the

[2]Richard Bevan Braithwaite, *An Empiricist's View of the Nature of Religious Belief* (Cambridge: Cambridge University Press, 1955); reprinted in B. Mitchell, ed., *The Philosophy of Religion* (London: Oxford University Press, 1971).

novels of Dostoevsky and Bunyan's *Pilgrim's Progress.*

Braithwaite's response to the challenge posed by the positivistic philosophers of language recalled the forgotten link between literature and religion. That link had been recognized by Matthew Arnold in the 19th century, but repudiated by most churchpeople. Braithwaite's recollection of it showed one way that religious convictions could be considered philosophically respectable, but more importantly suggested to theologians the significance of *stories* again. Naturally he has been criticized on a number of grounds —especially for conflating stories and statements, that is, treating stories as if they were clumps of statements linked logically rather than as events shaped by a plot moving toward an end. Nonetheless, R. B. Braithwaite, by his creative response to the challenge from the philosophers of language, has helped Christian theologians to become aware of the importance of stories for investigating and expressing religious faith.

The Narrative Quality of Human Experience

A second factor contributing to the rise of story theology was the recovery of the realization that *human* experience is *inherently* narrative in form. A now-classic articulation of and defense for this claim was an article by Stephen Crites whose essay guides this section. Rather than think of our experience as timeless points, events or occurrences (the logical outcome of construing experience as disconnected "flashes" or "moments" that happen), Crites claims we should think of experience as patterned in and through time. What this means, then, is that experience "is itself *an incipient story.*"[3]

Crites draws a parallel between experience and music to guide those who would follow his argument. Is it better to consider music as a group of tones combined into a whole,

[3]Stephen Crites, "The Narrative Quality of Experience," *Journal of the American Academy of Religion* XXXIX/3 (September, 1971), p. 297; emphasis added.

or as a whole piece divisible, when necessary, into tones? If a person can sing or play a piece "by sight," that performer will not break up the song into pieces *unless* a certain tone or note or progression presents difficulties.

Similarly, unless some event of our experience presents us with difficulties, we will not stop to analyze the experience we have. Ordinarily a performer (or hearer) of music will not stop to dissect and analyze a piece of music. Similarly, we will not stop to analyze an item of our experience. Ordinarily we allow our experience to remain a whole through time. This parallel suggests, then, that the typical philosophical way of thinking about experience — as single events happening to a person in the present moment — is based not in our ordinary way of treating experience, but in the way we treat our experience when "something's wrong." Is it better for philosophers to begin with experience as patterned and durational? Or is it better to begin with experience as momentary and present? What Crites wants us to see is that the question of the "right way" to think of experience is an open question, not a question that can be presumed to be settled. It may be the case that the philosophers who have begun with single, present events have put the cart before the horse. Maybe we need to begin the other way around.

Crites claims that it is better to think of human experience as *inherently durational*. To argue for this claim, he first asks what happens in each present moment. Well, that involves another question: what is the "present"? Do we not think of the present as that point at which the future meets the past? If we think of the present that way and then try to find it, we discover that "the present" disappears into something that has no duration and no location. If we try to break up our experience, we will discover that when we break it down as small as we can, it will all be past or future, never present, since the present doesn't last any time at all! Perhaps we would do better to think of our experience in a different way, as thinking about it as single events in the present moment gives us no time or place for experience.

Crites, having argued against the typical way to think of experience, secondly argues that there is a better way to think of experience, as concretely, inherently durational.

> The conscious present is that of a body impacted in a world and moving, in process, in that world. In this present action and experience meet. Memory is its depth, the depth of its experience in particular; anticipation is its trajectory, the trajectory of its action in particular.[4]

The problem with the other way of thinking of experience is that it denies the continuity through time of our experience. It ignores the fact that human experience is itself *through time*, intrinsically temporal and durational. When we abstract our experience from time and try to place it at a point where past meets future, we leave something essential behind: the enduring quality of our experience.

Crites, however, does not want to eliminate analysis of individual experience. Rather, his main point is that both ways of thinking about experience — durationally and analytically — are necessary *if* one remembers that human experience is basically durational and *if* one remembers that analysis is *abstraction from* (and distortion of) that experience *for a specific purpose*, not the basic way of human experiencing. In short, both ways of thinking about experience need to be held in a creative tension.

If our experience is basically durational, how can we talk of it? The answer fits perfectly: in narratives. Stories do tell of a "body impacted in a world." They portray experience through time. Of course stories without analysis and criticism are as dangerous as analysis without stories,[5] as we shall see in section four below. When we lose our critical abilities our stories may be deformed or false without our realizing what has gone wrong. When we lose our stories, our critical abilities run rampant and become vicious, as Crites has noted.[6] The better our story is, the better we are

[4]*Ibid.*, 303.   [5]*Ibid.*, 310.   [6]*Ibid.*

able "to recover a living past, to believe again in the future, to perform acts that have significance for the person who acts."[7] The main point, however, is that stories are the most fitting way to tell of human experience because human experience is essentially durational.

The implication of this view is that without a story that is both faithful to our ongoing experiences and actions, and examined critically for its truthfulness, we cannot be fully human. Yet someone might want to argue that all stories are phony, that they all are inevitably falsifications of our experience, that what we really do is to repeat stories to ourselves in order to make what is an incoherent and absurd world appear to us as coherent and meaningful. However, a person could not argue for that claim. For if one made an incoherent argument to support the claim, it would not be convincing. And if one made a coherent argument for the claim, it would imply the acceptance of coherence as a standard and thus an acceptance of what one finally was arguing to be an illusion. To argue that all stories are presentations of the illusion of coherence is impossible.

What would be a much more interesting attempt to undermine this claim would be for a skeptic to get a person to see that his or her story is an illusion, to get a person to see the difficulties in his or her own story so that s/he has to stop and analyze that story. But then, that would not be a good argument against Crites' persuasive claim that human experience is inherently narrative and needs stories to form and to report it.

The Evolution of Biblical Criticism

The evolution of modern methods of Bible study has contributed to the rise of narrative theology. Historically, Christian churches — and not only the "fundamentalist" ones by any means — have been wary of accepting the conclusions of biblical criticism. Sometimes those conclu-

---

[7]*Ibid.*, 311. The specific story Crites refers to here is the story of "revolution."

sions have shown that cherished traditional beliefs or practices cannot find their warrant in the Bible. Hence,
individual Christians have accused scholars of destroying
"God's word," and some churches have excommunicated
scholars whose conclusions were at variance with the established beliefs of those churches.

Yet criticism of the biblical texts can have positive results,
including some very well-founded insights into who Jesus
was, that help sharpen the sometimes-confused picture that
emerges from the difficult to reconcile (at best) statements
about him in the Bible. Although debate over what books
belong in the Bible and scholarly examination and interpretation of the texts has been part of Christianity since the
post-apostolic era, David Friedrich Strauss (1808-1874) is
usually considered the first biblical critic (in the modern
sense).

Strauss published *The Life of Jesus Critically Examined*
in 1835 and 1836. In it he claimed that much of what the
gospels say of the life of Jesus is not literally true, but the
product of myth-making imaginations. Although the book
made him famous and affected subsequent Protestant theology significantly, he lost his academic career once it was
published: Evangelical Church authorities, appalled at the
picture of Jesus emerging from his work, removed him from
his teaching position. Subsequent scholars have found his
approach to the Scriptures far too heavy-handed. Not only
did he let his philosophical beliefs control the results of his
historical investigations to an inappropriate extent, but also
his critical tools were far too undeveloped to allow him to
appreciate the nuances of the texts.

Since Strauss' time, scholars have developed ever more
subtle methods to try to portray what Jesus truly did and
taught more clearly. They have especially continued to seek
to distinguish what the writers of the Scriptures added to the
stories of Jesus as they expressed their unbounded faith in
him. This distinction — symbolized in the contrast of the
"Jesus of history" with the "Christ of faith" — lies behind
the scholars' *quest for the historical Jesus*. This "quest," a
dominant motif of nineteenth century Protestant theology,

especially in Germany, was a failure. As Alfred Loisy and Albert Schweitzer pointed out in the 1900's, the conclusions the questers reached resulted more from their own expectations than from the texts they were investigating.

The disappointing results of the quest led some critics to be sceptical of ever disentangling the threads of Jesus' life and thought from the embroidery of the authors of the New Testament. Yet new methods for studying biblical texts were developed, especially "form-historical" criticism. Finally, in the 1950's a "New Quest" for the historical Jesus began.

The New Quest acknowledged that it was practically impossible to reconstruct a chronology of the life of Jesus, to discover the inner-consciousness of Jesus, or to reach an unsurpassable understanding of Jesus' message. By recognizing the limits of their research, they hoped to have some definite, if limited, results. The New Questers believed that they could isolate some of the central and distinctive threads of Jesus' teaching, if they could find a test that they could apply to remove the embroidery. The principle they followed was that "whatever fits neither into Jewish thought nor the views of the later church can be regarded as authentic."[8] While rigorous application of this principle might well render some of Jesus' actual sayings historically dubitable, those sayings which passed the test well would provide a firm foundation on which to develop an understanding of the preaching and teaching of Jesus.

What the New Quest strongly reinforced was the view of a number of scholars that a central and distinctive part of the teaching of Jesus could be found in his parables. Hans Conzelmann, discussing Jesus' view of the Kingdom of God, put it this way:

> The parables form the given starting point for the reconstruction of Jesus' own view, since they contain an assured store of genuine tradition... Certainly they are painted over here and there with meanings given them by

[8]Hans Conzelmann, *Jesus*, trans. by J. Raymond Lord (Philadelphia: Fortress Press, 1973), p. 16.

the later church, but in many cases this secondary layer is easily removed (as demonstrated by the research of Jeremias). When this is done, the parables manifest a specific structure of mind toward the future: the kingdom is future, pressing near and now active in Jesus' deeds and preaching...This same structure is also manifested in a large number of logia [sayings], which are in the same form (J. M. Robinson). The genuineness of this core of material is proved not only through indications of form but also through the content, insofar as the connection of the future expectation with the person of Jesus presumes a unique, unrepeatable situation into which the post-Easter church could no longer retroject itself without further ado.[9]

That is, the parables appear most strongly to fulfill the requirements that show the central and distinctive teaching of Jesus himself: the connection of the coming kingdom with the words and deeds of Jesus (uncongenial to Jewish ideas at that time and to the later church).

Thus, recent biblical critics have highlighted the facts that we can recognize Jesus' teachings especially in his parables, that the gospels proclaiming and manifesting him are not written as history or biography, but as stories about him which express his effect on their tellers, and that the Jewish Bible, Christians' Old Testament, is not primarily composed of nascent science or divine commands merely illustrated by edifying stories, but is really the set of stories of God and his people. The fact that the Bible *contains* stories was supplanted by the recognition that the Bible is *composed of* stories — myths, legends, satires, allegories, histories, apocalyptic, parable, etc. This marks a significant shift in vision. The biblical narratives came to be seen not as secondary illustrations, but as the context in which the rest of the material was developed. Even the law codes would not really make sense except as part of the story of the Exodus. The rules and the "science" that occupied so much energy

[9]*Ibid.*, 74.

were not the main things, but rather abstractions from the main point — the stories.

Once one realizes, then, that "the ol' time religion," as the song has it, is a religion lived and told in story, one becomes much more interested in the stories of that religion. After all, if Jesus and his followers interpreted stories, revised stories, might what was "good enough for Paul and Silas" be good enough for contemporary theologians? Thus, biblical criticism contributes to the rise of story theology.

The Erosion of the Enlightenment Myths

A fourth factor significant for the emergence of story theology is the recent recognition that our basic notion of rationality is precipitated from a myth or set of myths about what it means to be human. As this myth constitutes our modern Western culture, to discuss it with clarity is difficult. As with many myths, it appears in various forms in different places and at different times. The rest of this section will discuss the four central convictions this myth grounds (human autonomy, evolutionary progress, the independent reality of the world, the separation of art from science) and conclude by showing the heart of the matter.

First, people who participate in this modern myth see each person as ideally or actually an autonomous individual. The ideal of autonomy peaks in the work of Ayn Rand. She sees rational self-interest as the only reasonable ethic. The characters in her novels proclaim the value of "I" as the only god worth worshipping and declare the only life worth living is a life for oneself. "I" is the ultimate value.

A rather different philosopher, John Rawls, defines acting autonomously as "acting from principles that we would consent to as free and equal rational beings."[10] Rawls claims that the *goal* of moral education is autonomy and that education to teach people to follow rules to which they

[10]John Rawls, *A Theory of Justice* (Cambridge, Mass.: Harvard University Press, 1971), p. 516.

consent is the center of morality. Rawls clearly values a person as a rule unto him or her self. What these two very different philosophers share — and exhibit in different forms — is an underlying presupposition that only the individual is ultimately the beneficiary of any action and that only the individual is the source of true value.

But are these presuppositions true? Can a Christian subscribe to autonomy as the *goal* of his or her morality? Many Christians would claim that *solidarity under God* is the proper goal. Others sensitive to ecological problems would claim that self-seeking is not a virtue, but a vice that has seriously harmed our environment. They might find *conservation* a virtue worth cultivating. Others might claim that seeing all humans as free, equal and rational will not help us find what is best for those who are truly enslaved or irrational or who do not have the possibility of determining their own goals. To adjudicate between these claims is beyond the scope of this book. But that they are debated shows the fragility of the modern myth of individual autonomy, the myth that only individuals can have or can make what is valuable by autonomous choices. That autonomy is the goal of morality is no longer the agreed-upon basis of ethical debate and moral choice.

The second conviction that comes out of the modern myths is the idea that evolution is progress. People as varied as Karl Marx, who thought human history was progressing to a social state of harmony and equality, and Pierre Teilhard de Chardin, who saw the cosmos evolving toward the goal of being all in Christ, have equated evolution with progress. Two spheres have been seen as the arenas of human progress: the moral and the intellectual. A clear articulation of this conviction comes in the work of the liberal (not Marxist), secular (not religious) philosophical position articulated by Charles Frankel. What he wrote in the following about the progress of morality can also be said of intellectual progress (with the proper adjustments):

In sum, although it is not possible to say in wholesale terms that there has been moral progress, it is possible to assert that the context of human behavior has changed and that the collective capacity to achieve human purposes, whether for good or ill, has enormously increased. The expectations which it is reasonable to impose on modern social arrangements are therefore justifiably higher than those that may have been reasonable in the past. In this modified but important sense it is fair to speak of moral progress.[11]

What Frankel evidently means by this is that we *can* now have more good *and* evil, and can now expect people together to do more good than in the past. Frankel supports, therefore, a "retail" view of moral, social, and intellectual progress.

But can we truly support the claim — whether wholesale or retail — that every day we are getting better and better? It presumes that our vast increase in data is an increase in wisdom. But that we have more data does not mean that we have a greater ability to cope with the world we live in than we used to have. In spite of the increase in data, nations have great trouble controlling mass violence; individuals are unable to "cope" with their world, in spite of more data. This view of progress also promotes the self-centered view that all those people and nations we dislike — in past and present — are backward. The view presumes that our progress in science is a truly human progress. It also presumes that we are approaching a goal, rather than wandering aimlessly. Yet the goal of "progress" is specified so differently by people like Teilhard de Chardin or Karl Marx, and so often not specified at all, that it is hard to see how one could warrant the claim that we are closer to our goal than our ancestors. This view presumes that we can identify our evolution as progress, not merely change, and while it may

[11]Charles Frankel, "Progress, The Idea of," in *The Encyclopedia of Philosophy*, ed. Paul Edwards (New York: Macmillan and Free Press, 1967), Vol. VI, p. 486; also see Robert Nisbet, *The History of the Idea of Progress* (New York: Basic Books, 1979).

be true that we have made progress in some areas, the presumptions ingredient in the myth of progress have become questioned so that many doubt them. The myth that equates change with progress needs to be validated or abandoned. It cannot be assumed.

The third conviction the myth(s) of modernity supports is the myth that there is a world "already-out-there-now-real" for us to become acquainted with. This conviction, hardly unique to modernity, leads us to believe that one of the most important problems we need to solve is to figure out how our *ideas* about what is there hook up with what *is* there really. Once we have figured that out, then we should be able to differentiate among those ideas that hook up with or mirror reality really well (and call them true) and those that don't (and call them false or distorted), for our true ideas will be the ones that we can see match the world and our false ones are those that we can see don't match or mirror reality. And since to know what our ideas are we must be able to express them, the central issue here is to see just how our language hooks onto the world. Once we see that, and see whether a specific statement does "hook on" in the correct manner, then we shall be able to see whether or not that statement is true.

But this account assumes that we can check the world directly to see if our statements match the world. It also assumes that we can see or know the world without having to be able to say anything about it. It assumes that we can know the world without talking about it. It is not so obvious that we *can* separate our language-about-the-world from the world so neatly. And even if we can make that separation, we are immediately re-involved with language if we are to say whether our *checking* is correct. And then we need to check our checking and check our checking of our checking and so on. . . . Finally, we cannot separate our talk of the world from the world. While there must be some sense in which reality is independent of what we say about it and know of it, we can no longer merely assume that we can check our language against the world. The problems with this view of the relation of language to reality may be soluble, but the fact that there are problems with this view suggests that the myth which grounds it may also have some problems which need to be solved.

The fourth conviction emerging from the myth(s) of modernity is that science is radically different from art. The former is cognitive, the latter imaginative. The former discovers, the latter creates. Science is HARD, art *soft*. Many find this disjunction tremendously important, for without it there seems no way to distinguish between matters of fact and matters of taste, between "objective" and "subjective," between "what is true" and "what I like."

But such a hard and fast distinction is as open to objection as much as the positivists' distinction between meaningful and meaningless language. We cannot assume that Galileo was *discovering* something about the universe. He may well have been *creating* scientific values.[12] The assumption that art is soft entails that Picasso's *Guernica* is either not art, or is soft, which is absurd. The assumption that they are radically different contrasts with Albert Einstein's belief that the most beautiful thing we can experience — the mysterious —is the source of both art and science. If we accept this distinction, we cannot explain how the best art *and* science reveal how the world is — and where we are in it — nor how the worst art *and* science conceal how things are. The problem, as John Dominic Crossan has diagnosed it, "is the very validity of the distinction itself." Crossan then continues:

> The most basic question for a theology...of story is whether there *is* any such direct, ordinary, objective, descriptive language as over against some other type, whether it is considered to be a higher or a lower type.[13]

While some of what we say and do is better than other things we say and do, to claim that this division coincides with the division between art and science is dubious, at best.

[12]Cf. Richard Rorty, *Philosophy and the Mirror of Nature* (Princeton: Princeton University Press, 1979), p. 331.

[13]John Dominic Crossan, *The Dark Interval: Towards a Theology of Story* (Niles, IL: Argus Communications, 1975), p. 26.

But what is this myth of modernity? The previous paragraphs have discussed the convictions that emerge from the myth, and by undermining these convictions' certainty have sought to bring the myth into question. The myth of modernity is *the story that kills stories.* Stanley Hauerwas and David Burrell tell the story in a precise way:

> The plot was given in capsule by Auguste Comte: first came religion in the form of stories, then philosophy in the form of metaphysical analysis, and then science with its exact methods. The story he tells in outline is set within another elaborated by Hegel, to show us how each of these ages supplanted the other as a refinement in the progressive development of reason. So stories are prescientific, according to the story legitimating the age which calls itself scientific. Yet if one overlooks that budding contradiction, or fails to spell it out because everyone knows that stories are out of favor anyway, then the subterfuge has been worked . . . . [14]

The myth of the enlightenment is a story that tells us we have outgrown stories. It tells us that narratives are irrelevant to truth and truth is irrelevant to narratives. It tells us that we are better off than our ancestors, for we are autonomous, we can distinguish truth from art, we know ourselves, and we know the world. They were inferior. However, it also tells us that these claims are not only clearly and simply true, but also not part of a story.

Are they true? Are they independent of narrative?

As Hauerwas and Burrell have shown, the myth of modernity condemns myth. Those who live within the modern world, yet fail to recognize how a paradoxical myth structures that world, are committed unwittingly to such a story. Of course, the haughty claims listed above might be true, but they are not independent of myth. The questions

[14]Stanley Hauerwas (with David B. Burrell), "From System to Story," in *Truthfulness and Tragedy: Further Investigations into Christian Ethics* (Notre Dame: University of Notre Dame Press, 1977), p. 25.

asked in this exposition do not overthrow the myth of progress. But there are *other* myths, countermyths and parables. In various ways, these render the status of the modern myth uncertain. Since we recognize the multiplicity of ways to construct a world, stories in which to live, and vehicles of meaning, we can take none for granted. We must be prepared to evaluate and appraise them.

Summary: *The Emergence of Narrative Theology*

We have seen how narrative theology has arisen. The churches and the churches' theologies have been shaken up. Critical philosophers have challenged believers to think through their faith and hinted at the centrality of narrative. The powerful arguments that sustain the claim that human experience is intrinsically durational in form have shown the need for narratives to report that experience. Biblical scholars have retrieved the centrality of the parables for the teaching of Jesus. Through the experience of the horrors of twentieth century wars and the critical arguments of various scholars, the myths of modernity have been unmasked.

All these movements and events have made the conditions right for a general resurgence of interest in myth and myth making over the last forty years. Constructive Christian theologians have naturally sought to tell the Christian stories in this context. So, a specifically Christian movement of narrative theology has emerged.

For Further Reading

For a general approach to the history, see James C. Livingston, *Modern Christian Thought: From the Enlightenment to Vatican II* (New York: Macmillan, 1971). In his concluding section, Livingston has practically nothing on narrative theology, although the background is portrayed in a balanced and readable way, with numerous excerpts from people discussed. A more radical approach is presented in the superb reader edited by William Miller, *The New Christianity* (New York: Dell Books, 1967). Miller's introductions to the excerpts provide an excellent approach to the theology that led up to and through the "death of god" movement. Perhaps the best comprehensive and balanced view of the general background can be discovered in the historical sections of Richard P. McBrien, *Catholicism* (Minneapolis: Winston Press, 1980). While McBrien's synthetic and propositional approach is very different from that of narrative theology (and thus I would disagree with him on many points), his encyclopedic text is a monumental achievement and the historical sections are especially clear and fair. A very broad historical treatment that takes narrative theology with full seriousness is William Clebsch, *Christianity in European History* (New York: Oxford University Press, 1979). His discussion of the modern epoch (chapter six) is very provocative and has influenced me greatly. His text is quite readable and nonetheless suggestive of novel approaches to religious history.

The challenge of the philosophy of language and the response to it by Christian theologians is the subject of T. W. Tilley, *Talking of God: An Introduction to Philosophical Analyses of Religious Language* (New York: Paulist, 1978). The notes and afterword of that text provide further reading suggestions. Although articles on aspects of religious language continue to appear in the journals, I see no real breakthroughs to new and better understandings from within the analytic tradition which is the subject of that book. The work of Paul Holmer, *The Grammar of Faith* (San Francisco: Harper and Row, 1978) is problematical as it stands, although his concentration on the formative power of narratives is very influential.

Stephen Crites has continued his work (see n. 3, above) in "Angels We Have Heard," in *Religion as Story*, ed. by James B. Wiggins (New York: Harper and Row, 1975), a varied set of short explorations of the significance of story for understanding religion. Wiggins' introduction is very helpful. In this vein the work of David Burrell, *Exercises in Religious Understanding* (Notre Dame: University of Notre Dame

Press, 1974) provides a group of narratives that help the reader to understand the lives of people who had deep religious convictions in different contexts.

A good basic history of the evolution of thought about the Bible is Dennis C. Duling, *Jesus Christ Through History* (New York: Harcourt, Brace, Jovanovich, 1979). Duling places the critical approach to biblical texts in the context of the history of biblical study from earliest Christianity to the present. A most important discussion of the loss of the understanding of the narrative structure of biblical texts is Hans W. Frei, *The Eclipse of the Biblical Narrative: A Study in Eighteenth and Nineteenth Century Hermeneutics* (New Haven: Yale University Press, 1974). Yet in the second half of the twentieth century that eclipse is surely waning. For example, Luis Alonzo-Schökel, *The Inspired Word: Scripture in the Light of Language and Literature* (New York: Herder and Herder, 1965) brings a complex theory of language to focus a study on the *text* of the Bible as the locus of inspiration. Alonzo-Schökel's work was in the vanguard of Catholic scholarship in approaching the Bible as a literary text. Frei's *The Identity of Jesus Christ: The Hermeneutical Bases of Dogmatic Theology* (Philadelphia: Fortress Press, 1975) naturally takes the narrative dimension of the text seriously.

The myth of the enlightenment is supported by Frankel (see n. 11 above and the works he cites). Nisbet (see n. 11) analyzes the various meanings of "progress." Richard Rorty and J. D. Crossan (see notes 12 and 13) attack the enlightenment myth in various ways, but the most sustained exploration and attack on it, with special attention to its moral implications is Alasdair MacIntyre, *After Virtue: A Study in Moral Theory* (Notre Dame: University of Notre Dame Press, 1981).

3

THE SHAPES OF STORIES

What I am calling a story *Matthew Arnold called
a* parable *and a* fairy tale. *Other terms which
might be used are* allegory, fable, tale, myth.
—R. B. Braithwaite[1]

Earliest narrative theology tended to lump together stories with a wide variety of form and function and to treat
them as if they were all the same. Some critics then dismissed all religious stories as "fairy-tales." But stories are far
more varied. The simplistic groupings of a Braithwaite and
the facile rejections of stories both should be rejected in
favor of a more nuanced approach to narrative theology.

The purpose of this chapter is to show the various shapes
of religious stories by taking representative samples from
the spectrum of stories. *Myths* are stories that set up worlds.
Their polar opposites are *parables*, stories that upset
worlds. Between these are *actions*, realistic stories set within
worlds. While some might prefer a more complex set of
analytical categories, for our purposes this structure will
provide us enough variety to avoid excessive amalgamation

---

[1]Richard Bevan Braithwaite, "An Empiricist's View of the Nature of Religious
Belief," in *Christian Ethics and Contemporary Philosophy*, ed. I. T. Ramsey
(London: SCM Press, 1966), p. 68.

and enough simplicity for a comprehensive exposition of the shapes stories take.

Stories That Set Up Worlds

In everyday talk, the word "myth" suggests a story which is false, pre-scientific, outdated, or for other reasons incredible. When some Christian theologians, such as Rudolf Bultmann, called for understanding the New Testament by "de-mythologizing" it, they were seeking to shuck the husk of the false, pre-scientific, outdated and incredible, from the kernel of the authentic teaching of Jesus. The success or failure of that program is irrelevant to our concerns here. For we shall use "myth" in a very different way.

A story is a myth if it "sets up" a world for people to dwell in or constitutes a tradition for people to live in. To label a story a myth in this sense is not to label it false (or true), but to recognize that the story does certain work and evokes certain sorts of responses. To understand that work and those responses, we can begin by considering a story taken from Nikos Kazantzakis' *Report to Greco*. The reporter in this somewhat autobiographical novel speaks in the following:

> Christ's every moment is a conflict and a victory. He conquered the invincible enchantment of simple human pleasures; He conquered every temptation, continually transubstantiated flesh into spirit, and ascended. Every obstacle in His journey became an occasion for further triumph, and then a landmark of that triumph. We have a model in front of us now, a model who opens the way for us and gives us strength.
>
> Blowing through heaven and earth, and in our hearts and the heart of every living thing, is a gigantic breath —a great Cry — which we call God. Plant life wished to continue its motionless sleep next to stagnant waters, but the Cry leaped up within it and violently shook its roots: "Away, let go of the earth, walk!" Had the tree been able

to think and judge, it would have cried, "I don't want to. What are you urging me to do! You are demanding the impossible!" But the Cry, without pity, kept shaking its roots and shouting, "Away, let go of the earth, walk!"

It shouted in this way for thousands of eons; and lo! as a result of desire and struggle, life escaped the motionless tree and was liberated.

Animals appeared — worms — making themselves at home in water and mud. "We're just fine here," they said. "We have peace and security; we're not budging!"

But the terrible Cry hammered itself pitilessly into their loins. "Leave the mud, stand up, give birth to your betters!"

"We don't want to! We can't!"

"You can't, but I can. Stand up!"

And lo! after thousands of eons man emerged, trembling on his still unsolid legs.

The human being is a centaur; his equine hoofs are planted in the ground, but his body from breast to head is worked on and tormented by the merciless Cry. He has been fighting again for thousands of eons, to draw himself, like a sword, out of his animalistic scabbard. He is also fighting — this is his new struggle — to draw himself out of his human scabbard. Man calls in despair, "Where can I go? I have reached the pinnacle. Beyond is the abyss." And the Cry answers, "I am beyond. Stand up!" All things are centaurs. If this were not the case, the world would rot into inertness and sterility.

As I walked hour after hour in the desert surrounding the monastery, God gradually began to liberate Himself from the priests. Thenceforth, the Lord for me was this Cry.[2]

This story *sets up a world*. It is a myth. The metaphor that is

[2]Nikos Kazantzakis, *Report to Greco*, trans. P. A. Bien (New York: Bantam Books, 1966), pp. 278-279. This is, of course, a very brief story, as are all the stories in this chapter. They are intended as examples rather than as full-blown representatives of their types. To be comprehensive would practically require another whole book.

the key to the story is "God is the Cry." Understanding *this* metaphor and accepting *this* myth reshapes the world in which the narrator lives and the life s/he leads.

Professor Joseph Campbell has analyzed the work that myths do into four areas. The first is a *religious* or *mythical* function. Myths "waken and maintain in the individual an experience of awe, humility, and respect, in recognition of that ultimate mystery, transcending names and forms, 'from which,' as we read in the Upanishads, 'words turn back.'"[3] In an era in which many cannot discern God acting in nature, Kazantzakis' story may construct a world in which a mystical or religious experience can again be possible in contemplating nature. But nature, for Kazantzakis, is not the tamed garden some Romantics and Transcendentalists of the nineteenth century admired. No, it is "red in tooth and claw," as Tennyson put it, threatening and awe-inspiring, demanding and upsetting. Nor is nature a Newtonian celestial machine spinning onward or a blind progress by survival of the fittest as Darwin put it. No, it is that lively sphere where entities develop by responding to a Cry which calls them to a challenging future. Kazantzakis' story may work as a myth as it construes the world so that a modern person can recognize its ultimate mystery.

The second function of a myth, according to Campbell, is its *cosmological* function. Simply, a myth must show where it all came from and where it all is going. Whether a myth is expressed as the creation of the world from a formless void by an ordering God, as the expansion of a primordial "Big Bang," or as the play of the gods, if a story purports to say where our world came from and where our world is going, it fulfills the cosmological function of a myth. In Kazantzakis' case, the world in which we live emerges in response to the Cry that is God. The world points us toward what the fearful perceive as an abyss, but what in reality is that Beyond where God is. In short, Kazantzakis' story exemplifies the

---

[3]Joseph Campbell, *The Masks of God: Creative Mythology* (New York: Penguin Books, 1976), p. 609. Campbell quotes from the Taittiriya Upanishad 2:9. He also calls this the mystical, metaphysical function of myth.

cosmological function of a myth as it construes the origin and destiny of the world.

The third function of myth is a *moral-social* function. Normally this is understood as "the validation and maintenance of an established order."[4] Traditional myths legitimate established forms of social government, promote the development of certain virtues and the avoidance of certain vices, and encourage obedience to certain rules. Which social structures, which virtues and which rules are established will vary from tradition to tradition. Clearly, however, Kazatzakis' story is not a traditional myth. It actually upsets one social structure, the Church: "As I walked hour after hour in the desert surrounding the monastery, God gradually began to liberate Himself from the priests." Nonetheless, it will promote a different form of life, a life of adventure. The virtues of the adventurous differ from the virtues of the monk. The rules to guide those who respond to the Cry are quite different from those which govern the folk who live in a different world with a different God. In short, while this myth encourages a certain style of morality and a certain adventurous social ethos, the order it maintains is significantly different from the order validated in more traditional Christian myths. That is not to say that Kazantzakis' story is not a myth, but merely that it is a myth that counters the myths we are used to encountering.

The fourth function of myth is a *psychological* one. An adequate mythology centers and harmonizes the life of an individual in the social structure which the myth has validated.[5] The myth gives a person a definite role to play in a society, a definite place to hold in the social structure, a specific orientation to harmonize the various aspects of his or her life. A traditional myth will provide definite and concrete models. One who follows the models is supported psychologically. However, in Kazantzakis' story, the role to be played is untraditional. The orientation is not to the structures in the society inherited from the past, as is typical

[4] *Ibid.*, p. 421.   [5] *Cf. ibid.*, p. 623.

in a conservative myth. Rather, the person constrained by
the inherited forms of the past ("the scabbard") must
voyage creatively and responsibly into the future. So that
the world will not "rot into inertness and sterility" the
challenge of novelty must be met. Naturally, this model is
not comfortable. Hence, the myth provides the support of
saying that one is not alone — not only have other humans
been cast in this role, but also the earlier forms of life have
played the role of respondent to the Cry. Thus, Kazantzakis'
story fulfills the fourth function of the myth by providing
cosmic support for the psyche likely to be troubled and
anxious at its plunge into the abyss or the beyond.

At this point, two likely demurs need to be mentioned.
The first is that we cannot compare the world-myth-sets-up
with the *world* (independent of any myth). John Shea, in his
discussion of what myths are and do, unfortunately seems to
imply that we can:

> Myth is that story or formulation which establishes the
> world within which we live and out of which we act. In P.
> L. Travers' instructive analogy — we live in myth "as an
> egg yolk in its albumen.". . . If a story or insight is to
> create world, it must introduce order into randomness
> and cast its shadow well beyond the temporal and spacial
> confines of its originating experience.[6]

While Shea begins well with his definition, his later claim
that myth orders randomness presumes that we can characterize the world (as random) *independent of myth*. This is
incorrect. In fact, the function of myth is not to order
randomness, but rather to show which events occur acciden-
tally, randomly or disorderedly, and which events are
planned, expected, or part of an order. Myths do give us the
patterns we see in the world. But that fact does not license us
to say that the world is without pattern. We simply *can't* say
that. The notions of pattern and randomness are interde-

---

[6]John Shea, *Stories of God: An Unauthorized Biography* (Chicago: Thomas
More Press, 1978), p. 52.

pendent. What they mean is specified in the context of myth. What the world *is* beyond myth can't be *said*.

The second is the claim that today we live in a world that is not structured by myth. In fact, as claimed in chapter two, one of the blights of the modern era is that we refuse to recognize that we live in a world constructed by myth. It is partly correct to attribute this view to the arrogance of the Enlightenment mindset. But another factor is the relativizing of all myths which has occurred in the modern era. Enlightenment critics came to see that no myth *as myth* could simply be accepted as true. This was because these thinkers were becoming aware of the many myths which set up many worlds in various cultures. As no one of them could be demonstrated as the true one — and the others as false — they saw all myths as useless.

This response was something unprecedented. In other times and places, a given community or tradition which became acquainted with myths counter to its own reacted rather differently. Usually a given culture (say the Jews) would hear the myths of another culture (say the Babylonians) only when these cultures collided with each other (as when the Babylonians carried off the Jews from Palestine to be slaves in Babylon during the sixth century B.C.E.). In a context of collision, one tradition has usually either *rejected* the other's as phony or mistaken, or has *revised* it for its own use (as the Jews reworked a Babylonian creation myth for their own [Genesis 1:1—2:4a]).

People of the Enlightenment, however, came to know other myths as scholars, rather than as soldiers or slaves. Rather than rejecting or adapting other myths, they began to create a world blind to the power of myth, for they were blind to the myth which constructed the Enlightened World. Within that world, however, are traditions which keep alive ancient myths, traditions which are faithful to fractured myths, and communities which seek to create new myths. The upshot is that the world in which we live is one in which many myths compete — sometimes subliminally and sometimes violently — to control the earth and the people on it.

In sum, a myth is a story that establishes a world. It directs people's religious awe, gives a sense of the whence and whither of the cosmos, establishes a social order, and provides psychological space. Not all myths succeed in performing all these duties; not all myths will be visible on the surface of a society (some will have to be uncovered); not all myths function equally well. Yet those who seek to live in a cosmos not established by myth will be unable to have a sense of who or where they are.

Stories That Upset Worlds

The polar opposite of myth is parable. A parable is a story which is set within a world created by myth and which functions to subvert the world in which it is set. A person will often be unnerved as a reaction to an effective parable. As John Dominic Crossan put it, "You can usually recognize a parable because your immediate reaction will be self-contradictory: 'I don't know what you mean by that story but I'm certain I don't like it.'"[7] As most of chapter five will be devoted to the parables of Jesus, here we can consider a story from a different story-teller:

The Master

And when the darkness came over the earth, Joseph of Arimathea, having lighted a torch of pine-wood, passed down from the hill into the valley. For he had business in his own home.

And kneeling on the flint stones of the Valley of Desolation he saw a young man who was naked and weeping. His hair was the colour of honey, and his body was as a white flower; but he had wounded his body with thorns, and on his hair he had set ashes as a crown.

And he who had great possessions said to the young man who was naked: "I do not wonder that your sorrow

[7]John Dominic Crossan, *The Dark Interval: Towards a Theology of Story* (Niles, IL: Argus Communications, 1975), p. 56.

is so great, for surely He was a just man."

And the young man answered: "It is not for Him that I am weeping, but for myself. I, too, have changed water into wine, and I have healed the leper and given sight to the blind. I have walked upon the waters, and from the dwellers in the tombs I have cast out devils. I have fed the hungry in the desert where there was no food, and I have raised the dead from their narrow houses; and at my bidding, and before a great multitude of people, a barren fig-tree withered away. All things that this man has done I have done also. And yet they have not crucified me."[8]

Can you make sense of the story? Are you baffled as to its significance? Does it annoy you? If so, then this story may have functioned as a parable for you.

For a story to work as a parable, the hearer has to accept the myth in which it is set. Here, the story presupposes the Christian myth of the uniqueness of Jesus' person and work. Could it be, the story hints, that Joseph of Arimathea might have met another just like Him had he been lucky? Could it be that He is recognized as a Messiah not because of what He did (which was common) but because of what was done to Him? Could other wonder-workers have been as just as He? Could it be that Christians might have believed in some other fellow as Savior had the circumstances been a bit otherwise? If this story has worked as a parable for you, then these sorts of questions which tend to subvert the Christian myth may arise. Or, to quote Crossan again: "You have built a lovely home, myth assures us; but, whispers parable, you are right above an earthquake fault."[9] Parables shake one's world to its foundations.

For a story to work as a parable, its hearer has to "get" it — much like "getting a joke." Yet even those who do not "get" a parable can understand how others might, just as scholars who do not accept a given myth can understand it

---

[8]Oscar Wilde, "The Master," in *Religion From Tolstoy to Camus*, selected, with an introduction and prefaces by Walter Kaufmann (New York: Harper and Row, 1964), pp. 259-260.

[9]Crossan, *The Dark Interval*, p. 57.

and see why others accept it. This is similar to seeing how a joke that flops in one context could be a side-splitter in another: "I can see that would be a really funny story at a fraternity party, but why he told it here in the convent, I'll never know." Even if one is not jolted by "The Master," because one is not a Christian or because one has heard it before or because one is not disturbed by that sort of story, one can see how it might subvert some people's worlds.

Parables must be distinguished from countermyths or antimyths. A countermyth or antimyth is a story that sets up a world in opposition to another myth. For example, presume that you live in a world structured by the traditional Christian myth of creation and redemption, or in a world constituted by the story above from *Report to Greco*. Then consider the following story:

> To Dr. Faustus in his study Mephistopheles told the history of the Creation, saying:
>
> "The endless praises of the choirs of angels had begun to grow wearisome; for after all, did he not deserve their praise? Had he not given them endless joy? Would it not be more amusing to obtain undeserved praise, to be worshipped by beings whom he tortured? He smiled inwardly, and resolved that the great drama should be performed.
>
> "For countless ages the hot nebula whirled aimlessly through space. At length it began to take shape, the central mass threw off planets, the planets cooled, boiling seas and burning mountains heaved and tossed, from black masses of cloud hot sheets of rain deluged the barely solid crust. And now the first germ of life grew in the depths of the ocean, and developed rapidly in the fructifying warmth into vast forest trees, huge ferns springing from the damp mould, sea monsters breeding, fighting, devouring, and passing away. And from the monsters, as the play unfolded itself, Man was born, with the power of thought, the knowledge of good and evil, and the cruel thirst for worship. And Man saw that all is passing in this mad, monstrous world, that all is strug-

gling to snatch, at any cost, a few brief moments of life before Death's inexorable decree. And Man said: 'There is a hidden purpose, could we but fathom it, and the purpose is good; for we must reverence something, and in the visible world there is nothing worthy of reverence.' And Man stood aside the struggle, resolving that God intended harmony to come out of chaos by human efforts. And when he followed the instincts which God had transmitted to him from his ancestry of beasts of prey, he called it Sin, and asked God to forgive him. But he doubted whether he could be justly forgiven, until he invented a divine Plan by which God's wrath was to have been appeased. And seeing the present was bad, he made it yet worse, that thereby the future might be better. And he gave God thanks for the strength that enabled him to forgo even the joys that were possible. And God smiled; and when he saw that Man had become perfect in renunciation and worship, he sent another sun through the sky, which crashed into Man's sun; and all returned again to nebula.

" 'Yes,' he murmured, 'it was a good play; I will have it performed again.' "

Such, in outline, but even more purposeless, more void of meaning is the world which Science presents for our belief. Amid such a world, if anywhere, our ideals henceforward must find a home.[10]

This story, while it may upset those whose worlds are constructed by other myths, is not a parable, but a countermyth.

Although the story utilizes terms and ideas from other, more traditional myths, it does not presuppose acceptance of them on the part of its hearers. Because it is told in rather straightforward terms, it does not have to be "gotten" as a joke does. Finally, it clearly fulfills the cosmological, social and psychological functions of a myth as its author shows in

---

[10]Bertrand Russell, "A Free Man's Worship" (1903) in *Mysticism and Logic* (Garden City, NY: Doubleday, n.d.), pp. 44-45.

subsequent paragraphs of his essay (and it may even have a perverse "mystical" or religious function). Hence, although it is a story intended to overthrow traditional religious views, it does not do so by working within the story, but by telling a new story and creating a new myth. Thus, it is not a parable, but a countermyth.

To distinguish countermyth from parable is crucial. A countermyth sets up a new world to compete with one created by the old myth. A parable rocks the foundations of the old myth by working within the world it structures. Once hearers "get" a parable, they may be able to see the new possibilities in their old myths and to uncover new insights generated by the unleashing of their tamed metaphors, if they are flexible enough to admit the new through the seams and edges of their worlds. If hearers are rigid, they will either reject the parable or be so startled as to have to reject their own myth because they are so unsettled. They will then have to set up a new one by discovering or creating a counter-myth. A countermyth is proposed as an alternative to the old myth. A parable proposes no alternatives, but leaves room either to see life in the old or to construct something new.

In sum, parables are stories which subvert the mythic world in which they are told. How people respond varies. Some people "get" them. Others don't. Some have their worlds transformed. Others have their worlds destroyed. Parables work to reveal the unexpected, subvert the normal, cast out certainty to make room for hope, and thus provoke various responses. They are dangerous stories.

Stories Set In Worlds

Actions are stories set within worlds. Unlike myths, actions do not set up worlds, but rather presume a world in which the story can take place. Unlike parables, actions do not subvert worlds, but explore what happens in a world. Most of the stories we tell and hear fit in this category. Generally, actions can be described as realistic narratives.

For most purposes, theorists break this category into two parts: factual stories and fictional stories. In the former part, histories, biographies and autobiographies are the major types. These are stories of the past, whether recent or distant. The latter category includes novels, allegories and fairy-tales. These are stories that may be time-irrelevant. The distinction between these is whether the story is intended to present the "significance" of life in a world. Hence, the standards by which one judges a good action story, for most purposes, differ: a good history will not be judged by the same criteria as a good fairy tale. A fairy tale has no specific "facts" to represent, while a history, by definition, does. To say that a fairy tale is not true (that is, doesn't present historical facts) does not count against the fairy-tale; to say the same thing about a history damns it.

For our purposes, however, such splintering of the category of *actions* is unnecessary. The point of an action story is to *reveal how things go in a world*, whether the form of the story is factual or fictional. This does not mean that a religious story can prescind from accurate representation of facts. When any story is presented as factual, it must represent facts adequately and accurately to be successful. But remember the fictional story about Sheppard and the factual story about Rubin. Both *primarily* intend to reveal the way things go in our world. *How* they reveal differentiates them. O'Connor constructed a fictional narrative. Whether their action stories do reveal the way things are is independent of *what* they reveal, an issue different from the form of the story. To illustrate this point consider the following stories:

> A rabbi, whose grandfather had been a pupil of Baal Shem Tov, was once asked to tell a story. "A story ought to be told," he said, "so that it is itself a help," and his story was this. "My grandfather was paralyzed. Once he was asked to tell a story about his teacher and he told how the holy Baal Shem Tov used to jump and dance when he was praying. My grandfather stood up while he was telling the story and the story carried him away so much that he had

to jump and dance to show how the master had done it. From that moment, he was healed. This is how stories ought to be told."[11]

"Listen, my child," [St. Francis] said, "each year at Easter I used to watch Christ's Resurrection. All the faithful would gather round His tomb and weep, weep inconsolably, beating on the ground to make it open. And behold! In the midst of our lamentations the tombstone crumbled to pieces and Christ sprang from the earth and ascended to heaven, smiling at us and waving a white banner. There was only one year I did not see Him resurrected. That year a theologian of consequence, a graduate of the University of Bologna, came to us. He mounted the pulpit in church and began to elucidate the Resurrection for hours on end. He explained and explained until our heads began to swim; and that year the tombstone did not crumble, and, I swear to you, no one saw the Resurrection."[12]

Each of these stories says something important about the world in which it is set. Each of them also has something important to say about stories. For these points, it makes no significant difference whether these actions are factual (historically true) or fictional (imaginatively constructed).

An action is a realistic narrative which helps a person to explore the contours of a world. Depending on the context in which it is told and the purposes for which it is told, its facticity may be irrelevant. Further, different people can understand the same story differently and appreciate it in different ways. When those understandings differ, people can expand their own understandings by exploring their differences and rethinking the world they share. Even when realistic narratives are differently interpreted, they help explore worlds.

[11]Martin Buber, *Werke* III (Munich, 1963), p. 71; cited from J. B. Metz, *Faith in History and Society: Toward a Practical Fundamental Theology*, trans. David Smith (New York: Seabury Press, 1980), pp. 207-208.

[12]Nikos Kazantzakis, *Saint Francis* (New York: Simon and Schuster, 1962), p. 231; cited from Shea, *Stories of God*, p. 69.

Summary: The Shapes of Christian Stories

The point of this chapter has been to differentiate among the types of stories by showing the different shapes stories take and the different functions each type has. If one tries to reduce stories to "all one type" or to use the term "story" indiscriminately, one will produce a theology simply inadequate to account for all the work stories do. A narrative theology of myth without parable would be stifling; of parable without myth would be baffling; of action alone would be boring. Narrative theology must attend to all the types of stories.

For Further Reading

The present chapter has been deeply influenced by the work of John Dominic Crossan (n. 7, above and chapter five, *passim*). Crossan's important contribution, all too often neglected by narrative theologians, is his exploration of the function of parable in relation to myth. Crossan also breaks up "actions" into three types: apologues (stories which defend worlds), actions (stories which investigate worlds) and satires (stories which attack worlds), following Sheldon Sacks, *Fiction and the Shape of Belief: A Study of Henry Fielding with Glances at Swift, Johnson and Richardson* (Chicago: University of Chicago Press, 1964). However, as these are generally categories of fiction and as many theological stories claim to be factual, such a complex division of realistic narratives is not needed here.

By contrast, John Navone tends to treat all stories as if they were actions. *The Jesus Story: Our Life as Story in Christ* (Collegeville, MN: The Liturgical Press, 1979) and *Tellers of the World* (New York: Le Jacq Publishing, 1981), with Thomas Cooper, both neglect the mythic and parabolic functions of some stories, and the fact that we have many stories of Christ. As exploration of the shape of Christian lives, however, *The Jesus Story* provides an interesting analysis and theology of action stories and a section devoted to useful summaries of some other theologians concerned with narrative. As exploration of how narrative theology can be an expression of transcendental Thomist cognitional theory, *Tellers of the World* provides clear conceptual links with more traditional forms of propositional theology.

J. B. Metz sees the relation of transcendental Thomism and narrative theology very differently. In *Faith in History and Society* (n. 11 below), he offers a plea for a narrative theology as the way to free transcendental theology from tautologous wordspinning (154-168). Yet Metz also includes the work of Rahner in a positive way (205-228). So although narrative theology is in tension with propositional-transcendental theology, Metz finds that tension creative and politically important as well. The political implications of narrative theology and the social aspects of narrative theology appear in his *Followers of Christ* (New York: Paulist Press, 1978).

Some of the finest stories from religions of the Biblical tradition appear in the works of Martin Buber and Elie Wiesel: Martin Buber, *Tales of the Hasidim*, Two Volumes (New York: Schocken Books, 1961) and Elie Wiesel, *Souls on Fire* (New York: Random House, 1972) and *Messengers of God* (New York: Random House, 1976).

4

STORIES OF "THE END": ESCHATOLOGY

Oh, when the moon drips red with blood,
Oh, when the moon drips red with blood,
Lord, I want to be in that number,
When the moon drips red with blood.
—a verse of "When the Saints Go Marchin' In"

The problem of understanding the meanings of stories of the end of time has perplexed Christians for millennia. Often they have tried to discover whether they would be counted among the saints in the final days or on which day the final judgment or the Second Coming would occur by discovering a key to unlock the mysteries of these eschatological stories. The results of such attempts have been wildly divergent. This chapter undertakes an extended exercise in this difficult area in order to show the strengths and necessity of narrative theology. We will not be able to tell the "final story" in this chapter, but will show how to understand eschatological stories and why the *stories* are important. The first section lays out a theory of interpreting stories of the end, based in the work of Karl Rahner. The second section applies the theory to an eschatological story from the New Testament. The final section criticizes the work of some contemporary theologians who ignore the logic of story.

The Hermeneutics of Eschatological Assertions

The mouth-filling title of this section is the title of an important article by the late Roman Catholic theologian, Karl Rahner. The principles of interpretation (hermeneutics) for statements or propositions (assertions) about the events of the final end of individuals and humanity collectively (eschatology) which Rahner developed must be adapted to interpret stories, but can still serve as a guide. This section could be titled, *how to puzzle out stories of the end.*

Many Christians have believed that the Bible reveals certainly some events which will occur at the end of time. Usually they have extracted specific *sentences* from the biblical stories and construed them as Divine Statements Infallibly Revealing The Course of Future Events. By doing this, however, they have extracted an assertion or metaphor from the narrative in which it was embedded and which determined what it could mean. When this connection is lost, losing the original force of the utterance is risked because this extraction makes the meaning of the removed assertion or metaphor independent of the story. Such loose assertions can then come to mean almost anything and free metaphors can come to carry incredible implications.

For example, the force of many of the central utterances in eschatological stories in the Bible is that of *threat.* "If you keep on doing what you're doing," the story-teller warns, "you'll be in trouble with God!" These stories are often fables or fantastic images of the future either in or out of this world. Yet when sentences used as threats are extracted from the stories, they can become *predictions.* Then they are read back into the stories as predictions, and the stories are read as coded glimpses of the future, shown to the authors who had to write in code at God's dictation.

Then, people attempt to interpret the hidden meaning of the Scriptures, sure that if they can but break the code, they will come to know all about the future events. Such a process leads some today to claim that the picture of Armageddon (Rev 16) is a code for the nuclear holocaust that threatens the earth. Yet not only does such a procedure loosen a metaphor or saying from a story, reinterpret it without any warrant, and then read it back into the story to change the narrative's meaning, but also this "method" has a long history of use.

The story of William Miller (1782-1849) is just one illustration of such interpretation. This devout Baptist farmer and preacher intensely studied the apocalyptic books of the Bible and concluded that the second coming of Christ would occur between March 21, 1843 and March 21, 1844. In the 1830's his preaching in New York and New England stirred up quite a fervor in some of the evangelical churches. The movement blossomed throughout the U.S. It did, however, lose some of its intensity in 1845. It split up into various sects, including the Adventist churches, which today still remind us that the end is coming — something worth remembering. They have left off, however, being so specific as to the date of the end.

While one may admire the intensity and sincerity of literal millennialists and pre-millennialists like Miller and rejoice over the long-term effects of their ideas, this sort of interpretation involves serious theological problems. Two stand out. First, if God could reveal the day of the End, then why did he reveal it so obscurely that so many good people throughout history have mistaken the day and the time? Why was God not more plain? The typical answer is that God did reveal the secrets, but in a manner so that only the right people could figure them out. This response resurrects the heresy of gnosticism, that by having a "secret knowledge" one could be saved. However, resurrecting heresy has not been a concern to literal millennialists or pre-millennialists.

Second, what we know is determined not only by that

which is known or by the person who reveals something to us, but also by our capacity to understand what we know or the person who speaks. A brilliant theologian may know a great deal about her or his research area. But what s/he can communicate to an audience will depend partly on the capacity they have to hear and absorb what s/he says. Even if God told the Seer of Patmos that two hundred 20-megaton nuclear bombs would devastate the earth in 1987, the Seer's own conceptual and linguistic limitations would make it impossible for him to make sense out of what God said. Further, if people presume that God did speak directly to the Seer, that the Seer was inspired by God, and that the Seer could not make God's message clearer and speak more plainly, they must also believe that they are either more inspired or more intelligent than the Seer if they try to translate the Divine Message into more comprehensible terms. They therefore place themselves in a more exalted position than the biblical text. They imply that the Bible is not really final. We need to find an approach less vicious, one that seeks to discern what a writer meant when he wrote, and to apply — if possible — his meaning in our time, rather than one that degrades the Seer beneath the interpreter.

In order to understand the forces of stories of the future properly, an interpreter also needs to take seriously the fantastic aspects integral to them. They are *not* stories about the world in which we live, but are quite "out of this world." In fact, they are stories of another world. This means that we cannot presume that the principles for interpreting them are the same as the principles for interpreting stories set in the world in which we ordinarily live. To assume that the world in which these stories are set is a world like the ordinary is "false and primitive."[1] We cannot reduce these narratives or the fantastic worlds which they presume to the ordinary world. We cannot assume that they are a continuation of the ordinary. Nor can we assume that they are merely a code for the ordinary and everyday present. They are both *future* and

---

[1] Karl Rahner, "Hermeneutics of Eschatological Assertions," *Theological Investigations* IV (Baltimore: Helicon Press, 1966), p. 324.

extraordinary, and those aspects cannot be dismissed from the story.

A more useful way to interpret stories of the future begins by setting the limits within which we can attempt to understand such texts. Rahner finds two limiting principles important: (1) "It is certain from scripture that God has *not* revealed to man the day of the end"; and (2) that man is essentially historical, "a being involved in history."[2] This implies a distinction between eschatology and apocalyptic. Apocalyptic takes stories of the future as spectator's reports of events at the end of time, somehow beamed back. This denies the hiddenness of the future affirmed in (1). Eschatology takes stories of the future as speculations about the future which grow out of the present. This properly preserves the hiddenness of the future.

Since humans are intrinsically historical, Rahner suggests that our "knowledge of the future, insofar as it is still to come is an inner moment of the self-understanding of man in his present hour of existence — *and grows out of it*."[3] Our understanding of what *will be* must be rooted in what *is*. Our stories of the future must make explicit the fact that the present-we-are-in leads to the future-that-will-be, and suggest what sort of future can arise from the present. We also cannot imply that we can control the future, for we can't. We can only prepare for it. Apocalyptic suggests either we can control the future or our present life has no real impact on the real future, thus denying (2), that humans are intrinsically historical. Eschatology warns us to prepare always for the future, for the future will emerge from our present. Rahner summarizes this nicely:

> The apocalyptic suggestion is either phantasy or gnosticism; it does not merely suppose, as Christians also must, that the future only exists in the inaccessible mystery of God as such, which remains within the light inaccessible; it also unwittingly supposes that the future already leads of itself a supra-temporal existence, of which history is

[2] *Ibid.*, p. 329, 330.   [3] *Ibid.*, p. 331.

> only the projection on the screen of worthless time, and
> that time is not the real ground from which the eternal
> validity of man emerges, but a nothingness which is
> unmasked and really eliminated in this gnostic contact
> with true reality, called apocalypsis.[4]

Apocalyptic destroys the meaning of the world in which we
live and which Christians believe Christ redeems. It asserts
that the future is beyond the grace of God, fixed and immu-
table. An apocalyptic reading of stories of the future is
incompatible, therefore, with the faith portrayed by the
central stories of Christianity. Apocalypticists (in the sense
discussed) and millennialists have been flirting with heresy
because they read their own favorite story wrong, because
they raise it to the level of a single absolute, and because they
neglect the more central stories of redemption in the Christian tradition.

Eschatological Judgment: Separating Sheep from Goats

In the New Testament, only one story portrays a *final*
judgment. While many scholars think that this story had
been elaborated upon during the period from the time of
Jesus' teaching to the time of Matthew's writing (some fifty
years), the judgment of T. W. Manson cannot be reasonably
disputed: "Whether or not it belongs as a whole and in all its
details to the authentic teaching of Jesus, it certainly contains features of such startling originality that it is difficult
to credit this to anyone but the Master Himself."[5] It provides a test case for our principles of interpreting eschatological stories.

> When the Son of man comes in his glory, and all the
> angels with him, then he will sit on his glorious throne.

[4] *Ibid.*, p. 337.

[5] T. W. Manson, *The Sayings of Jesus* (London: SCM Press, 1967 [original
edition, 1937]), p. 249.

Before him will be gathered all the nations, and he will separate them one from another as a shepherd separates the sheep from the goats, and he will place the sheep at his right hand, but the goats at the left. Then the King will say to those at his right hand, "Come, O blessed of my Father, inherit the kingdom prepared for you from the foundation of the world; for I was hungry and you gave me food, I was thirsty and you gave me drink, I was a stranger and you welcomed me, I was naked and you clothed me, I was sick and you visited me, I was in prison and you came to me." Then the righteous will answer him, "Lord, when did we see thee hungry and feed thee, or thirsty and give thee drink? And when did we see thee a stranger and welcome thee, or naked and clothe thee?" And the King will answer them, "Truly, I say to you, as you did it to the least of these my brethren, you did it to me." Then he will say to those at his left hand, "Depart from me, you cursed, into the eternal fire prepared for the devil and his angels; for I was hungry and you gave me no food, I was thirsty and you gave me no drink, I was a stranger and you did not welcome me, naked and you did not clothe me, sick and in prison and you did not visit me." Then they also will answer, "Lord, when did we see thee hungry or thirsty or a stranger or naked or sick or in prison and did not minister to thee?" Then, he will answer them, "Truly, I say to you, as you did it not to one of the least of these, you did it not to me." And they will go away into eternal punishment, but the righteous into eternal life (Matt 25:31-46, RSV).

There is much to be interpreted in this vivid story, with its suggestions of *threat* and *promise*, its fantastic imagery, and its eschatological motifs.

To understand this story, it must be placed, as must all eschatological stories in the New Testament, against the background of the Hebrew Scriptures. Simply put, the hope of Israel was that the covenant God had made with one nation would be expanded to encompass all the nations of the earth. Thus the God of Israel would rule all the earth.

During Jesus' time, these hopes were often expressed in the language of apocalyptic imagery, images of "terrors and woes preceding the coming of the Messiah, the convulsions of nature, the frightful battle between angelic hosts and the legions of Satan." The final outcome of these cataclysms would be "the establishment of a temporal reign of the righteous, the resurrection of the dead, the final judgment, the punishment of the wicked, and the creation of a new heaven and earth."[6] Scholars continue to debate to which popular or scriptural writings this story alludes, and which ideas were prominent while Jesus was teaching. However, the primary point of this utterance is the expression of the hope for the coming of the reign of God over all.

Given this context and the hermeneutical principles discussed above, this story cannot be interpreted as merely referring to the present or to the decisions that people must make. Nor can it be understood as communicating sure knowledge about a future event or state of affairs. Yet this story has often been understood as providing a picture of the last days, seen through a "telescope through time" which gives the viewers a glimpse of something-that-already-exists-in-the-future which can't be changed. Some have thought this "proves" the reality of a heaven and a hell, a claim that goes far beyond the story as told. If we are to avoid such apocalyptic interpretation, how can we interpret the story?

The first point to get clear on is where Jesus appears in the story. The obvious place to see him is on the judgment throne. But that place is future to us — the final judgment is not here and now. Yet from that point, the King identifies where he was *all the time*, in every present. If Jesus is to be identified with the King, and the King declares his identification with the deprived, the suffering, the lonely, and the outcast, then Jesus is to be found there, too. This eschatological story speaks from the imagined future to every person who would find Jesus in every present.

---

[6]Van A. Harvey, "Eschatology," *A Handbook of Theological Terms* (New York: Macmillan, 1964), p. 81.

Second, the actions the King performs in that imagined future speak to each moment. The sheep and the goats are separated on the basis of what they *do* in *every* present, on the basis of what *acts* they perform. The typical — and badly strained — interpretation of the significance of what the sheep and the goats have done is "that the decisions made by man now in relation to Jesus are determinative of their destiny in the age to come."[7] Such a reading is correct in that it sees that *what we do now* conditions *what we will be*. But this is not the point of the story. The king does not separate the sheep from the goats on the basis of their *decisions*. The repeated question, "When did we *see thee*?" suggests that the problem is not one of decision. No one would decide against the king if s/he could see him. Rather, the problem is one of *vision*.

Thus, if we were to take this to be an apocalyptic picture of the future, we would have to conclude that the king's judgment is rather capricious. He blesses those who didn't know him, but somehow did right anyway, and curses those who didn't know him and failed to do right. Now if we take the judgment of the king as based on the decisions they made, we can eliminate the arbitrariness. But this reading ignores the perplexity of the sheep and the goats — a perplexity which they share. To take this story as a *picture* of what will happen to people in the future undermines the story. Either the king is capricious or the perplexity of the animals (people?) is incomprehensible.

Rather, the story is to be understood neither as a picture nor as a prediction, but as a *threat* and a *warning*. Whoever is blind to the identification of the king with the suffering will get what the goats got. Whoever can see the king in the suffering people and act well will both see and do what is right. The story warns against being either sheep or goats. Christians can be saved the fate of being blind sheep or blind and foolish goats if they can see where the king is. The story does not predict what will happen in the end, but warns us

[7]Howard Clark Kee, "The Gospel According to Matthew," *The Interpreter's One Volume Commentary on the Bible*, edited by Charles M. Laymon (Nashville: Abingdon Press, 1971), p. 639.

that we need to learn to see if we want to avoid the predicament the story presents: a seemingly capricious judgment. It alerts us that our future grows out of not only what we decide to do, but also what we see in the present.

Further, this story functions as a parable which must startle the hearer and reveal the unexpected. It must reveal the hidden place of the king in this present world, and that place must be a surprise. As John R. Donahue concludes, this eschatological parable warns "Christians of all ages that they must discover not only what the doing of justice is but where justice is to be located. As in the Old Testament the marginal ones become the touchstone for the doing of justice."[8] This story is not a *myth* in that it does not create a world for people to inhabit, but presumes the world created by the apocalyptic expressions of hope of Jesus' time. Nor is this story an *action* set in the future. It is a true *parable* which, if it is to work, must so challenge our perceptions of the present that we can see our world anew. The point of the story is to reveal what happens if we walk our paths in blindness. Yet those who will see the King where he is here and now will see him then and there, too.

Modern Eschatologies: Some Critical Notes

The frequent recurrences of apocalyptic millennialism in the Christian traditions give eloquent witness to people's desire to have answers to questions about the ultimate destiny of each and of all. The Bible provides no answers about the time and place of the End. Biblical interpreters may be even less helpful than the text itself. Yet the questions do not go away and Christian theologians have tried to answer them. In the present section two recent views of "the End of humanity" proferred by propositional theologians Karl Rahner and John Hick are evaluated from the perspective provided by narrative theology.

---

[8]John R. Donahue, "Biblical Perspectives on Justice," *The Faith That Does Justice,* edited by John C. Haughey (New York: Paulist Press, 1977), p. 105.

In his magisterial *Foundations of Christian Faith*, Karl Rahner, S.J., asserts that Christian eschatology can and must say what a Christian view of humanity says — no more and no less. Rahner considers both the destiny of the individual and the destiny of humanity. His position is complex and subtle.

Regarding individual salvation, Rahner makes four negative claims. First, Christians cannot understand heaven and hell as parallel destinies at the end of each person's life. They are better considered as possible ends each might reach. Although they are radically different, they should not be thought of as "two sides to the same coin." Second, Christians cannot resolve the ambiguities of the present situation by a doctrine of universal salvation. While "universal salvation" can properly answer one question, e.g., "What does God want for humanity?" that does not imply what *my* own end will be. Third, Christians cannot declare that any person is certainly lost. To declare that would mean that the declarer knew the limits of God's unlimited love — a presumptuous and unchristian view. Fourth, eternal life is not merely "changing horses at death" and riding on. Rather, death and eternal life must be considered to be "time's own mature fruit," what happens when time is full and fulfilled.[9]

Rahner also draws four positive conclusions about the end of individuals from the Bible. First, in the biblical tradition, every person is valuable enough to become eternal. Unlike the tradition of Greek tragedies, where only the leaders are made immortal, the Bible renders everyone valuable. Second, in the Johannine tradition, the notion of eternity is not something added to history, but grows from within history. Hence, "eternal life" is not merely something postponed until after death, but is a quality of life that begins in the present life. Third, the content of the life of the dead is given only in images in the Scripture. These images, I would add, are metaphors alive in stories. And there is no way to get behind those stories to God who is "absolute

---

[9]Karl Rahner, *Foundations of Christian Faith*, translated by William V. Dych (New York: Seabury Press, 1978), p. 437.

mystery."[10] Finally, those who are alive and have not died in the Lord can let those images and stories speak of that ineffable happiness, for nothing can be said that tells us any more than those stories do.

In response to the question of the salvation of humanity, Rahner has a precisely nuanced answer which Eugene Kennedy has preserved:

> Rahner has consistently described a vision of the universe in which all men and women ultimately will be saved by a loving God who is beyond our comprehension.
>
> "An orthodox theologian," Rahner says dryly, "is forbidden to teach that everybody will be saved. But we are allowed to *hope* that all will be saved. If I hope to be saved, it is necessary to hope that for all men as well. If you have reason to love another, you can hope that all will be saved."[11]

The doctrine of universal salvation does not express what an orthodox Christian believes. It answers the question of what s/he hopes.

If Rahner is to meet his own hermeneutical standards, his reflections on the destiny of humanity must be relevant to the present situation and grow out of it. He shows this in his reflection upon the unity and difference of loving God and loving humanity. There can be no love of God without loving the neighbor, although love of God cannot be reduced to loving the neighbor. In the active love of neighbor, "the miracle of the love and of the self-communication in which God gives himself to man" happens. Loving God and loving the neighbor are connected in Christology: "man and God are not the same, but neither are they ever separate."[12] Thus, Rahner takes seriously not only the practice recommended in Matthew 25, but also the Christology

---

[10]*Ibid.*, p. 441.

[11]Eugene Kennedy, "Quiet Mover of the Catholic Church," *New York Times Magazine*, September 23, 1979, pp. 66-67.

[12]Cf. Rahner, *Foundations*, p. 447.

suggested by that eschatological parable. When humans recognize needs and act on the basis of that recognition, they are fully with God. In short, eternal life, life with God, grows out of historical life.

I would argue that Rahner uses the propositions of systematic theology as a type of "literary criticism." His work provides both positive and negative guides for understanding the images of the End and stories of the future. He neither pretends to know the "Real Truth" lurking behind the stories nor seeks to remove the End from the present or reduce the End to the present. Because he treats eschatological assertions as irreducible images and stories, his propositional theology interprets, but does not supplant, those images and stories. In sum, Rahner's propositional theology derives from and respects the integrity of the narratives which are the core of the Christian tradition.

John Hick takes a rather different approach. In *Death and Eternal Life*, he attempts to write a "global theology" that integrates and unifies as far as possible all the various strands of religious belief on this globe. After an extensive survey (nearly 400 pages) of the beliefs of the religions and humanisms of the world, he reaches the conclusion that "the persisting self-conscious ego will continue to exist after bodily death. We shall not, however, in most cases attain immediately to the final 'heavenly' state."[13] Most of us will have to go through an intermediate state in which the last vestiges of our selfishness are cast off. In short, a liberal Protestant theologian has resurrected a doctrine of purgatory from the limbo to which Protestants consigned it centuries ago in order to assemble a collage of the End of humanity.

Hick claims that in our present state, we see each other only "through the slits of separate ego-masks." Inspired by the one-in-threeness and three-in-oneness of the doctrine of the Trinity, the final state will be one of "total community which is one-in-many and many-in-one, existing in a state

---

[13] John Hick, *Death and Eternal Life* (San Francisco: Harper and Row, 1980 [first published, 1976]), p. 399.

which is probably not embodied and probably not in time."[14] Now we are selfish and separate. In the end we will be selfless sharers of ourselves, without bodies and without time.

Like Rahner, Hick sees Christology as a key. But the Christology is quite different. For Hick, Jesus was the perfect man, love incarnate who lived "in ideal relationship to Ultimate Reality so far as this is possible for a single individual prior to the perfecting of humanity as a whole."[15] This "overcautious, rationalistic humanism"[16] allows Hick to declare that the Christians' mystical Body of Christ, the Hindus' universal Atman which we all are, and the Mahayana Buddhists' self-transcending unity in the Dharma Body of the Buddha all really mean the same thing: "the wholeness of ultimately perfected humanity beyond the existence of separate egos."[17]

But unlike Rahner, Hick seeks to supplant the images and stories which structure the religious traditions and neglects to respect their narrative integrity. First, Hick's interpretation of eschatology is apocalypticizing. He takes the *stories* as ultimately *pictures* of the future, rather than as narratives extrapolating to the future. He then tries to assemble these pictures he has drawn from the traditions into a complete, global canvas. He thus loses the narrative quality of the stories and their ability to express hope and fear and to be used to warn. Although the content differs, Hick makes the same basic move as the millennialists in interpreting eschatological stories: the stories are construed as pictures of the future.

Second, Hick's syncretism removes what is distinctive and interesting from the various eschatological stories told by the many religious traditions on this globe. For instance, he conflates the Dharma-body of the Buddha (which is a

---

[14]*Ibid.*, p. 464.   [15]*Ibid.*

[16]William H. Thompson, "The Hope for Humanity: Rahner's Eschatology," *A World of Grace: An Introduction to the Themes and Foundations of Karl Rahner's Theology,* edited by Leo J. O'Donovan (New York: Seabury Press, 1980), p. 156.

[17]Hick, *Death and Eternal Life,* p. 464.

spiritual abstraction) with the Mystical Body of Christ (which is a tamed metaphor for the Church). Now both use "body" as a central metaphor. But the Dharma body could never be or go wrong. Yet the body of Christ as the Church, the community of Christians, can go wrong — as Paul often pointed out to the Corinthians. To conflate these two images because they use the same word as a constituent of their central metaphors obscures the fact that there are serious differences in the stories and the doctrines derived from the stories which structure those religious traditions. In fact, Hick evacuates his notions of any specifiable meaning because they can be used to mean anything.

Third, while it may be the case that Christians should hope that God will eventually save all humanity, one does not have to forsake the claims of the Council of Chalcedon or to construe people's hopes and wishes to be an *argument* for life after death to support that hope, as Hick does.[18] While many contemporary Christian theologians want to reinterpret the "true divinity and true humanity" of Jesus in categories more appropriate today, Hick has abandoned the formula altogether. Traditional theologians have roundly criticized this tactic. There is also a huge logical gap between what people *hope* and *believe* to be true to a claim about the *actuality* of the states of affairs represented in those hopes and beliefs. That people do hope for a variously described Beyond makes no argument for the actuality of the Beyond however described.

Finally, Hick has tried to construct a "master myth," a story to end all stories. But such a story undercuts the narratives which structure Christianity — not to mention other traditions. If narratives are the basis of structuring and understanding human experience and religious traditions, then Hick's "global theology" can understand neither. By seeking to say what is beyond and behind all narratives, Hick reduces narratives to propositions. This finally clashes with that basic Christian claim that God is beyond all myths, a claim rooted in and sustained by the stories of and about Jesus.

[18]Cf. *ibid.*, p. 166.

Conclusions

Having completed an exercise in narrative theology, we can evaluate some of the claims made in chapter one for the primacy of narrative theology. First, stories give meaning to the central ideas — metaphors, doctrines, concepts, titles, codewords — of Christianity. When a theologian attempts to abstract doctrines from stories and insert them into other contexts, s/he evacuates those doctrines from any definite meaning. To move metaphors (be they live or dead) from one story to another necessarily changes the meaning of those metaphors. John Hick's treating stories as replaceable by a "global theology" fails to do justice to the distinctive claims and life of Christianity.

Second, narrative theology can incorporate the insights of propositional theologians. The use of Karl Rahner's work is an instance of that process. Moreover, the basic insight of Hick, that of an ultimate optimism for all, can be incorporated fully as well, without sacrificing the distinctiveness of Christianity.

Third, narrative theology can uncover, transform, and proclaim Christian faith more powerfully than propositional theology. This claim is not yet sustained, for a single metaphor or story about one issue is not enough to make that claim good. The many stories which give meaning to the central ideas of Christianity and shape to the lives of Christians must be explored to warrant this third claim.

For Further Reading

Karl Rahner's work on eschatology is best seen in his *Foundations* (see n. 9 above) which incorporates in part the article cited in note 1. A commentary on his work, *A World of Grace* (n. 16 above), offers valuable help for understanding Rahner's sometimes obscure formulae. A contrasting approach is Rudolf Bultmann, *History and Eschatology: The Presence of Eternity* (New York: Harper and Row, 1962). Whether Bultmann has de-eschatologized Christianity or not, his reading of various theories of history is provocative and his contrast between religious and philosophical understandings is very helpful.

Monika Hellwig, *What Are They Saying About Death and Christian Hope?* (New York: Paulist, 1978) offers a general overview of individual eschatology. She includes research and reflection from non-Christian authors, but has avoided the temptation to write a "global theology." Hans Küng, *Eternal Life? Life After Death as a Medical, Philosophical and Theological Problem*, translated by Edward Quinn (New York: Doubleday, 1984) is an exhaustive discussion of the question which sees eternal life as an expression of human hope and of a trustful vision of the cosmos. Küng responds forcefully to those critics who see hope for life after death as demeaning of the present life.

Apocalyptic themes throughout the history of literature provide J. Frank Kermode, *The Sense of an Ending: Studies in the Theory of Fiction* (New York: Oxford University Press, 1967), material for provocative reflection on images of history in literature. Kermode helpfully distinguishes "fictions" from "myths," but also denigrates myth as necessarily damaging and obscurantist. Apocalyptic expectations and their political importance are discussed in Norman Cohn, *The Pursuit of the Millennium* (New York: Harper and Row, 1961), and in Rosemary Ruether, *The Radical Kingdom: The Western Experience of Messianic Hope* (New York: Harper and Row, 1970). Both recognize apocalyptic as one of the cries of the oppressed, and find Christian apocalypses behind the revolutionary movements of the 19th and early 20th centuries. Ruether carries the story into the 1960's and also discusses other views of social change and hope.

Apocalyptic literature has always been popular, i.e., literature of the people, not of the academics. Our contemporary versions of apocalyptic appear primarily in science fiction, literature at the margin of our culture, found in pulp magazines and paperbacks, but rarely in leather-bound first editions. The connection between religious apocalyptic and contemporary s.f. is made in Frederick A. Kreuziger, *Apoc-*

alypse and Science Fiction: A Dialectic of Religious and Secular Soteriologies (Chico, CA: Scholars Press, 1982). This able Ph.D. dissertation does justice to both the varieties of s.f. literature and to the appreciation of religious texts. Unlike Küng, who dismisses science fiction in a few sentences in *Eternal Life*, Kreuziger treats s.f. seriously and shows why liberal (as opposed to radical) theologians and mainstream (as opposed to marginal) churches tend to neglect both s.f. and serious apocalyptic. Kreuziger does not, however, distinguish the functions of s.f. literature so clearly as he should. There are s.f. myths (e.g., the *Dune* series by Frank Herbert, the *Riverworld* series of P.J. Farmer) which set up alien worlds, s.f. actions (e.g. stories by Robert Heinlein, Arthur Clarke, Isaac Asimov) which explore and critique the world in which we live by highlighting tendencies in our society, and s.f. parables (e.g., some works by Ursula K. LeGuin, Michael Moorcock, Kurt Vonnegut, and the brilliant 1952 book of Frederick Pohl and C.M. Kornbluth, *The Space Merchants*) which are truly upsetting of our presuppositions. Kreuziger's bibliography is very helpful for literary and theological resources, but rather anemic in its listing of s.f. and fantasy literature. Browsing in a local bookshop — especially a branch of a national chain — will provide one with a better feeling for the literature itself.

5

THE STORIES OF JESUS: I

God became man because he loves to share stories.

To appreciate the stories of Jesus we need to retrieve them
from the biblical texts which report them. The first section
of this chapter sketches some of the problems with retrieving Jesus' stories, shows why some attempted resolutions of
those problems by declaring Jesus' actual words and deeds
irrelevant are inadequate, and suggests that there are ways
to go beyond those inadequate views. The second section of
the chapter centers on those stories which contain some of
Jesus' central and distinctive teaching — his *parables.*

The Need for Biblical Criticism

Ordinarily, when a Christian reads the Bible, s/he will
read through a story and meditate on it, or read one book of
the Bible straight through, or follow a reading being done in
church. Usually a Christian will not notice that there are a
remarkable number of points upon which the Bible offers
inconclusive — and sometimes self-contradictory —
reports. Moreover, when one lays the texts of the four
gospels, for instance, side by side, one discovers some

remarkable disagreements. Starting from the end, the Resurrection appearances in the gospels are remarkably dissimilar, even concerning the basic locale of the appearances. At the tomb? In Jerusalem? Far from Jerusalem (seven miles)? The last words that Jesus spoke before his death are given with three very different formulations. Was he despairing or quoting Ps. 22 as Mark and Matthew have? Was he at the last committing himself to his Father, as Luke has it? Was he finally finished with whatever he was doing, as John has it? What were his last words? What did the centurion say? Did Jesus speak in parables as the first three gospels have him speaking? Did he talk in long, boring discourses as John has him? Did he institute the Eucharist at the Last Supper? If so, why does John not mention it? If not, why do the other three make it central? Did the Passion happen before the Passover or during it? Did Jesus spend one Passover in Jerusalem, or three? Was Jesus in Jerusalem shortly after his birth as Luke has it, or was he taken to Egypt, as Matthew writes? What was his paternal grandfather's name? If one asks these questions of an introductory class and then directs them to the appropriate texts, they will come to see that the Bible gives various answers for all of these questions. When people look at the text we have, and ask it questions, they will discover irreconcilable answers in the text.

Yet the Christian community has offered reconciliations of the texts. Two ways stand out. The first of these is a "harmony of the gospels" which puts together almost all the events mentioned by the four gospels into an order chosen by the harmonizer. A classic example of this is the *Diatessaron* composed by Tatian in the second century. The results are very harmonious, but the procedure is a problem for it treats the gospels as picture puzzles with some pieces duplicated, some needing cutting to fit the other pieces, and some not really fitting at all. But the gospels are not picture puzzles. Each has an integrity of its own in its witness. And if the gospels or their writers are "inspired," can a "scissors-and-paste" harmony composed by other people improve on the inspired authors' approach? If one accepts a harmony, one must answer this question "yes." Because the harmonies assume that their composers can tell the stories better than the biblical narrators and because the harmonies can offer no justification for preferring one harmonious scheme over another, this attempt to resolve the surface contradictions in the gospel texts must be rejected.

The second way of reconciliation in the Christian community has been to cut the texts in such a way for use in liturgy that the discrepancies aren't noted. When one celebrates Christmas, for example, one hears and tells stories which have been carefully edited for liturgical use. The readings are sequenced to include visits to Jesus from both shepherds and magi, both flight from Palestine and circumcision in Jerusalem, both angelic appearances to Mary and angelic dreams of Joseph, in something of a "liturgical diatessaron." We celebrate our feasts by telling stories which manifest our joy — but we must remember that we, as celebrating community, adapt, we edit, we construct our celebratory stories from somewhat different ones.

Yet harmonies and liturgies abstract elements from the narratives and put them together in new ways. Hence, they do not really *resolve* the disagreements between the biblical texts, but *reconstruct* the stories. A different approach is to use scholarly analysis. We do not need to rehearse the sketch of the development of biblical criticism in the modern era from chapter two, but merely to recall that critics, too, had (and have) their faults. The early critics often neglected the narrative structure of the texts. They also were not self-critical enough; as one Catholic noted, the Liberal Protestants' Biblical Christ "looking back through nineteen centuries of Catholic darkness, is only the reflection of a Liberal Protestant face, seen at the bottom of a deep well."[1]

More recent critics have come to recognize that even if the word of God is not timebound, Jesus was a man of his times, and that the gospel texts are compilations of earlier sources by their final writers. This has led some scholars to be

[1] George Tyrrell, *Christianity at the Crossroads* (London: Allen and Unwin, 1963 [first published, 1909]), p. 49.

skeptical about retrieving anything substantial about Jesus' actual life and teaching. The reasons for this worry can be summarized in five points. (1) The New Testament was written by people who were convinced of Jesus' Lordship over them and the presence of the risen Christ in their communities. Thus not only must the historian cope with attempting to recover the earliest oral traditions behind the written texts, but also must discount all of it because the sources are biased by that faith and because the earliest communities may not have differentiated what Jesus said when he was alive and what the present Christ was saying through them. Thus, Jesus as he actually existed is inaccessible to us for our sources simply do not have a picture of the historical Jesus to retrieve. (2) Even if one discounts the equation of Jesus with Christ in the believing communities, the New Testament was composed by people who were quoting reports of reports of reports of what Jesus said. This distance from the source will demand a very critical eye to distinguish the embroidery from the original fabric of Jesus' teaching and actions. (3) The New Testament was never composed as a history in the modern sense of "history." It is *proclamation* of the wonderful work of God in and through Jesus as the Christ. Thus, when moderns ask historical questions of the text, we are forcing out of it an account radically foreign to its own style. This may easily introduce serious distortions if we take their proclamations as answers to our historical questions. (4) The New Testament was written in communities and cultures radically different from ours. To understand the significance of the texts without imposing our ideas on them is difficult. Indeed, even asking historical questions of the text, as noted above, may impose a framework so foreign on the texts that we will likely also impose our ideas on the text. (5) Beyond the problems that are attendant upon oral transmission of the sources, the text of the New Testament was passed down in handwritten manuscripts. The various manuscripts we have differ from one another at important points, so we have to decide which text is more nearly faithful to the tradition or most reliable at the points at which the texts vary. In sum, there are tremendous problems attendant upon any attempt to retrieve Jesus "as he really was" and represent him today.

In view of these problems, some theologians deny the necessity of knowing about the actual Jesus. They believe the important thing is not what Jesus said or did or who he thought himself to be. What makes Jesus decisive is that God has acted in him, the infinite God has acted through a finite man. This is the radical stumbling block, the scandal of Christian faith (1 Cor 1:23). This act of God cannot be seen through the eyes of the questioning historian. It cannot be demonstrated by the inquiries of the critic. It can only be accepted by faith through grace. Historical work on Jesus of Nazareth pales in comparison with what is truly important: responding in faithful obedience to God's call. The great biblical scholar, Rudolf Bultmann, says it elegantly:

> It is therefore illegitimate to go behind the kerygma, using it as a "source," in order to reconstruct a "historical Jesus" with his "messianic consciousness," his "inner life" or his "heroism." That would be merely "Christ after the flesh," who is no longer. It is not the historical Jesus, but Jesus Christ, the Christ preached, who is the Lord.[2]

In sum, what is important to us is not Jesus who lived, but Christ who lives because no knowledge of Jesus will save us for only faith under Christ's lordship can do so.

But two objections need to be made at this point to this claim. Theologically, the separation of the Jesus of history from the Christ of faith is terribly problematical. It suggests that even if Jesus never existed we might still have Christianity or that even if the New Testament were a pack of lies, the faith it proclaims would be saving truth. Although there is always the danger of substituting human accomplishments for divine grace or of idolizing our own work, there is also the danger of obscurantism or of evacuating Christian faith of historical content. A Christian theologian needs to avoid

---

[2]Rudolf Bultmann, "The Historical Jesus and the Theology of Paul," *Faith and Understanding*, edited by R. W. Funk, translated by L. P. Smith (New York: Harper and Row, 1969 [first German edition, 1933]), p. 268.

both problems, and a Bultmannian approach of separating Jesus of history from the Christ of faith may well fall into the trap of evacuating Christian claims of any distinctiveness.

Second, the evidence does not warrant such skepticism historically. Biblical scholars have come to agree on a vast number of variant textual readings and have a general consensus on almost all the biblical text. Historians and archaeologists have used other ancient texts to establish facts once thought completely unavailable, e.g., the location of the city of Troy. That the texts were not intended as historical documents in our sense of "historical" does not imply that we can never recover historical data from those texts. In sum, there is insufficient evidence to warrant a claim that we cannot recover the proclamation *of* Jesus, or aspects of it, by investigating the proclamation about Jesus in the New Testament.

In fact, using techniques not available to nineteenth century historians, and taking seriously the problems enumerated above, biblical critics have untangled many of the threads of the Christian tradition to disclose some that came from Jesus, some whose origin is uncertain, and some which likely came from other sources. The threads of the fabric of early Christianity we will begin with are the stories Jesus told; his parables provide a reliable key to his central and distinctive teaching.

Jesus' Stories

The words that begin Jesus' public ministry provide a brief summary of Jesus' teaching: "The time is fulfilled; repent, the Kingdom of God is at hand" (Mk 1:15).[3] The question is what this brief prophetic challenge summarizes. The answer is to be found in the stories of Jesus.

---

[3]Unless indicated otherwise, scriptural quotations in this chapter roughly follow the RSV, save that material probably or certainly added to Jesus' original stories is excluded and verses possibly added are bracketed (save for the parable of the Good Samaritan, as I will explain there).

The first question one wants to ask about the summary, is what the *kingdom* is. Jesus never gave a direct, literal answer to this question as far as we know. Rather he told stories to let one see what the kingdom is:

> For the kingdom of heaven is like a householder who went out early in the morning to hire laborers for his vineyard. After agreeing with the laborers for a denarius a day, he sent them out into his vineyard. And going out about the third hour he saw others standing idle in the market place; and to them he said, "You go into the vineyard too, and whatever is right I will give you." So they went. Going out again about the sixth hour and the ninth hour, he did the same. And about the eleventh hour he went out and found others standing; and he said to them, "Why do you stand here idle all day?" They said to him, "Because no one has hired us." He said to them, "You go into the vineyard too." And when evening came, the owner of the vineyard said to his steward, "Call the laborers and pay them their wages, beginning with the last, up to the first." And when those hired about the eleventh hour came, each of them received a denarius. Now when the first came, they thought they would receive more; but each of them also received a denarius. And on receiving it they grumbled at the householder, saying, "These last worked only one hour, and you have made them equal to us who have borne the burden of the day and the scorching heat." But he replied to one of them, "Friend, I am doing you no wrong; did you not agree with me for a denarius?"[Take what belongs to you, and go; I choose to give to this last as I give to you. Am I not allowed to do what I choose with what belongs to me? Or do you begrudge my generosity?"] (Mt 20:1-15).

Whether the bracketed verses are part of the original parable or not,[4] this parable is quite a surprise. One might expect

---

[4]John Dominic Crossan, *In Parables: The Challenge of the Historical Jesus* (New York: Harper and Row, 1973) argues well for excising verses 14 and 15; see pp. 111-114.

the householder to be generous. Then why was he generous to those who got to work in the cool of the evening for a short time but not generous to those who worked all day long through the hot sun? That's not even generosity. One might expect the householder to be legalistic. Then why did he not pay each by the part of the day worked as he did the first? But he seems neither generous nor legalistic, but both ungenerous and unlegalistic!

The kingdom of God reverses all our expectations. We can understand a generous householder or a precisionist one. We can't understand this one. What we expect from a precisionist (each person getting *just what* s/he deserves) or an altruist (each person getting *more than* s/he deserves) are incompatible. We can't imagine both strict justice and great mercy. So much the worse for us. That is the point of the parable: don't expect that the kingdom of God will be what you want it to be. You don't know what happens in God's kingdom. Neither do I.

Commentators on this parable take it as a response of Jesus to a challenge that attacked him for befriending the tax-collectors and sinners, the people who were the outcasts of their society. The former had sold out to the Romans ("quislings"); the latter gave up on the religious traditions. But Jesus responds, in this view, with the claim that these outcasts are God's people. Even if this is not the actual situation in which the story was told, at least one of its main points is clear: the justice and mercy of the kingdom of God are beyond anything we would expect.

The surprise gets even stronger with the parables of the leaven and the sower, but especially with the parable of the mustard seed:

> With what can we compare the kingdom of God, or what parable shall we use for it? It is like a grain of mustard seed...which grows up and becomes the greatest of all the shrubs and puts forth large branches (Mk 4:30-32).

In the present form, this parable does not seem very surprising. Yet its irony has been brought out by John Dominic Crossan.[5]

A proper metaphor for the kingdom of God would be a great oak or a cedar of Lebanon, as in Daniel 4, Ezekiel 17 or Ezekiel 21. The great branches, the towering heights, the deep roots are all metaphorical implicates of such a tree: such is the kingdom of God. But Jesus rather uses the tiny mustard seed. It sprouts up quickly, produces a large ungainly weed, and cannot hold up birds' nests. Now many would find the speed of growth and the size achieved to be worth commenting on. But this misses the satiric thrust of the parable. Given the expectation that *God's* kingdom would be magnificent, Jesus lampoons that idea. God's kingdom is not a great tree, but a weed. When one expects a kingdom ruled in stately majesty, one gets a kingdom which sprawls sloppily. Not only does the kingdom of God upset expectations, but also God's kingdom is hardly recognizable. So we should be upset and worried about it, no?

No.

> Or what woman, having ten silver coins, if she loses one coin, does not light a lamp and sweep the house and seek diligently until she finds it? And when she has found it, she calls together her friends and her neighbors, saying, "Rejoice with me, for I have found the coin which I had lost" (Lk 15:8-9).

Almost all scholars agree that the verse that follows this one is an editorial comment.

What do we seek? If we are Jews hearing Jesus, we seek the kingdom of God. What do we do when we find it? We rejoice, for we find what we had lost. Although there are numerous interpretations of this parable — as recovery of sinner, as indication of the need to act immediately, as expressing the joy over the coming of the kingdom — it is

---

[5]J. D. Crossan, *The Dark Interval: Towards a Theology of Story* (Niles, IL: Argus Communications, 1975), p. 95.

clear that the motif of *joy* is one which those who are in or who find the kingdom are to share. The unexpectedness of God's kingdom shouldn't be frightening. Rather, it is a kingdom that will make you *overjoyed*, surprised with delight, not dreadful or worrisome. Whether the woman in the story is God rejoicing over a lost sinner or whether the woman is I or whether the woman is Jesus or whether this parable has some other interpretation that is more appropriate than any yet discovered, we can rejoice with her.

There is something quite curious about Jesus' teaching about the kingdom. Every time we think we have a grasp on it, it slips out of our grasp. Jesus' treasure parable provides an example: "The kingdom of heaven is like a treasure hidden in a field, which a man found and covered up; then in his joy he goes and sells all that he has and buys the field" (Mt 13:44, RSV). In this parable, the speaker promises to tell us what the Kingdom of God is like. Then, as John Dominic Crossan points out, we are never told what the kingdom of God is like. And it is in this *failure* to represent the kingdom that is the *success* of the parable. It is as if the speaker is saying, "Watch carefully how and as I fail to do so and learn that it cannot be done. Have you seen my failure? If you have, then I have succeeded. And the more magnificent my failure, the greater my success."[6] Crossan calls this a *metaparable* which shows that the kingdom of God is beyond our imagination. Jesus' parables call us to go beyond anything we have imagined; if we can imagine it, it isn't God's kingdom.

If we can't capture or know or imagine the Kingdom, can we say anything of the second element of Jesus' call, *God*? Conzelmann summarizes the usual view as follows:

> Jesus wished to formulate no new doctrine of God. He believed in the God of Israel, the Creator and Ruler, Lawgiver and Judge. He did not define God's "essence," but brought his lordship to bear in its absoluteness; and

[6]J. D. Crossan, *Finding is the First Act* (Philadelphia: Fortress Press and Missoula: Scholars' Press, 1979), p. 120.

this absoluteness is salvation. Naturally, God . . . is righteous and good — indeed the only good One. . . . All
assertions about God include at once the hearer who is
addressed: He is Father.[7]

Jesus calls God *abba*. We translate this Aramaic word as
"father," although it suggests the intimacy of "papa" or
"dad." Although Jesus is not unique in addressing God this
way, it is surely a distinctive and central piece of Jesus'
prayer.

The question becomes what *sort* of "father" is God?

The following parable is often taken by critics (for example, Jeremias, Linnemann) as being a response of Jesus to
those who criticized him for consorting with the wicked. Yet
that doesn't seem to get to the *point* of the story. Others treat
it as exemplifying the forgiveness of sins (Perrin) or as a
typical "reversing-our-expectations" parable (Crossan). Yet
this is the only parable in the New Testament in which the
chief protagonist is the *father*. Although we have called it by
another title, consider this story of a *father* who had two
sons. The following translation is Clarence Jordan's.
Although it is idiomatic — as Jesus' teaching likely was — it
is faithful to the sense of the New Testament.

> He went on to say, "A man had two sons. The younger
> one said to his father, "Dad, give me my share of the
> business." So he split up the business between them. Not
> so long after that the younger one packed up all his stuff
> and took off for a foreign land, where he threw his money
> away living like a fool. Soon he ran out of cash, and on
> top of that, the country was in a deep depression. So he
> was really hard up. He finally landed a job with one of the
> citizens of the country, who sent him into the fields to feed
> *hogs*! And he was hungry enough to tank up on the slop
> the hogs were eating. Nobody was giving him even a
> hand-out.

[7] Hans Conzelmann, *Jesus*, translated by J. R. Lord (Philadelphia: Fortress
Press, 1973 [first German edition, 1959]), p. 54.

"One day an idea bowled him over. 'A lot of my father's hired hands have more than enough bread to eat, and out here I'm starving in this depression. I'm gonna get up and go to my father and say, 'Dad, I've sinned against God and you, and am no longer fit to be called your son — just make me one of your hired hands.'

"So he got up and came to his father. While he was some distance down the road, his father saw him and was moved to tears. He ran to him and hugged him and kissed him and kissed him.

"The boy said, 'Dad, I've sinned against God and you, and I'm not fit to be your son anymore—' But the father said to his servants, 'You all run quick and get the best suit you can find and put it on him. Get his family ring for his hand and some dress shoes for his feet. Then I want you to bring that stall-fed steer and butcher it, and let's all eat and whoop it up, because this son of mine was given up for dead, and he's alive; he was lost and is now found.' And they began to whoop it up.

"But his older son was out in the field. When he came in and got almost home, he heard the music and the dancing, and he called one of the little boys and asked him what in the world was going on. The little boy said, 'Why, your brother has come home, and your daddy has butchered the stall-fed steer, because he got him back safe and sound.' At this he blew his top and wouldn't go in. His father went out and pleaded with him. But he answered his father, 'Look here, all these years I've slaved for you, and never once went contrary to your orders. And yet, at no time have you ever given me so much as a baby goat with which to pitch a party for my friends. But when this son of yours — who has squandered the business on whores — comes home, you butcher for him the stall-fed steer,' But he said to him, 'My boy, my dear boy, you are with me all the time, and what's mine is yours. But I just can't *help* getting happy and whooping it up, because *this brother of yours* was dead and is alive; he was lost and has been found'" (Lk 15:11-32, CPV).

This longest and richest of Jesus' parables is surely open to many interpretations. Not only do we hear many ideas in it, but the first hearers likely did, too. I think that it is indubitable that this parable makes allusions not only to the people whom Jesus consorted with, but also to the free forgiveness of sins. It also reverses one's expectations in that the father *freely* forgives the son who was lost and bestows on him gifts to celebrate with joy his return. But let's look at what the father *does*.

First, he splits up the property with his younger son. Since Jewish law provided for inheritance rights only to the older son, this was not an unexpected procedure. Apparently many families did this to provide the younger son with some capital. Nothing exceptional here.

Second, he saw his prodigal son returning and was moved to tears. This father has a heart. But, then, that is not unusual. Most fathers would rejoice at the return of a son who had wandered. Most fathers would see him coming down the road, be overjoyed with the return, and sit and wait for the son to apologize and then forgive the one who has asked forgiveness.

It is the third action that is unexpected here and was likely unexpected then. Instead of sitting and waiting, the father ran to him, embraced him and received him before he said anything. Then, when the son tries to recite his prepared apologetic request, the father interrupts him and gets ready to throw a party! A clear modern parallel is to imagine a teenager, driving the family car home about three in the morning after an evening of riotous partying, being greeted by an anxious parent who sweeps the prodigal up in his arms, whirls him around, and bursts out, "Thank God you're home! Let's have a party to celebrate!" The action of the father in Jesus' story is just as bewildering.

The final thing the father does is also crucial. The elder brother is outside, complaining and moaning as the story notes (imagine a hard-working brother getting home from the graveyard shift about five in the morning doing the same thing). Again the father gets up and goes out to him. He does not leave him in the cold. He does not demand that the elder brother enter. He not only doesn't issue commands from his chair, but also goes out and pleads with him, too, explains the situation, and tries to draw him in. The father also performs an unexpected gracious action for the elder brother as well. Again an unexpected action.

It would be allegorization — reading the parable as if it were an allegory — to say that the father in this story stands for the Father of All. Yet this is the only parable of Jesus which presents a father interacting with his children. Jesus' disciples may have heard this parable as revealing the actions of Jesus' Father. If this sort of hearing reveals the distinctiveness of the parable and fits the parable as well as other interpretations, then it is one legitimate way to hear it. And then, may a Christian at least *hope* that this is the way a heavenly Father will act, too?

The third element of Jesus' prophetic challenge is *repentance*. What repentance is for Jesus is hard to characterize: it surely means to change one's life in response to the reign of God, but just how that change is to take place or what the results are remain resistant to formulation. One story which contextualizes the notion is the eschatological parable of the sheep and the goats. However, another way of contextualizing it is to consider the sayings of Jesus that are collected as his "beatitudes." These appear in two forms in the New Testament, but for present purposes, consider the tougher sayings of Jesus, as reported by Luke in his version of this material from his "Sermon on the Plain":

> And he lifted up his eyes on his disciples and said:
> Blessed are you poor, for yours is the kingdom of God.
> Blessed are you that hunger now, for you shall be satisfied.
> Blessed are you that weep now, for you shall laugh.
> Blessed are you when men hate you, and when they exclude you and revile you, and cast out your name as evil, on account of the Son of man! Rejoice in that day, and leap for joy, for behold, your reward is great in heaven; for so their fathers did to the prophets.

But woe to you that are rich, for you have received your consolation.

Woe to you that are full now, for you shall hunger.

Woe to you that laugh now, for you shall mourn and weep.

Woe to you, when all men speak well of you, for so their fathers did to the false prophets.

But I say to you that hear, Love your enemies, do good to those who hate you, bless those who curse you, pray for those who abuse you. To him who strikes you on the cheek, offer the other also; and from him who takes away your cloak do not withold your coat as well. Give to everyone who begs from you; and of him who takes away your goods do not ask them again. And as you wish that men would·do to you, do so to them (Lk 6:20-31, RSV).

Which of these collected sayings originates from Jesus and which have been added or transformed by the community is open for debate. But the general form of these sayings, the "eschatological reversal," that is, when the kingdom is here, it will be the opposite of the way it is now, is from Jesus.

But as with the eschatological stories in the previous chapter, so with the eschatological promises and threats here. These are admonitions addressed to those here-and-now, suggesting that the way things are here-and-now will lead to something just the opposite in the kingdom. What we need to do in response, it seems, is to *change* the here-and-now from what it *is* into what it *should be*. And when that unimaginable task is complete, the Kingdom will be here!

Thus, to repent means to turn one's life around, to orient oneself to the kingdom of God, and to do what is proper for a disciple who would be in the kingdom. If the kingdom upsets all our expectations, then to participate in the kingdom means to upset our ordinary ways and to live extraordinarily. We are to have confidence in God and to live not for ourselves but for the kingdom. And then we will truly find our selves.

Two parables are generally associated with what we must do to participate in the kingdom. The parable of the great supper, preserved in very elaborated versions by Matthew (22:1-14) and Luke (14:16-24), suggests that we need to respond *now*:

> "A man once gave a great banquet, and invited many; and at the time for the banquet he sent his servant to say to those who had been invited, 'Come; for all is now ready.' But they all alike began to make excuses. The first said to him, 'I have bought a field, and I must go out and see it; I pray you, have me excused.' And another said, 'I have married a wife, and therefore cannot come.' So the servant came and reported this to his master. And the master said to the servant, 'Go out to the highways and hedges, and compel people to come in, that my house may be filled.'" (Lk 14:16-21a, 23).

If a person refuses to respond to the invitation, and to respond *now*, that person will be left out. But that does not mean the banquet table will be empty. No, the banquet will get along quite nicely with the uninvited guests and without those who have been invited, if they refuse to come.

(A digression: what sort of banquet is it that is the banquet of the kingdom? Luke suggests a Eucharistic banquet [22:30]. Matthew describes a banquet in heaven [8:11]. A Catholic missionary returning from China was once asked, Maureen Tilley has told me, how he explained heaven and hell to the Chinese. He responded, "Hell is like a great banquet at which everyone is given four-foot-long chopsticks so nobody can feed himself; heaven is like a great banquet at which everyone is given four-foot-long chopsticks and everybody feeds each other." Or maybe all of the above sorts of banquets and more!)[8]

[8]The present digression was introduced into the text to illustrate what the gospel writers themselves sometimes did. A key word, e.g., "banquet," would link these two stories metaphorically. The writers would then link them in their text as they set down what they had been told. Similarly a story so apt for the occasion would be introduced into the text since it *must* have come from Jesus. (Had chopsticks been

Secondly, the parable of the Good Samaritan is often thought to show *to whom* we need to respond:

[And behold, a lawyer stood up to put him to the test, saying, "Teacher, what shall I do to inherit eternal life?" He said to him, "What is written in the law? How do you read?" And he answered, "You shall love the Lord your God with all your heart, and with all your soul, and with all your strength, and with all your mind; and your neighbor as yourself." And he said to him, "You have answered right; do this and you will live."

But he, desiring to justify himself, said to Jesus, "And who is my neighbor?"] Jesus replied, "A man was going down from Jerusalem to Jericho, and he fell among robbers, who stripped him and beat him, and departed, leaving him half dead. Now by chance a priest was going down that road; and when he saw him he passed by on the other side. So likewise a Levite, when he came to the place and saw him, passed by on the other side. But a Samaritan, as he journeyed, came to where he was; and when he saw him, he had compassion, and went to him and bound up his wounds, pouring on oil and wine; then he set him on his own beast and brought him to an inn, and took care of him. And the next day he took out two denarii and gave them to the innkeeper, saying, 'Take care of him; and whatever more you spend, I will repay you when I come back.' [Which of these three, do you think, proved neighbor to the man who fell among robbers?"] [He said, "The one who showed mercy on him." And Jesus said to him, "Go and do likewise."] (Lk 10:25-37, RSV)

used in the Biblical communities and had the origin of the missionary's story been lost, I strongly suspect that an evangelist might well have included it into his text as a story of Jesus). The evangelists made no distinction, apparently, between the words the actual Jesus said and the inspiration of Christ in the community. The *origin* of the story did not matter to them. What mattered was whether it served to keep his memory alive and furthered the Christian cause.

I have unfortunately not been able to trace this story to its source: context and author remain unknown to me.

This parable has been extensively discussed in recent years. The following interpretation has benefitted from these debates.[9]

(a) What is the *story*? As you can see from the brackets, the text has been elaborated. Luke first gave it a context (as we might put a frame on a painting): the confrontation between Jesus and the lawyer. Although many find the parables to be responses to challenges, most scholars agree that Luke here inserted this story into a challenge-context. If it were the case that Jesus often responded this way and Luke knew a good story, then it would be a "natural" to combine the two. Second, by giving the story this *context*, Luke limited the *significance* of the story. For Luke, the story is a didactic device that teaches the hearer how far his responsibility extends, how far the law applies, and how negligent one is in not recognizing the Samaritan as his neighbor. Thus, by setting the story within the context indicated above by the first and last set of brackets in the text (verses 25-29, 37) Luke has made this a moralizing story. Although it is true that a good parable often carries a moral point, it cannot be limited to a moralizing meaning, and so most critics now see the story as told by Jesus as definitely independent of the specific context Luke gave it.

A second problem is the question whether the bracketed rhetorical question near the end of the story (v. 36) belongs to the original story setting. If it does, then in all likelihood, the question, "Who is my neighbor?" in verse 29 belongs to the original setting as well, although the lead-in to the story with the lawyer and the closing moralizing verse are still Luke's framework. As a rhetorical question is a *great* way to end a parabolic story, some think that the actual story extends from verse 29b to verse 36.

Yet there are two reasons to conclude that verses 29b and 36 are part of the "inner frame" or the "matting" surrounding the original picture. First, the story itself, verses 10-35

---

[9]The following paragraphs are deeply indebted to Norman Perrin, *Jesus and the Language of the Kingdom* (Philadelphia: Fortress Press, 1976), chapter three, especially pp. 168-181.

(the unbracketed central section above), is *by itself* a good story, and in fact by itself a good *parable*. The expectations of the hearer are reversed, his world is upset when it is not his fellow-Jew but his despised Samaritan half-brother and ritual outcast who performs the merciful act. The central story itself works as a parable *without any reference to the "neighbor question."* Thus, there is some reason to believe that the "neighbor issue" is an expansion of the original story likely told by Jesus, and a very clever one that shows how the story reverses a good Jew's expectations. And, second, we have a good explanation of how this "inner frame" came to be placed around the story. Eta Linnemann expresses it perfectly: "Verse 36 belongs to the story as a signpost does to a crossroads. It is to ensure attention for what matters to the narrator in the story."[10] This frame "highlights" the picture *in a specific way* and gets us to notice *specific things*. In so doing, it makes the story a different story!

Thus, we actually have *three* stories here: vv. 30-35, vv. 29b-36, and vv. 25-37 are all different stories. Verses 29b and 36 reform the inner story, to tell the story so as to highlight a crucial point of the story and to make a point with the story about what it means to be a neighbor. And when Luke decided "to write an orderly account for you, most excellent Theophilus [literally, God-lover]" (Lk 1:3b, RSV), he placed it so that his hearers could also hear the story in spite of the fact that they were Gentiles (for the most part) and might be unfamiliar with the specific original setting of the hostility between Jews and Samaritans.

(b) How is it possible for us to interpret the stories? Three guidelines are crucial here. First, we cannot interpret the story in any way we choose to do so. "Free" interpretation is the most "false" interpretation of all: it is false to the story we have preserved in the tradition, it is false to those who have told and interpreted the story before us, and it is thus in

---

[10]Eta Linnemann, *The Parables of Jesus: Introduction and Exposition*, trans. by John Sturdy (London: S.P.C.K., 1966 [first German edition, 1961; translation from the third edition of 1964]), p. 155.

danger of falsifying what is revealed in and from the story. While new insights into the meaning of a narrative can never be ruled out, interpreting a narrative that belongs to a tradition without regard for that tradition effectively removes that story from the tradition, which is disastrous for a religion constituted by an ongoing tradition. Second, we must interpret a story in a way faithful to the community that tells the story. We cannot merely parrot the interpretations of the past nor merely tell the story as it was first told. Our present telling and interpreting a story must be indebted to our past, but not enslaved to it. In short, present interpretation must avoid the Scylla of slavish adherence to the rock of the past and the Charybdis of fanciful interpretation cut off from our past. Finally, no interpreter can presume to have the final word on any story s/he is interpreting. No one can claim to have the absolute method or the deepest insight, unsurpassably correct. Each interpreter must do the best s/he can today. And each interpreter should also hope that someone else will do it better tomorrow, for all our sakes. This stance of courageous humility is implicit in the notion of the "development of doctrine" beloved of Catholics. It is also something that the history of interpretation of the parables can teach us, as Norman Perrin has noted, reflecting only on the modern period:

> When one looks at the story of the modern interpretation of the parables one is struck by the sheer *impact* of the new developments in the discussion. Julicher's demonstration that the parables were not allegories, Dodd's that they had to be illuminated by an ability to set them in their original cultural-historical context, Via's original insistence on understanding them as literary-aesthetic objects, Crossan's on understanding them as poetic metaphors — all of these developments confront the interpreter and are obviously relevant to his task.[11]

We can interpret the stories because we *must*; otherwise the stories would die out. But even when we do our best, a better

[11]Perrin, *Jesus and the Language of the Kingdom*, p. 181.

will come along, who will be even more faithful to the story itself and the enduring community that has interpreted it than we have been.

(c) How *do we* interpret the story of the Good Samaritan? The first interpretation of the story of the Good Samaritan is found in Scripture. It interprets the story as illuminating what it means to be a neighbor. This interpretation, the inner frame of the story noted above, incorporates the original story into a new story and has become the standard interpretation and telling of the story. Joachim Jeremias' discussion of the question in v. 29 shows this well:

> Jesus was not being asked for a definition of the term "friend" [Jeremias' translation of the word we ordinarily translate as neighbor], but for an indication as to where, within the community, the limits of the duty of loving were to be drawn. How far does my responsibility extend?[12]

The traditional interpretation is that it extends even to your enemies and the outcast — definitely in line with Matthew 5:43-48 or Luke 6:27-30 (see above, p. 87). The usual application is to admonish those in the community who have not recognized their neighbors and who have not seen how far their duty extends.

A second interpretation of the story is also contained in Scripture. It is the "outer frame" of Luke, vv. 25-28, 37. This interpretation suggests that it is our moral responsibility, if we are to fulfill the law of God, to go out and "do likewise," to take care of people who are in trouble. If the first interpretation is an admonitory one, the second is an exemplary one. Unlike the first interpretation, this interpretation interjects *us* into the story: *we* are supposed to take the place of the Samaritan, *we* are supposed to do what *he* does. This is certainly upsetting. This story, told today in a Northern Irish Protestant church, would have the three figures in the

---

[12]Joachim Jeremias, *The Parables of Jesus,* Second Revised Edition, trans. S. H. Hooke (New York: Scribner's, 1972 [first German edition, 1947; translated from the eighth edition of 1970]), p. 203.

story as a minister, a choir leader, and an IRA terrorist. Bad enough to hear that one of the *enemy* did something for a person. But to be told to go out and do likewise? That's outrageous! How could a preacher dare suggest that one ought to imitate a *terrorist*. That is the suggestion of the "second story" which includes the "outer frame" as part of the story and injects us into it in this way.

Yet these two ways of telling the story are in some tension with each other. In the "admonitory story" (verses 29b-36) we feel sympathy with the man in the ditch. We are, *if* we are in the story at all, in the ditch.[13] In the "exemplary story" (verses 25-37), we are inserted into the story as the Samaritan (or terrorist or whoever we find "distasteful" or "enemy"). The main point of the admonitory story is to get us to *see* who our friends are and how far our duty extends. In the exemplary story, the main point is to get us to *do* acts of kindness and compassion for those who are in trouble whenever we stumble across them. While these two stories are not directly contradictory, they are significantly different and in tension with each other. What is important, however, is that both stories are found woven into the text of Luke's gospel; neither single story alone was good enough. Not only a multiplicity of interpretations are found in the text, but also a number of different stories are found there. No final story is told. No final interpretation is given. Rather, the text itself invites us to carry on the process for ourselves as members of the ongoing community that cherishes these stories.

A contemporary interpretation of the story, on which a large number of American New Testament scholars have come to agree, tells the story as a thoroughgoing *parable*, shattering the expectations of those who hear it. Norman Perrin, following the work of John Dominic Crossan, summarizes this:

---

[13]This sort of reading of the parable has been offered by Robert W. Funk, "The Good Samaritan as Metaphor," *Semeia* II (1974), pp. 74-81. Perrin has suggested that the original hearers (and the present ones, I think) of the parable must have felt some significant tensions over whom to identify with. See *Jesus and the Language of the Kingdom*, pp. 177-179.

If Jesus had wanted to teach love of neighbor in distress, then it would have been sufficient to talk of one person, a second person and a third person. If he had wanted to add a jibe against the clerical circles in Jerusalem he could have mentioned priest, Levite, and Jewish lay-person. If he had wanted to inculcate love of one's enemies, then "it would have been radical enough to have a Jewish person stop and assist a wounded Samaritan," because to the Jews at the time of Jesus a Samaritan was a "socio-religious outcast." But the story has the *Samaritan* help the traveler, so that "the internal structure of the story and the historical setting of Jesus' time agree that the literal point of the story challenges the hearer to put together two *impossible and contradictory* words for the same person: "Samaritan" (10:33) and "neighbor" (10:36)." As told by a Jewish Jesus to a Jewish audience, "the whole thrust of the story demands that one say what cannot be said, what is a contradiction in terms: Good + Samaritan." The story is a story of reversal, because "when good (clerics) and bad (Samaritan) become, re-spectively, bad and good, a world is being challenged and we are faced with polar reversal."[14]

The world of the hearer is turned upside down by the story told as a *parable*. Neither admonition nor exemplification stories do this, nor does taking the story in these ways adequately explain the radical reversal of the "innermost story" and the reason each of the persons in *that* story is cast as he is. This understanding also explains why the parable can be so powerful when modern roles are substituted in retelling the story (a terrorist?!), and why the story can upset the worlds of its hearers when the story is told well again (as it does not if the terrorist is in the ditch).

This contemporary interpretation is licensed by the tradi-tion as it explains the power of the inner story (verses 30-35) by recognizing its structure, but also accounts for the other interpretations and stories in a constructive manner. By

---

[14]Perrin, *Jesus and the Language of the Kingdom*, p. 164; emphasis added.

freeing the inner story from its frames, the contemporary interpretation allows that story to speak for itself and to show how rich the stor*ies* of the Good Samaritan really are.

Yet I think that this understanding of the story can be deepened further. When one studies the words of the Greek text as scholars accept it today, one gets no surprises *except when one examines what the Samaritan does first*. The first reaction of the Samaritan to the stranger in the ditch is "he had compassion [on him]." The Greek verb behind this translation is *splanchnízomai*. It is used eleven times in the New Testament in addition to the use here.[15] Eight times Jesus "has compassion." One time Jesus is asked to "have compassion." One time the king in a parable of the kingdom "has compassion." One time the Father in the parable of the "prodigal son" "has compassion" ("was moved to tears" in the CPV, p. 84 above). Is there a pattern here? Who in the New Testament has compassion? As whom does he act? Is it possible that the parable of the Samaritan and the traveler is not only intended to put together Good + Samaritan, but Jesus + Samaritan? Is this parable not only attempting to reconstruct our beliefs about our friends and our enemies, but also to shatter our myths about who is Friend and Enemy? Are we to see a terrorist act as Jesus acted? In sum, **the parable of the Good Samaritan should shatter our worlds even more than Crossan and Perrin think: where IS Jesus and WHO is having compassion?**

[15]The forms are all finite or participial. They can be found in Matthew 9:36, 14:14, 15:32, 18:27, 20:34; Mark 1:41, 6:34, 8:2, 9:22; Luke 7:13, 15:20 and the present Luke 10:33. For a discussion of the significance of the word, see *Theological Dictionary of the New Testament*, ed. G. Kittel and G. Friedrich, trans. by G. W. Bromiley (Grand Rapids: Eerdmans, 1971), Volume VII, pp. 553-555. I find the division of the two uses of the verb in the New Testament unwarranted on historical grounds and suspect that (1) there may be a closer connection than the article suggests between the two uses and that (2) the distinction drawn between the two uses is based in distinguishing Jesus from the figures in the parables on theological more than philological grounds. While we can distinguish the strata in which the verb occurs, that does not mean we must separate their meanings.

A Concluding Reflection

We came to the story of the Good Samaritan expecting to find an answer to questions about how Christians are to repent, to participate in the kingdom, or to act so that the reign of God will be realized. But when we examined this story, it became clear that it was not one story, but three. And none of them answered the questions we brought to the story. No matter how we take it, the parable turns the tables on us and forces *us* to answer. The key is not "who is the Samaritan?" but "what do we see in the Samaritan?" This then leads us to ask not "what did Jesus tell us to do?" but "where do we fit in his story?" The parable does not tell us the answer, but asks us to rethink our questions, review our visions, and reengage our imaginations.[16]

What is true of the long parables of the Good Samaritan and the Father with Two Sons is true of all Jesus' parables. They are more surprising than readers or hearers expect them to be. They ask more of their audience than their audience seeks of them. When his parables are freed from the crust of fossilized understandings to work on their readers, the audience can begin to be surprised into turning around, into repenting, into reconsidering the false certainties that structure all our lives in order to make room for the hope of the kingdom. The best biblical scholarship allows readers to read Jesus' stories anew and to free those stories to turn the reader around.

For Further Reading

For general overviews of the history of biblical criticism, the works of Livingston, O'Brien, and especially Duling, discussed in the "For Further Reading" section of chapter

---

[16]A. C. McGill also believed that the radical view of the parable of the Good Samaritan identified him as Jesus. See *Suffering: A Test of Theological Method* (Philadelphia: Westminster, 1982 [1968]), pp. 108-111 for his independent argument.

two, are helpful. In addition to these, those interested in
how and why the New Testament assumed its content will
find C. F. D. Moule, *The Birth of the New Testament* (New
York: Harper and Row, 1962) a good overview. Also useful
are Robert C. Grant, *The Formation of the New Testament*
(London: Hutchinson, 1965) and Willi Marxsen, *The New
Testament as the Church's Book* (Philadelphia: Fortress,
1972).

The first section of the chapter reflects many of the concerns and insights of the most important biblical scholar of
this century, Rudolf Bultmann. Two works which present
the major themes of his scholarship accessibly are *Jesus and
the Word*, translated by L. P. Smith and E. H. Lambro (New
York: Scribner's, 1958 [first German edition, 1926]) and
Jesus Christ and Mythology (New York: Scribner's, 1958).
The latter presents his program of demythologizing the New
Testament and is very readable. The key essay for Bultmann's project of demythologizing, "The New Testament
and Mythology" (1941) is published along with a number of
critiques and Bultmann's responses to criticisms in *Kerygma and Myth*, ed. H. W. Bartsch, revised translation by
R. H. Fuller (New York: Harper and Row, 1961).

The secondary literature on Bultmann is enormous. A
good general introduction is Norman Perrin, *The Promise
of Bultmann* (Philadelphia: Fortress Press, 1978 [first published, 1959]). *The Theology of Rudolf Bultmann*, edited by
C. W. Kegley (New York: Harper and Row, 1966) collects
critical essays by many scholars and includes a complete
bibliography of Bultmann's writings up to 1965. *Rudolf
Bultmann in Catholic Thought*, edited by T. O'Meara and
D. Weisser (New York: Herder and Herder, 1968) collects
essays which appreciatively and critically respond to Bultmann's work. Influential critical studies include Schubert
M. Ogden, *Christ Without Myth* (New York: Harper and
Row, 1961) and the very different work of John MacQuarrie, *The Scope of Demythologizing* (New York: Harper and
Row, 1960). Ogden seeks to bring Bultmann's program up
to date in *The Point of Christology* (San Francisco: Harper
and Row, 1982).

Although Bultmann was skeptical about retrieving much reliable information about the actual Jesus, others have been more sanguine. James M. Robinson, *A New Quest of the Historical Jesus* (Naperville, IL: Allenson; and London: SCM Press, 1959) offers not only a view of the new quest but also a solid history of the movements of thought that led to the new quest, including a critical reading of the 19th century quest. A number of the essays in *The Historical Jesus and the Kerygmatic Christ,* edited by C. E. Braaten and R. A. Harrison (Nashville: Abingdon, 1964) are constructively critical of the new quest and others provide some afterthoughts from those who engaged in the quest.

Scholarship on the parables is extensive. Warren S. Kissinger, *The Parables of Jesus: A History of Interpretation and Bibliography,* A.T.L.A. Bibliography Series 4 (New York: Scarecrow Press, 1979) provides a history that is very useful for pre-modern interpretation and sets of bibliographies arranged by parable which are exceedingly helpful in research. Yet scholarship on the parables of Jesus is most conveniently divisible into linguistic/geographical areas.

In the British tradition, two key works are T. W. Manson, *The Sayings of Jesus* (Cambridge: Cambridge University Press, 1931) and C. H. Dodd, *The Parables of the Kingdom* (London: Nisbet, 1935). The latter is especially important and, in the opinion of Joachim Jeremias, sets down some bases of interpretation which it would be unimaginable to repudiate.

The single most important book on the parables, whose wealth of insight has been confirmed throughout the years, is that of Joachim Jeremias, *The Parables of Jesus* (n. 12 above). Although conservative in his interpretations and criticism, Jeremias provides the standard: a scholar whose interpretation of a parable differs from Jeremias' must bear the burden of proof. Representative of recent German work is Eta Linnemann, *The Parables of Jesus* (see no. 10 above), which is quite readable and definitely accessible to the "educated adult"; it also provides some new insights into the parables recognized by fellow-scholars.

It is the Americans, however, who have made tremendous

strides in parable interpretation over the last fifteen years or so. Godfather to the movement is Amos Niven Wilder whose *Early Christian Rhetoric: The Language of the Gospel*, revised edition (Cambridge, MA: Harvard University Press, 1971 [first edition, 1964] has influenced subsequent scholarship with its literary-critical approach. The late Norman Perrin was a student of Jeremias and influenced by Wilder. His *Jesus and the Language of the Kingdom* (see n. 9 above) surveys and evaluates very helpfully the work done on parable interpretation in the context of Jesus' preaching of the kingdom. It extends his earlier *The Kingdom of God in the Teaching of Jesus* (Philadelphia: Westminster Press, 1963) and his *Rediscovering the Teaching of Jesus* (New York: Harper and Row, 1967) which I have found very helpful. Equally important is the work of Dan Otto Via, *The Parables: Their Literary and Existential Dimension* (Philadelphia: Fortress Press, 1967) and *Kerygma and Comedy in the New Testament* (Philadelphia: Fortress, 1975). His initial interest in literary analysis has moved into the area of structuralist approaches to the text, as has the interest of John Dominic Crossan. Although I find his discussion of language desultory, Crossan's *The Dark Interval* (see n. 5 above) is a very useful text to open students up to story theology. His works on parables (see n. 4 above) and his expansion of his work to comparative folktales (see n. 6) offer exciting adventures in interpretation. Within the next decade or so, I expect the great English text of Dodd and the magisterial German text of Jeremias to be joined by a revolutionary text from American parable scholarship.

6

THE STORIES OF JESUS: II

He went about doing good and healing.
—Acts 10:38

The verse cited above is a summary of the actions of Jesus. We have already considered some of his central and distinctive acts — his proclaiming the coming of God's reign and his challenging people's settled expectations by teaching in parables. In this chapter we consider the central and distinctive *actions* of Jesus.

On Reading New Testament Stories

Great care must be taken to uncover the central and distinctive actions of Jesus. People often have wanted a "life of Jesus" to answer their questions about who Jesus was. But the failure of the Old Quest for the Historical Jesus showed that a biography of Jesus is unretrievable from the biblical texts. Nevertheless, if proper care is taken, we can uncover some of the central and distinctive actions of Jesus. Three general guidelines must be observed.

First, modern interpreters must recognize how different their goal and context is from that of the ancient tellers and writers of stories.[1] Their goal was not to tell the truth by reporting the news like a newspaper writer or television commentator. Rather, they sought to tell the truth by confronting the hearers with a story that turned them on and made the hearers the active subjects of a new story. Their goal was not to report facts, but to manifest the good news so that the hearers could come to tell the stories as their own stories. Ancient storytellers did not seek to communicate facts but to convert hearers. Hence, if we are interested in the actions Jesus actually performed, we must ferret them out, recognizing that the contexts in which the ancient storytellers worked and the goals that they had may be quite different from ours.

Second, modern interpreters must note how differently contemporary and ancient people *hear* stories. Ancient hearers recognized the stories they were told as proposals for them to adopt or reject, not as "news" to be remembered or forgotten. The evangelists must be understood as people of their time who produced literature according to the conventions of their time. Since they were transcribing the good news they had heard preached and since they were working in different contexts, the stories they told differed and the interpretation of events' significance differed. As Edward Schillebeeckx put it, "Hence the difference in the characters of Jesus, of the Jews and of his disciples, the differences also in their actions, according to whether it is Mark, Matthew, Luke or John telling the story."[2] Because they had heard the stories in different contexts, the final writers of the gospels, having become proclaimers of the stories, inevitably composed divergent accounts when they sought to convert new hearers.

Third, modern interpreters must be aware of just what their procedures are and just what their goals are. This is often summarized as separating the stories of the "Christ of

---

[1] In this section, I am relying heavily on the discussion in Edward Schillebeeckx, *Jesus: An Experiment in Christology*, translated by Hubert Hoskins (New York: Seabury Press, 1979), p. 77.

[2] *Ibid.*, p. 78.

faith" from the stories of the "Jesus of history," of separating fact from propaganda. However, this formulation of the historian's task is very misleading.

The formula "Jesus of history/Christ of faith" is appealing because it recognizes that historians read the texts with a goal very different from that of the original writers and readers: the historian is not accepting or rejecting the stories as his or her own, but investigating them to discover the facts they contain. However, it is sometimes misleading for the terms used are ambiguous. "Jesus of history" may refer "both to the *actual* Jesus and to the Jesus that is *now recoverable by historical means*."[3] The results of historical investigation cannot put people in touch with the actual man from Nazareth, but can only clarify, verify or falsify the stories about him. As there is much about the actual man that is *not* recoverable by historical means, one cannot equate the "historian's Jesus" with the actual man, as sometimes happens. "Christ of faith" is often equated with propaganda. But we have *no* stories of Jesus that are not stories of the Christ of faith. All the stories are told by those who came to have faith in him. Stories of the Christ of faith are not so facilely separable from stories of the Jesus of history. The task of the historian is not to separate the two, but rather to show how the stories we have were altered, transformed and developed "under the influence of the theological interpretation of the actual Jesus by the Christian community,"[4] as a preliminary to reconstructing, as far as possible, "how things actually were for persons in past times and distant places"[5] in a manner comprehensible today.

In sum, historical criticism can clarify the doctrines Christians use to symbolize their faith, modify the exaggerations sometimes present in Christians' understanding, and reveal the multiplicity of stories about and understandings of Jesus as preserved in the New Testament. Historians

[3]Van A. Harvey, *The Historian and the Believer* (New York: Macmillan, 1966), p. 268; emphasis added.

[4]*Ibid.*

[5]William A. Clebsch, *Christianity in European History* (New York: Oxford University Press, 1979), p. 26.

cannot write a biography of Jesus. They cannot discover everything he did and taught, for Jesus did things not recorded in the Bible. They cannot give a definitive judgment on the reliability of every story or saying in the New Testament. They cannot provide a faith or a theology. But the actions reliably attributable to the actual Jesus provide a touchstone for all our theological reflection. Historians can provide *that*.

The Actions of Jesus

Norman Perrin provided a framework for our investigations by summarizing what can be reliably attributed to the actual Jesus:

> [Jesus] was baptized by John the Baptist, and the beginning of his ministry was in some way linked with that of the Baptist. In his own ministry, Jesus was above all the one who proclaimed the Kingdom of God and who challenged his hearers to respond to the reality he was proclaiming. The authority and effectiveness of Jesus as proclaimer of the Kingdom of God was reinforced by an apparently deserved reputation as an exorcist. In a world that believed in gods, in powers of good and evil, and in demons, he was able, in the name of God and his Kingdom, to help those who believed themselves to be possessed by demons.
>
> A fundamental concern of Jesus was to bring together into a unified group those who responded to his proclamation of the Kingdom of God irrespective of their sex, previous background or history. A central feature of the life of this group was eating together, sharing a common meal that celebrated their unity in the new relationship with God, which they enjoyed on the basis of their response to Jesus' proclamation. Jesus challenged the tendency of the Jewish community of his day to fragment itself and in the name of God to reject certain of its own members. This aroused a deep-rooted opposition to him,

which reached a climax during a Passover celebration in Jerusalem when he was arrested, tried by the Jewish authorities on a charge of blasphemy and by the Romans on a charge of sedition, and crucified. During his lifetime he had chosen from among his followers a small group of disciples who had exhibited in their work in his name something of his power and authority.[6]

Within this framework, then, we can seek to understand the stories of the central and distinctive actions of Jesus.

No less than his parables, Jesus' other actions focus attention on the kingdom of God. Two sorts of actions especially stand out: his healings (especially his exorcisms) and his sharing of meals or "table-fellowship." The centering of Jesus' actions on God's active ruling can be seen in the context of one of the exorcism stories in the New Testament:

> Now he was casting out a demon that was dumb; when the demon had gone out, the dumb man spoke, and the people marveled. But some of them said, "He casts out demons by Beelzebul, the prince of demons"; [while others, to test him, sought from him a sign from heaven]. But he, knowing their thoughts, said to them, "Every kingdom divided against itself is laid waste, and house falls

[6]Norman Perrin, *The New Testament: An Introduction* (New York: Harcourt Brace Jovanovich, Inc., 1974), pp. 277-278. This text was revised by Dennis Duling, and in the second edition, published in 1982, Duling has expanded this outline. At the beginning, he inserts: "Jesus was born about 4 B.C. to Joseph, a carpenter from Nazareth of Galilee and his wife Mary. He had brothers, one of whom (James) became prominent in the Palestinian church, and sisters (Mk 6:3). He grew up and was educated in the environment of the rural village life of Galilee, and his native tongue was the language of Palestine, Aramaic." At the end of the first paragraph he adds: "Thus, he moved from village to village, from town to town, preaching the Kingdom, exorcising demons, healing the sick, and offering hope to the poor. The general portrait of Jesus here is that of a spirit-filled ("charismatic") prophet, preacher, exorcist, and healer, often unconcerned about, or willing to break with, the legal-ritual traditions of purity which so concerned most of his fellow Jews." To the end of the sketch he appends, "Thus arose a 'Jesus movement,' spearheaded by a band of itinerant radicals who, like Jesus, moved about the villages and towns of Palestine, preaching and healing in his name" (pp. 411-412). Whether this expansion exhibits a desire to construct a biography of Jesus in a way Bultmann warned against is moot.

> upon house. And if Satan also is divided against himself,
> how will his kingdom stand? For you say that I cast out
> demons by Beelzebul. And if I cast out demons by Beel-
> zebul, by whom do your sons cast them out? Therefore,
> they shall be your judges. But if it is by the finger of God
> that I cast out demons, then the kingdom of God has
> come upon you (Lk 11:14-20).

The story here can be split into two parts — likely two parts
that Luke and/or his source put together. The first part is
the abbreviated discussion of the healing in a sentence. The
second part of the story is the controversy about by whose
power the healing is done. As with the story of the Good
Samaritan, multiple stories have been rolled into one.

The simple story of the exorcism is emblematic of Jesus'
ministry. As J. Ramsey Michaels puts it:

> Exorcism is clearly an integral and essential part of
> Jesus' ministry. References to demon possession and
> exorcism are embedded in every stratum of the Gospel
> tradition — Mark, the Q source, the distinctive material
> in Matthew and Luke, and the Gospel of John.[7]

Some of the stories are simply told in such a compressed
way that exorcisms seem taken for granted (see Mark 1:32-
34). Most of the stories, however, when they are told at
length, are combined with other material, so as to make the
story serve a specific point by expanding the exorcism story
with other material, as in our present story.

This longer story suggests two important items. First, it is
clear that Jesus is not the only exorcist or the only healer
working in Palestine at this time. His comparison of his
ministry with that of others ("by whom do your sons cast
them out") indicates this here. Since his challenge is that
they will be tarring their sons with the same brush which tars
him, we can assume that there were other exorcists to be

---

[7]J. Ramsey Michaels, *Servant and Son: Jesus in Parable and Gospel* (Atlanta:
John Knox Press, 1981), p. 154.

tarred. Second, it also seems that some of the people were opposed to Jesus' healings: why else would there be such a ruckus about them and about "by whose power" these acts were performed? If exorcisms were fairly common, at least among some "preachers," why did Jesus' exorcisms cause such a fuss?

Although a conclusive answer to this question may not be possible, Paul W. Hollenbach has suggested that Jesus' uniqueness consists in his exorcising in a way that would upset the established social structure. Hollenbach notes that "Jesus not only explicitly stated that exorcisms are the central act of God in the world (Lk 11:20), but he also sent out his followers on an exorcising mission (Mk 3:14-15), which also indicates the central importance he attached to exorcisms."[8] Thus, he interprets exorcism as indicating the kingdom of God being at hand.

Jesus' practice of exorcism also upset the Pharisees and the tetrarch of Galilee. Both responded hostilely to him because his exorcising demoniacs was a threat to the established political and social structure wherein demoniacs had a specific place. Although it was acceptable for demoniacs to exist and for professional exorcists to "ply their art; but it was not all right for an unauthorized exorcist to make so much over demon possession and demoniacs that he identified their healing with God's saving presence."[9] Jesus was the center of a widespread healing practice carried on outside the usual established practices. Hence, his attracting a large number of followers necessarily challenged "the prevailing social system and its underlying value system. . . . Jesus as an exorcist struck out directly into the vortex of the social turmoil of his day."[10] In short, Jesus' explanation of his exorcising activity as by the finger of God and his practice outside the established structures challenge the previously established rules.

---

[8]Paul W. Hollenbach, "Jesus, Demoniacs, and Public Authorities: A Socio-Historical Study," *Journal of the American Academy of Religion* XLIX/4 (December, 1981), p. 582.

[9]*Ibid.*, p. 583.   [10]*Ibid.*, p. 580.

However, this action is not merely a "moral" reminder or a "spiritual" restitution. It is a truly *political* action that challenges the whole socio-political system. "Possession by demons" is not only as a manner of representing physical or mental illness in a society more primitive — medically speaking — than ours. "Possession" by demons may have served "not only as a means for the oppressed to express their degradation, but also. . .as a means for the dominant classes to subdue those who protested against their oppressors."[11] For what better way to silence the voices of the oppressed than by accusing them of demon possession and loosing the power of a religiously sanctioned establishment on them to bring those demons into line. And Jesus was "curing" them of possession and thus allowing them to speak and to act. Now, not all demoniacs were poor and oppressed; some were from the upper classes. Yet by "curing demoniacs" Jesus was freeing people not only from their emotional or physical illnesses, but also from the system which gave rise to their illnesses. He was loosing energies which might serve to upset the present structure. No wonder, then, they accused him of using demonic power to "cast out devils."

In effect, Jesus' exorcisms are parabolic actions, acts which upset the presuppositions of those around him and which even subvert the social and political structures of his time. If we are to understand his acts today, we need to see how the stories of his actions fit into the myths that structured his times: and the way they fit into those myths is "parabolically." This is brought out clearly by another of the healing stories:

> And when he returned to Capernaum after some days, it was reported that he was at home. And many were gathered together, so that there was no longer room for them, not even about the door; and he was preaching the word to them. And they came, bringing to him a paralytic carried by four men. And when they could not get near

[11] *Ibid.*, p. 581.

him because of the crowd, they removed the roof above
him; and when they had made an opening, they let down
the pallet on which the paralytic lay. And when Jesus saw
their faith, he said to the paralytic, "My son, your sins are
forgiven."

Now some of the scribes were sitting there, questioning
in their hearts, "Why does this man speak thus? It is
blasphemy! Who can forgive sins but God alone?" And
immediately Jesus, perceiving in his spirit that they thus
questioned within themselves, said to them, "Why do you
question thus in your hearts? Which is easier, to say to the
paralytic, 'Your sins are forgiven,' or to say, 'Rise, take up
your pallet and walk'? But that you may know that the
Son of man has authority on earth to forgive sins" — he
said to the paralytic — "I say to you, rise, take up your
pallet and go home." And he rose, and immediately took
up the pallet and went out before them all; so that they
were all amazed and glorified God, saying, "We never saw
anything like this!" (Mk 2:1-12, RSV)

If Bultmann is correct,[12] we again have two stories rolled
together into a third. Roughly the material between the two
occurrences of "he said to the paralytic" is one story, and the
material outside of those two occurrences is another story,
and the writer of Mark (or his source) has combined these
two stories into our present story.

Yet our present story brings out the connection between
healing and forgiveness. But forgiveness of sins at that time
was seen as a prerogative of God — only God had that
power. Hence, what Jesus is perceived as doing — whether
during his ministry or after his death we can no longer know
for sure in the present case — is again to attribute the power
to heal to a force beyond the contemporary social and
political structure, by his connecting that healing with
forgiveness. In other words, Jesus' healing is presented here
as an act which is parabolic, subversive of the expectations

---

[12]Rudolf Bultmann, *The History of the Synoptic Tradition,* trans. John Marsh,
rev. ed. (New York: Harper and Row, 1976), pp. 14-16, 331.

of "the scribes" (conveniently introduced), an act undertaken not only on behalf of the paralyzed man, but also outside of the "normal" structure. Even Jesus' healings are parabolic acts.

The final distinctive action of Jesus is his table-fellowship, a meal shared perhaps as a realization or anticipation of the coming of the kingdom of God, as the "banquet" parables discussed in chapter five suggest. This table-fellowship also provides a background for the celebration of the Lord's Supper, the Communion of the community. Yet the bare facts of this table-fellowship, noted in the summary which began this section, need fleshing out.

> And as he sat at table in his house, many tax collectors and sinners were sitting with Jesus and his disciples; for there were many who followed him. And the scribes of the Pharisees, when they saw that he was eating with sinners and tax collectors, said to his disciples, "Why does he eat with tax collectors and sinners? And when Jesus heard it, he said to them, "Those who are well have no need of a physician, but those who are sick; I came not to call the righteous, but sinners." (Mk 2:15-17, RSV)

What is curious about this story is that it does not really hang together well. The question is why Jesus commits the religiously proscribed act of *eating with* outcasts. The answer is that he has come to *call* them. This lack of direct meeting of question and reply indicates that the story we have is a composite. But it shows us that not only did Jesus befriend and associate with "tax collectors and sinners" (a point attested to in all layers of the synoptic tradition), but that he also ate with them.

But who were these people? As J. Ramsey Michaels notes, "sinners" seems to be a group term for tax collectors who profited from the Roman occupation, prostitutes whose serving the occupying armies violated sexual mores, Gentiles who were ritually unclean as they were not even Jews, and also perhaps Roman soldiers, shepherds, and Samaritans.[13] Once we understand the range of the people Jesus shared his meal with we can see what he is really doing, as John R. Donahue notes:

> By his fellowship with the toll collectors and sinners Jesus makes present the love and saving mercy of God to those whom the social structures of his time would classify as unjust and beyond the pale of God's loving concern. Jesus' association with these groups is a form of symbolic activity which proclaims that those ritual laws which were designed to protect the sanctity and justice of God concealed the revelation of the true God. In associating with these groups Jesus is a parable of God's justice where mercy (hesed) and justice (s^{c}dāqāh) are not in opposition, but in paradoxical agreement.[14]

Thus, in sharing *his* meal with the social and religious outcasts of his time, Jesus was subverting the beliefs of his contemporaries who thought that God's mercy and justice would be visited upon those who followed the Law in a scrupulously ritualistic manner. Even his meals were remembered as parabolic actions.

Concluding Reflections

The exploration of these stories which present Jesus' central and distinctive actions leads to three conclusions. The first is that there is an intimate connection between parables and actions in the material which we can retrieve about Jesus. This especially is important for those who are interested in sacramental theology today, as Johannes Baptist Metz has pointed out:

---

[13] Michaels, *Servant and Son*, p. 207.

[14] John R. Donahue, S.J., "Biblical Perspectives on Justice," *The Faith That Does Justice*, ed. John C. Haughey. S.J. (New York: Paulist Press, 1977), p. 87.

> I am convinced that it is very important to bring out
> this narrative aspect of the sacrament more clearly. If this
> is done, the relationship between word and sacrament
> may be more fully elaborated theologically. Above all, it
> should also be possible to relate the sacramental action
> more closely to stories of life and suffering and to reveal it
> as a saving narrative.[15]

What Metz recognizes here is the need for a narrative context to make sense of a symbolic action. If one has no idea of
the context in which a sacramental or other symbolic action
is performed, then one cannot understand that action.
When the evangelists relate Jesus' story, the symbolic and
sacramental actions are woven into stories of justice and
righteousness so deeply that to separate the bare symbolic
or sacramental action from this context is to distort that
action. This suggests, then, that a contemporary Eucharistic
theology needs to pay close attention to the context in which
that symbolic or sacramental action is placed.

Second, it seems obvious that the material which we can
retrieve about Jesus as he actually was suggests that he was
revolutionary in both his words and his deeds. In the sense
that all parables are subversive and all parable tellers are
subversives, Jesus may well deserve the title "revolutionary." His words and actions call for radical change ("repentance") not only in individuals' consciousness and actions,
but also in the social structures which deform people into
outcasts and demoniacs. This warrants the claim that the
gospel of Jesus is a politically relevant message placed in the
context of politically relevant actions. As José Miranda has
written, "[T]he thesis that the message of Jesus does not get
involved in politics is simply outrageous. This thesis implies
a complete misunderstanding of the prophets and a complete misunderstanding of Christ's intransigent condemna-

---

[15]Johannes Baptist Metz, *Faith in History and Society: Toward a Practical
Fundamental Theology,* trans. David Smith (New York: Seabury Press, 1980), p.
208.

tion of the rich."[16] While one may disagree with Miranda on the extent and focus of Jesus' political activity, it is clear that his teaching and his actions led Jewish authorities to condemn him for blasphemy and Roman authorities to try him for sedition. It seems that Jesus' actions were *perceived* as revolutionary and that they led to his conviction and execution as a rebel or bandit.[17] Hence, to claim today that Christians' thought and action should not turn to the political sphere is dubious at best.

Third, the claim that Jesus was a violent revolutionary who advocated armed revolt or resistance simply cannot be warranted. A few scholars have tried to show from the biblical texts that Jesus either advocated or participated in attempts to overthrow violently the political authorities. However, their claims tend to be "too interested in proving a thesis to be convincing."[18] Jesus' movement was surely polit-

---

[16]José Porfirio Miranda, *Communism in the Bible*, trans. Robert R. Barr (Maryknoll: Orbis Books, 1982), p. 69. It is not clear to me that Miranda's attribution of opposition to the rich on the part of Jesus can be warranted, at least not in such a bald formulation.

[17]The passion and death of Jesus has been discussed at length in recent years in order to try to discover the historical strands in this heavily embroidered material. A. E. Harvey, *Jesus and the Constraints of History* (Philadelphia: Westminster, 1982) argues that either the gospels are a through-and-through cover-up and Jesus was a Zealot (cf. Brandon's work noted in the "for further reading" section) or that the gospels are basically correct in reporting that Jesus was "handed over" by the Jews to the Romans. Ellis Rivkin, *What Crucified Jesus? The Political Execution of a Charismatic* (Nashville: Abingdon, 1984) argues that Jesus was a victim of the political circumstances of the time in which the high priests were puppets of the Roman procurator who wanted nothing but quiet order and saw any charismatic preacher as a threat to the system. Both Harvey and Rivkin reject Brandon's thesis and recognize the political nature of the Sanhedrin's action in handing Jesus over. But they disagree on whether the Sanhedrin was also representative of the religious groups in Judaism. For Harvey, it is assumed. For Rivkin, a "puppet Sanhedrin" must be distinguished from the "courts" of the Scribes and Pharisees which were religious and a-political. The arguments given by these — and other — scholars in this area are so contested that the brief summary in the text seems to me all that is securely warranted. What *actions* Jesus performed in the midst of his passion may never be historically warrantable since that sort of investigation presumes a consensus on the legal and political context in which he acted and on the actual events of the "trials" of Jesus, a consensus unavailable given the conditions of the sources and the divergences in the readings of the evidence.

[18]John Howard Yoder, *The Politics of Jesus* (Grand Rapids: Eerdmans, 1972), p. 47.

ically involved and surely subversive of the structures of power in his social world, but that movement cannot be understood as a violent one.

Thus, the sort of subversion in which Jesus was engaged was parabolic. While we cannot finally specify the full range of this parabolic activity, we have seen hints about it in this chapter. Perrin mentions that the disciples were brought together regardless of sex, previous background or history. Hollenbach, Donahue and Michaels have noted Jesus' healing of and eating with the poor and the outcast. Elisabeth Schüssler Fiorenza has clarified this by centering on Jesus' encouraging a discipleship of equals. The very structuring of the earliest Christian communities as communities of equals (cf. Gal 3:28) implies a critique of the established socio-political relationships between rich and poor, men and women, free and slave, by "envisioning a different future and different human relationships on the grounds that *all* persons in Israel are created and elected by the gracious goodness" of God.[19] The revolution that Jesus brings is liberation from those socio-political structures which deform people. This "liberation from patriarchal structures is not only explicitly articulated by Jesus but is in fact at the heart of the proclamation of the *basileia* [kingdom] of God."[20]

The way for us to say what his revolution meant and means is three-fold. We must retrieve, reinterpret, and retell the stories of his acts. We must celebrate in sacrament the acts that he and his disciples undertook (including the disciple who anoints Jesus in Mark 14).[21] We must perform in his memory those sorts of actions that constitute the parabolic subversion of structures of oppression by creating alternative ways to live together. Christians who do this follow the earliest disciples of Jesus; as we shall see in chapter seven,

---

[19]Elisabeth Schüssler Fiorenza, *In Memory of Her* (New York: Crossroads, 1983), p. 142.

[20]*Ibid.*, p. 151.

[21]Cf. *ibid.*, xiii-xiv, 128-130, 152-153 *et passim*.

they had to explain his significance and his power in spite of the fact that, in terms of power accepted in the socio-political world in which he lived, he lost and the established authorities won.

For Further Reading

Most of the books discussing the actions of Jesus also discuss his significance. These are reviewed in the "for further reading" section after chapter seven. Among those which focus significantly on Jesus' actions are Hans Conzelmann, *Jesus*, translated by J. Raymond Lord (Philadelphia: Fortress Press, 1973); C. H. Dodd, *The Founder of Christianity* (New York: Macmillan, 1970) which presents a clear and rather traditional study; Günther Bornkamm, *Jesus of Nazareth*, translated by I. and F. McCluskey with J. M. Robinson (New York: Harper and Row, 1960) which is a detailed position deriving from the "new quest"; Raymond E. Brown, *Jesus: God and Man* (Milwaukee: Bruce, 1967) which presents the position of a moderate Catholic biblical scholar. A very helpful teaching text is Anthony Tambasco, *In the Days of Jesus* (New York: Paulist Press, 1983), which is excellently written and includes clear, simple maps.

A number of books focus clearly on Jesus' actions. John Howard Yoder, *The Politics of Jesus* (see n. 17 above) supports a pacifist, yet politically radical and activist, reading of Jesus' actions. J. Ramsey Michaels, *Servant and Son: Jesus in Parable and Gospel* (see n. 7 above) offers a post-critical reconstruction of the religion of Jesus as portrayed in his actions and his parables. The classic text for construing Jesus as a member of the revolutionary Zealot group is S. G. F. Brandon, *Jesus and the Zealots* (New York: Charles Scribner's Sons, 1967). A more recent manifesto is José Porfirio Miranda's *Communism in the Bible* (see n. 16 above). Although Miranda's thesis is provocative and interesting, his claim, that Jesus was a violent revolutionary whom Christians should emulate by overthrowing (in whatever sort of revolution is necessary) all the structures of oppression, is weakened by unwarrantedly selective readings of the texts.

A very different view of Jesus' central and distinctive actions, one more in agreement with the work of Yoder and the position of the present chapter is Frederick Houk Borsch, *Power in Weakness: New Hearing for Gospel Stories of Healing and Discipleship* (Philadelphia: Fortress Press, 1983). Although Borsch is writing more for pastors and layfolk than for scholars, his scholarship is meticulous (as the excellent notes indicate), and his retelling of the stories powerful.

However, the most provocative recent work is the feminist approach of Elisabeth Schüssler Fiorenza (see n. 19 above). She has brilliantly raised the discussion of Christian origins to a new level by combining skill in classic historico-critical Biblical interpretation, sociological analysis, liberation hermeneutics, and inclusive feminist presuppositions about the androcentrism of the written texts. Even if some of her specific theological claims (e.g., identifying Jesus' view of God with that of the wisdom traditions) are controvertible, the story of early Christianity will have to be revised in light of her work.

7

THE STORIES OF JESUS: III

God has made him both Lord and Christ,
this Jesus whom you crucified.
—Acts 2:36

Jesus proclaimed the reign of God in his words and manifested it in his deeds. These actions inspired his followers to proclaim *him* in story and sacrament and to manifest his presence through their own actions. In order to proclaim his significance, they adopted and adapted the *myths* of the world in which they lived. Those myths — stories which structure worlds — provide the context for understanding the various metaphors which are central to the early Christians' proclaiming him. These metaphors were drawn from various places. In the Christians' hands, they became titles and names for Jesus. To understand these titles requires understanding the stories in which they were set, the uses which the New Testament writers made of those metaphors and stories, and the significance they have in the canonical Scriptures. That is the task of this chapter.

Examining these metaphors and titles and the stories which provide their meaning by giving them a context can reveal if there are any Christian mythologies centering on Jesus. If myths faithfully and critically tell his story, they ground the quest that Edward Schillebeeckx, among others, sees as leading to the goal of reflection on Jesus: "...Christology must end up as a story about Jesus, a narrative Christology, and not as an all-embracing, theoretical 'Christological system.'"[1] The chapter then concludes by discussing the kind of myth appropriate for stories about Jesus.

The Son of Man

"Son of man" may have been the first title applied to Jesus. It is surely an early one, as it is found in all the strata of the traditions that were composed as our gospels. The title is used over 80 times in the gospels, and only once in the New Testament outside of the gospels (Acts 7:56). Scholars continue to debate not only the meaning of the term, but also whether Jesus used the term as a title for himself, or whether it was first used of him by his followers and retrojected into remembrance of his sayings.

While say it can be used merely as a circumlocution for "I" in Aramaic, a use that seems to be reflected in many New Testament texts, "son of man" is also used in more significant ways. John McKenzie has summarized these ways into five thematic categories: (a) texts which refer to Jesus' human condition, his participating in ordinary life; (b) texts which claim divinely-given powers for Jesus; (c) texts which tell of Jesus' mission; (d) texts in which the son of man suffers and dies; (e) texts in which the son of man comes on the clouds of heaven.[2] This last apocalyptic way provides a most important story for contextualizing the title "son of man." One example is Mark 13:

> But in those days, after that tribulation, the sun will be darkened, and the moon will not give its light, and the

---

[1]Edward Schillebeeckx, *Jesus: An Experiment in Christology*, trans. by Hubert Hoskins (New York: Seabury, 1979), p. 77.

[2]John McKenzie, *The New Testament Without Illusion* (Chicago: Thomas More Press, 1980), pp. 117-118.

stars will be falling from heaven, and the powers in the heavens will be shaken. And then they will see the Son of man coming in clouds with great power and glory. And then he will send out the angels, and gather his elect from the four corners of the earth to the ends of heaven (Mk 13:24-27, RSV).

In Mark's gospel, this material is spoken by Jesus in the context of warning about that future hour in which the times will be fulfilled and about which no one knows. Mark places this immediately before the passion narrative and by doing so may be suggesting that the passion is that hour.

This story is not original to the New Testament. In order to understand its meaning, we need first to see the earlier story that has been adopted here to apply to Jesus. It is the dream of Daniel:

> I saw in the night visions,
> and behold, with the clouds of heaven
>   there came one like a son of man,
> and he came to the Ancient of Days
>   and was presented before him.
> And to him was given dominion
>   and glory and kingdom,
> that all peoples, nations, and languages
>   should serve him;
> his dominion is an everlasting dominion
>   which shall not pass away
> and his kingdom one
>   that shall not be destroyed. (Dan 7:13-14, RSV)

In order to understand what it meant to talk of Jesus as the son of man, we need to know how the dream of Daniel was understood when the gospels were being composed, for it stands behind the distinctive and significant uses of the title.

The dream can be categorized as an apocalyptic myth expressing the hopes of Israel for that future time in which the present political yoke of foreign oppression would be thrown off. But how the story was understood changed through the course of the first century.

People of Jesus' time understood the myth as looking to a time in which Israel and Israel's God would be vindicated.[3] They took the son of man in the story as a symbol standing for the community of Israel which would be liberated when the Jews would be able to determine their own destiny under God. The son of man was *not* understood to be an individual, not even a hoped-for Messiah. The story expresses the hope of the community and the son of man stands for that community.

Yet in the Christian scriptures the story is told so that the son of man is a specific individual, Jesus. The meaning of the story has been transformed to show, for the first time, that an individual person, Jesus, is the hope of Israel, the coming Judge (as in the story of the sheep and the goats, discussed on pp. 60-64) and the son of man. In the New Testament, a creative reinterpretation of the dream of Daniel appears, transforming the story from one centering on the community of Israel to one centering on Jesus of Nazareth.

The creative reinterpretation of the dream of Daniel did not stop there. Later, probably after the Romans destroyed the Temple in Jerusalem in the year 70 C.E., Jewish speculative writers began to apply the phrase "son of man" to the Messiah they hoped for. They were likely influenced by the Christian interpretation of the son of man as applying to an individual. They also began to think of the son of man not only as a figure who would come in the future, but also as a "pre-existent son of man." This development of the understanding of Daniel's dream also may have influenced the way Matthew's and John's gospels used the term. In short, apparently "son of man" first symbolized the community,

---

[3]In what follows, I am adapting the work of James D. G. Dunn, *Christology in the Making: A New Testament Inquiry into the Origins of the Doctrine of the Incarnation* (Philadelphia: Westminster, 1980), pp. 65-97. (One of the great debates of recent biblical scholarship is whether Jesus actually referred to himself as or presented himself as the son of man in any significant sense. While I think that the evidence is open to affirming that the actual Jesus did creatively interpret Daniel 7 to apply to himself, that affirmation would be contested by more biblical scholars than would support it.)

then referred to a present individual (Mark), then applied to a future messiah who "pre-existed" (Jewish speculation) and then probably meant, among other things, the present Messiah (in Matthew and John).

This complex history shows that identifying a thematic category of a title or a story is not sufficient to provide it with a single meaning. Like Jesus' parables, the stories which express his significance and the titles derived from them do not have a fixed meaning. As the contexts change, the meaning of the story changes and the significance of the title which is found in the story changes. The apparently simple claim that Jesus is the son of man is in fact multiple. The evolution of the interpretation of the story forces the development of the understanding of the title.

As the Christian community developed, the title "son of man" became used independently of the distinctive apocalyptic context in which it arose. It thus faded into the pale, but significant, claim that Jesus was truly human. Other stories were told to portray his significance for the developing community.

The Son of God

The most important single title for Jesus in the Christian tradition is "son of God." Yet this metaphor, whose meaning theologians debate constantly, cannot be understood unless we can see the narratives which give rise to it. When the writers of the New Testament applied this title to Jesus, they used it against the background of the Jewish Scriptures, alluding to one or both of the following:

> I will tell of the decree of the Lord:
> He said to me, "You are my son,
>   today I have begotten you." (Ps 2:7).

> (The Lord instructs Nathan to tell David:) "When your days are fulfilled and you lie down with your fathers, I will raise up your offspring from you, who shall come forth from your body, and I will establish his kingdom.

> He shall build a house for my name, and I will establish
> the throne of his kingdom forever. I will be his father and
> he shall be my son." (2 Sam 7:12-14, RSV).

With these as inspiration and in light of the very important
and widely known tradition that Jesus addressed God as
abba, it appears that a number of stories were told by the
writers of the New Testament which express the meaning of
claiming Jesus to be God's son. In fact, at least five stories
show what "son of God" means.[4]

(a) The earliest written stories of Jesus as the Son of God
are summarized in the following:

> Paul, a servant of Jesus Christ, called to be an apostle,
> set apart for the gospel of God which he promised before-
> hand through his prophets in the holy scriptures, the
> gospel concerning his Son who was descended from
> David according to the flesh and designated Son of God
> in power according to the Spirit of holiness by his resur-
> rection from the dead, Jesus Christ our Lord...(Rom
> 1:1-4, RSV).

> "And we bring you the good news that what God prom-
> ised to the fathers, this he has fulfilled to us their children
> by raising Jesus; as also it is written in the second psalm,
> 'Thou art my Son, today I have begotten thee.'"(a speech
> attributed to Paul by Luke in Acts 13:32-33, RSV).

In both these passages, the story of the Resurrection of
Jesus by God shows what it means to say that Jesus is God's
son. James D. G. Dunn discusses the significance of contextualizing the title "son of God" in this story:

> [T]he first Christians thought of Jesus' divine sonship
> principally as a role and status he had entered upon, been
> appointed to at his resurrection. Whether they thought of
> him as already God's son during his earthly ministry we

---

[4]See Reginald H. Fuller, *The Foundations of New Testament Christology* (n.p.:
Collins, 1976), pp. 164-167.

cannot say. But even if they did recall his "*abba-relationship*" with God while on earth, they nevertheless regarded Jesus' resurrection as introducing him into a relationship with God decisively new, eschatologically distinct, perhaps we should even say qualitatively different from what he had enjoyed before...[5]

This new regard for Jesus' sonship emerges in the context of a story of what God had done for him. To be raised from the dead is to fulfill the hope for the final days, for the coming of the eschaton. And that hope has been realized in Jesus. The day on which Jesus is raised from the dead, according to this apocalyptically based story, is the day on which Jesus is "designated" or "begotten" as son of God.

(b) A second story which provides the meaning of the title "son of God" is the story of the redemption of humanity by the crucifixion of Jesus. This story is told dramatically by Mark and didactically by Paul.

The story of Jesus' passion and death forms a key focus for Mark's drama. Mark centers his gospel on the passion and crucifixion of Jesus. He concludes the crucifixion scene with a minor character declaiming the key words that express the point of the gospel according to Mark: "And when the centurion, who stood facing him, saw that he thus breathed his last, he said, "'Truly this man was the Son of God!'" (Mk 15:39, RSV). Surprisingly, someone identified as a stranger — not a Jew or follower of Jesus, but a Roman soldier — recognized Jesus as son of God when Jesus died. Interestingly, except for a man possessed by a demon (or a demon speaking through a man), no other person in the gospel of Mark labels Jesus as son of God. Rather, only his death makes it possible for ordinary folk to see him as son of God.

Paul's version of the story is more explicitly theological than Mark's:

---

[5]Dunn, *Christology*, p. 36; emphasis deleted. It should be noted that the story of the resurrection as the context of "son of God" antedates Paul's use of it in Romans.

> While we were yet helpless, at the right time Christ died
> for the ungodly. Why, one will hardly die for a righteous
> man — though perhaps for a good man one will dare even
> to die. But God shows his love for us in that while we were
> yet sinners Christ died for us. Since, therefore, we are now
> justified by his blood, much more shall we be saved by
> him from the wrath of God. For if while we were enemies
> we were reconciled to God by the death of his Son, much
> more, now that we are reconciled, shall we be saved by his
> life. Not only so, but we also rejoice in God through our
> Lord Jesus Christ, through whom we have now received
> our reconciliation (Rom 5:6-11, RSV).

Paul understands the crucifixion explicitly as the death of
God's son for us. In contrast to the Resurrection story, an
eschatological story of hope and glory, the crucifixion story
is a scandalous story of passion and death for God's son.

These two ways of presenting Jesus' crucifixion each give
a context for "son of God" different from that of the Resurrection story. They also provide the story from which
important later doctrinal claims will arise. Both the doctrines of who Christ is (Christology) and what Christ did for
us (soteriology) can be developed from the crucifixion stories. In fact, these stories construct a world in which the
story of the crucifixion of Jesus *is* the story of human
redemption by God. The Christian stories are centrally
based in both the crucifixion narratives and the resurrection
narratives, which provide very different meanings for the
title "son of God."

(c) A third story suggests that the key to the understanding of Jesus as "son of God" is neither the story of the
crucifixion nor the story of the resurrection. Rather, Jesus is
recognized as (or recognizes himself as) the son of God in his
Baptism:

> In those days Jesus came from Nazareth of Galilee and
> was baptized by John in the Jordan. And when he came
> up out of the water, immediately he saw the heavens
> opened and the Spirit descending upon him like a dove;

and a voice came from heaven, "Thou art my beloved Son; with thee I am well pleased" (Mt 1:9-11, RSV).

Whether Jesus saw the heavens open (as Mark's story has it), or John the Baptist saw it (as John's story has it) or all present apparently saw it (as Matthew and Luke suggest in their development), it is clear that it is on this day at the beginning of his ministry that Jesus is "begotten" or "recognized" as God's son.

(d) A fourth story that gives rise to the claim that Jesus is God's son is the story of Jesus' conception as the son of God. Both Matthew and Luke suggest this, in somewhat different ways (which need not concern us here).[6] Matthew's story traces Jesus' genealogy from Abraham through David (perhaps recalling 2 Sam 7) to Joseph. The story then continues:

> Now the birth of Jesus Christ took place in this way. When his mother Mary had been betrothed to Joseph, before they came together she was found to be with child of the Holy Spirit; and her husband Joseph, being a just man and unwilling to put her to shame, resolved to send her away quietly. But as he considered this, behold, an angel of the Lord appeared to him in a dream, saying, "Joseph, son of David, do not fear to take Mary your wife, for that which is conceived in her is of the Holy Spirit; she will bear a son and you shall call his name Jesus, for he will save his people from their sins." (Mt 1:18-20, RSV).

This story has made it clear that Jesus was conceived as God's son.

These four stories provide a spectrum of meanings for calling Jesus "son of God." More importantly, each of the stories attributes a different day as the day referred to in "this day I have begotten thee." Story (a) sees Jesus made or

---

[6]Raymond E. Brown, *The Birth of the Messiah: A Commentary on the Infancy Narratives of Matthew and Luke* (Garden City: Doubleday, 1977) discusses these at length.

recognized as God's son on the day of his Resurrection. Story (b) moves it back to his crucifixion, story (c) to the inauguration of his ministry, and story (d) to his conception. This suggests that the early Christian writers piled story upon story, to show that story (a) is not to be taken as a story in which Jesus is "adopted" as God's son. Finally, they tell a story in which "God's creative action in the conception of Jesus (attested negatively by the absence of human fatherhood) begets Jesus as God's Son."[7]

This use of different stories in the Christian tradition to show what it means to call Jesus "son of God" means that there is no single myth which can express fully the meaning of that phrase. All the stories function as myths. They construct worlds in which God has entered into history and *made a man his son*. But each portrays a different way for God to enter the world. These myths jostle against one another, not functioning as a set of countermyths (see pp. 48-50 above), but as a set of authentic stories. In short, the title "son of God" is found in many different stories and thus, it means many different things to call Jesus God's son.

A fifth story presents a yet different view, one in which God *makes his son a man*. This story provides a complex attempt to fuse elements from the stories discussed above into one brilliant and comprehensive story. It is a myth that has structured most subsequent Christian theology. John's gospel tells of the incarnation of a pre-existent Son who enters a world to redeem it:

> For God so loved the world that he gave his only Son, that whoever believes in him should not perish but have eternal life. For God sent his Son into the world, not to condemn the world, but that the world might be saved through him. He who believes in him is not condemned; he who does not believe is condemned already, because he has not believed in the name of the only Son of God (Jn 3:16-18, RSV).

[7]Brown, *The Birth of the Messiah*, p. 141.

For John, the primary story is not the story of *events in time* like Resurrection, Cross or Baptism of Jesus. Rather, it is the story of an event *out of time* that makes these events truly meaningful. For Jesus to be truly the Son of God, the framework of the story must be that God makes his son a man. The other stories can then be placed within an Incarnation story, thus avoiding the suggestion that God made a man his son. John thus presents a story of God's son which has a radically different structure and meaning from the others.

Each of these five stories gives a different context to the claim that Jesus is the son of God. Thus, the metaphor "son of God" varies in meaning. However, the purpose of these stories remains constant: to say what God has done through Jesus.

The differences in contexts, structures, and foci of the stories raise the question of what it means to say that Jesus is the son of God. But rather than canonizing one story as *the* story, Christians must recognize all of them as properly different ways to tell the story of God's son. No single story will suffice. All of them are appropriate.

However, that does not mean that *any* story or interpretation will suffice. The Ecumenical Council of Chalcedon in the year 451 reflected on the stories told of and the claims made about Jesus as the son of God and son of man. The council proclaimed that Jesus Christ is "truly human and truly divine." It did not set a single story as the only right story. Rather, it excluded inadequate stories and interpretations of stories. Those which deny either Jesus' true humanity or his true divinity were found to be inappropriate for expressing Christian faith. In short, the proper expression of Christian faith must include all those stories which are found in the traditions and all those interpretations which are faithful to the standards the tradition has developed.[8]

---

[8]For the text of the Chalcedonian definition, see *Documents of the Christian Church*, ed. Henry Bettenson (London and New York: Oxford University Press, 1961 [1943]), pp. 72-73. For a discussion of the developments in doctrine which led to the formulation, see Maurice Wiles, *The Christian Fathers* (London: SCM Press, 1977 [1966]), pp. 55-82.

The New Adam

A third phrase gives Jesus the title of a "New Adam," a "last Adam" or a "Second Adam." The story grows out of St. Paul's experience of the power of Jesus Christ transforming his life. It has clear eschatological overtones, yet tells not only of the end, but also of a new beginning, of human life both with and without the salvation Jesus brings:

> Therefore as sin came into the world through one man (Adam) and death through sin, and so death spread to all men because all men sinned — sin indeed was in the world before the law was given, but sin is not counted where there is no law. Yet death reigned from Adam to Moses, even over those whose sins were not like the transgression of Adam, who was a type of the one who was to come. But the free gift is not like the trespass. For if many died through one man's trespass, much more have the grace of God and the free gift in the grace of that one man Jesus Christ abounded for many. And the free gift is not like the effect of that man's sin. For the judgment following one trespass brought condemnation, but the free gift following many trespasses brings justification. If, because of one man's trespass, death reigned through that one man, much more will those who receive the abundance of grace and the free gift of righteousness reign in life through the one man Jesus Christ (Rom 5:12-17, RSV).

The story portrays Christ as the one man who reverses the trend begun by one other man.

The background for Paul's story is the second myth in Genesis. It tells of the fall into sin of Adam, the prototypical human or "everyman." After Adam, each human life is fractured, wretched and sinful. All participate in sin; all lives are fractured.

Jesus Christ, however, reverses the matter. As Adam brought sin into the world at the beginning, so Christ frees the world from sin at the end. But in so doing, Christ incorporates humanity into himself. As Adam initiated humanity, so Christ initiates a new humanity, a renewed humanity. Dennis Duling shows the significance of this story and the title associated with it:

> This new humanity brought about a new community of those "in Christ," or "in the body of Christ," which share a mutual love and responsibility. The Christian was initiated into this community by baptism, and by it the Christian was sustained, sharing in the body, especially through participation in the Lord's Supper.[9]

The last Adam story involves all Christians as members of the body of Christ.

As all humans participate in Adam, so all Christians participate in Christ. And to be part of Christ's body is to extend his reconciliation throughout the world, to act as he did.

Yet the "last Adam" story and its implication of present incorporation of Christians into Christ has been overwhelmed by the Incarnation story and its concern for what happened in the past. This development is not very happy. James D. G. Dunn discusses what happens when Christians stop balancing the story of the Incarnation of the Son with the story of the Redemption of people in the last Adam:

> [I]ncarnation became steadily more central as the decisive christological moment which determined the character of the redeemer figure — now seen as the divine being who united humanity with his deity, rather than as one who conquered where Adam failed, who died and rose again where Adam ended only in death. Likewise incarnation became steadily more central as the decisive act of redemption...so that later theology had to look for meaning in Christ's death more as the paying of a ransom to the devil than as the ending of the first Adam that last Adam might come to be. . . .[I]t is certainly arguable that all these subsequent developments are the consequence in

---

[9]Dennis C. Duling, *Jesus Christ Through History* (New York: Harcourt Brace Jovanovich, 1979), p. 57.

part at least of losing sight of the original meaning and intention of the Adam christology, that is, as one of the earliest attempts to spell out the sense of eschatological newness, of participating in a new humanity which was God's original intention for man but which now could be enjoyed only through sharing in the life from death of the risen Christ, the last Adam.[10]

When a community allows one story to take over another story, when people allow the significance of the person and work of Jesus Christ to be narrated in only one way, the significance of the overwhelmed story is lost. Christian theologians were forced to develop outlandish theories and absurd stories to account for the atonement, the work of Christ, as Ian T. Ramsey has so elegantly shown.[11] Yet if we can retrieve the story of Christ as the "last Adam," the "eschatological man," we can again see what it is to be a member of Christ's body and to participate in his saving work. But that is work for chapter eight.

The Suffering Servant

Although scholars disagree about how old this story is, the story of Jesus as the suffering servant is a central one in the New Testament. The early Christians took the story of the servant of the Lord, a figure who appears in Isaiah 40-55, and applied it to Jesus. Whether this is as complex and creative an interpretation as that of the "son of man" story is unknown. The figure in Isaiah may represent a specific individual or type of individual (such as prophet or king) or it may be a symbol for the community (or part of it)

---

[10]Dunn, *Christology*, p. 128. Dunn also interprets the kenosis hymn in Philippians 2 as expressive of the Final Adam Christology rather than of Incarnation Christology. Even if Dunn's novel interpretation of the hymn cannot be sustained, his argument is interesting, and the points made here still stand.

[11]See Ian T. Ramsey, *Christian Discourse: Some Logical Explorations* (London: Oxford University Press, 1965), ch. 2.

which remained faithful to the Lord and was vindicated. Yet 1 Peter 2:21-25 is a story which meditates on Isaiah 53, a story applying that hymn to Jesus.

> For to this you have been called, because Christ also suffered for you, leaving you an example, that you should follow his steps. He committed no sin; no guile was found on his lips. When he was reviled, he did not revile in return; when he suffered, he did not threaten; but he trusted to him who judges justly. He himself bore our sins in his body on the tree, that we might die to sin and live to righteousness. By his wounds you have been healed. For you were straying like sheep, but have now returned to the Shepherd and Guardian of your souls. (1 Pet 2:21-25, RSV)[12]

This reflection implies that the crucifixion is the fulfillment of the prophecy in Isaiah.

This story needs to be understood in the context of, or in juxtaposition with, the other stories of the cross, of Final Adam, and of the recognition of the son of God. At various points in the New Testament, the story of the despised and rejected one, one who was righteous and meek and died for us, is told as a story of who Jesus is and what he did. In 1 Peter, however, it becomes explicit that not only is this what Jesus did and was, but also that this is what Christians who profess faith in him must do and be. In short, the prophecy of Isaiah provides the framework for a story of Jesus *and* his followers, for whoever are *accounted* righteous and healing by the Suffering Servant must become righteous and healing suffering servants, too.

---

[12]Although 1 Peter is one of the late documents of the New Testament, the story itself seems taken from an earlier tradition. Some scholars would also see a connection with the suffering son of man sayings (e.g., Mk 8:31; see p. 118 above) here. The present analysis is indebted to Norman Perrin, and Dennis Duling, *The New Testament: An Introduction*, second ed. (New York: Harcourt Brace Jovanovich, 1982), p. 378 which suggests the "meditation" in this context.

The New Moses

The stories of Moses' leading the Exodus and receiving the commandments of the Law inspire and constitute the Jewish world. Matthew's gospel presents Jesus as the New Moses. First, Jesus is the New Interpreter of God's law. This is suggested especially by the frequent antitheses in Matthew, "You have heard that it was said..., but I say unto you..." especially in the Sermon on the Mount. The law Jesus gives, however, is tougher than the old law, for Jesus intensifies the Mosaic law at its most important points, yet minimizes the routine and less important commands.

Second, Jesus is the founder of the Church. Just as the nation of Israel followed the path that Moses pointed out, so the church must walk the way that Jesus has marked out. But, as Howard Clark Kee has pointed out, Matthew's adapting, developing, and restating the teaching of Jesus when he wrote his gospel half a century after Jesus' ministry is his way of remaining true to Jesus' teaching:

> From the standpoint of the modern historian, one could say that Matthew has falsified the account by depicting Jesus as warning his disciples that they will be required to appear at hearings before kings and governors (10:18), since these circumstances did not arise until apostolic times and even later. But Matthew is making precisely the opposite point: The Living Christ is present and active in his church in apostolic times. It is not a matter of placing the history of the church back into the ministry of Jesus, but of placing the history of Jesus within the ongoing life of the Church.[13]

Hence, Matthew models his story of Jesus and the Church on the story of Moses and Israel, but with the crucial differences that Jesus the leader remains with the community and his law demands a higher, more perfect obedience.

[13]Howard Clark Kee, *Jesus in History*, Second Edition (New York: Harcourt Brace Jovanovich, 1977), p. 180.

The Word of God

A sixth title for Jesus that has been important in all Christian theology is the word or *logos* or wisdom of God. This phrase has its context in a myth of the incarnation of the pre-existent wisdom or word. In John's gospel, the myth of the pre-existent word is incorporated into the hymn which forms the prologue to the gospel:[14]

> In the beginning was the Word and the Word was with God and the Word was God. He was in the beginning with God; and all things were made through him, and without him was not anything made that was made. In him was life and the life was the light of men. The light shines in the darkness and the darkness has not overcome it.
>
> He was in the world, and the world was made through him, yet the world knew him not. He came to his own home, and his own people received him not. But to all who received him, who believed in his name, he gave power to become children of God;
>
> And the Word became flesh and dwelt among us, full of grace and truth; [we have beheld his glory, glory as of the only Son of the Father. . .] And from his fulness we have received grace upon grace (Jn 1:1-16, RSV).

A few verses of the gospel have been omitted here in order to present the hymn without John's commentary.[15]

The hymn itself has four elements. First, the *word* was with God from the beginning. The word existed before the creation of the world. Second, the world was *created* through the word. The word is the mediator or agent of creation, and even present in creation, in spite of the presence of darkness (sin?) in the world. Third, those who can

[14]Some scholars believe that the same myth informs Paul's quotation of wisdom hymns as well. See Dunn, *Christology*, chapters six and seven.

[15]See Raymond E. Brown, *The Gospel According to John I-XII*, The Anchor Bible 29 (Garden City, NY: Doubleday, 1966), p. 3-4, 21-36.

recognize him can become children of God. While this may refer to the presence of God in the world, it probably alludes to the preaching and teaching of Jesus. Fourth, we have seen the glory by hearing the preaching, believing in him, and have thereby *received* grace upon grace.

The hymn was part of the worship of the Christian community. It sings of creation and incarnation, and of the worshiper's response to the present, creative power of God's word. Whether the bracketed phrase is part of the commentary or part of the hymn is unimportant. It merely makes explicit what is implicit in the rest of the text: the Word descended and became flesh. The Word through which the world was made has become human in Jesus.

Yet the final author of the gospel has added not only remarks which amplify the hymn and comment on John the Baptist, but also a fifth element to complete the four in the hymn: "For the law was given through Moses; grace and truth came through Jesus Christ. No one has ever seen God; the only Son, who is in the bosom of the Father, he has made him known" (Jn 1:18, RSV). The first phrases of this addition allude to either — or both — Matthew's story of Jesus as the New Moses or Paul's story of Jesus who redeems people as the Last Adam. "That the Son has made the unknown God known" recaps the hymn. So the final movement in the story is the return, the ascent to the bosom of the Father. Thus, the structure of the myth in the text as we have it is:

1. The pre-existence of the Word as or with God.
2. The creation of the world in/through the Word.
3. The presence of the Word in the world.
4. The response to the Word which redeems us.
5. The Presence of the Son (Word) with the Father (God).

The question is how this myth is to be understood.[16]

---

[16]The history of this hymn and this story before John included it in his gospel is disputed. Most likely early Christian worshiping communities refashioned earlier myths about Wisdom ("logos" in Greek) from Jewish traditions or about the Logos (which we usually translate as "word") in order to sing of Jesus. Some may have transformed contemporary myths about a divine man into a hymn about the Son of the Father. Whatever this narrative's background is, it is complex.

The most popular reading of the myth has followed the descent/ascent motif. This reads the story as telling of the *descent* of the Word (3 in the structure above) and the *ascent* of the Son (5). This reads the myth as basically a story of the Incarnation of the Son of God (as the story discussed on pp. 126-127 above), completed by an ascent (appropriate in the light of the Ascension story in Acts 1:6-11).

Yet this popular reading has a major problem. It ignores the part of the story told in step 4. By leaving out the response of those who can see and become the children of God, this popular reading understands the story as a four-part story:

1. Pre-existence
2. Creation
3. Descent
4. Ascent

This reading has dominated much of subsequent Christology. Yet it reflects neither the structure of the original hymn nor the structure of the canonical prologue. It also ignores the terminological shifts in the text (Word, Son; God, Father) and the involvement, in either basic reading, of the hearers of the Word. This popular reading is inadequate to tell the whole story.

The popular reading has provoked an opposite reading, an existentialist reading. This takes the structure of the story as:

1. The response to the Word which redeems us.

It takes the prologue as the preview of the theology of the gospel of John and makes it sound terribly contemporary. In this reading cosmic or social history is irrelevant. It is the decision of the self in each moment that is crucial. Death, resurrection and judgment are not future events, but events of every instant. They are the call of the individual by Jesus to attend to God. Hence,

> John does not deny that there will be a resurrection or a judgment in the future, but the anxiety is removed from these future events by the belief that the decisive factor is the decision of faith that is made in the present moment.

Using the form of historical narrative and locating the
goal of history in the moment of decision, John succeeds
in presenting his theology as history.[17]

This reading of the story is just the converse of the popular
one. Instead of reading it as 1-2-3-5, the existentialist reading reads it as *4*. This is an inadequate approach, too. It is
the sort of de-eschatologizing and de-historicizing interpretation that was rejected, following Rahner, in chapter four.
It so collapses the story of the Word that there remains no
story, only timeless decisions.

Both popular and existentialistic readings are one-sided.
Both ignore the narrative structure of the gospel myth.
Neither can stand alone to tell the story. While they are
historically important readings they represent defective
understandings of the myth. In the end, telling the myth of
the word becoming flesh must include talking both of the
response to the word, and the response to the *word become
flesh*. In short, to tell of Jesus as the Word, Wisdom or *Logos*
of God, is to tell the *whole* story of response to the Incarnate
Word.

The Messiah

The last title we will consider here is "messiah." What
does it mean to call Jesus "the anointed one" (in Hebrew
māŝîah and in Greek, *Christos*)? What sort of Messiah or
Christ is Jesus? In one sense, all the myths, parables, and
actions of the New Testament can be understood as contributing to answering this question. Although in its following form the present story has been carefully crafted by its
author from a number of sources, it tells *what kind* of Christ
or Messiah Jesus is:

And Jesus went with his disciples to the villages of
Caesarea Philippi; and on the way he asked his disciples,
"Who do men say that I am?" And they told him, "John

[17]Kee, *Jesus in History*, p. 256.

the Baptist; and others say Elijah; and others one of the prophets." And he asked them, "But who do you say that I am?" Peter answered him, "You are the Christ." And he charged them to tell no one about him.

And he began to teach them that the Son of man must suffer many things, and be rejected by the elders and the chief priests and the scribes, and be killed, (and after three days rise again). And he said this plainly. And Peter took him and began to rebuke him. But turning and seeing his disciples, he rebuked Peter, and said, "Get behind me, Satan! For you are not on the side of God, but of men."

And he called to him (the multitude with) his disciples, and said to them, "If any man would come after me, let him deny himself and take up his cross and follow me. For whoever would save his life will lose it; and whoever loses his life for my sake (and the gospel's) will save it. For what does it profit a man, to gain the whole world and forfeit his life? For what can a man give in return for his life? For whoever is ashamed of me and of my words in this adulterous and sinful generation, of him will the Son of man also be ashamed, when he comes in the glory of his Father with the holy angels." And he said to them, "Truly, I say to you, there are some standing here who will not taste death before they see the kingdom of God come with power." (Mk 8:27—9:1, RSV).

The parentheses in the present quotation indicate *only* phrases that the story would make better sense without. If Jesus had referred to the Resurrection, why would Peter be so perplexed? If this is addressed to others besides the disciples, why is their reaction not recorded? If there is no difference between losing one's life for Jesus' sake and for the gospel's sake, is the reduplication necessary?[18]

---

[18]For the debate over this story, see Rudolf Bultmann, *The History of the Synoptic Tradition*, trans. by John Marsh (New York: Harper and Row, 1976), pp. 257-259; Oscar Cullmann, *The Christology of the New Testament*, Revised Edition, trans. by S. C. Guthrie and C. A. M. Hall (Philadelphia: Westminster, 1963), pp. 122-25; Fuller, *Foundations*, pp. 109-111. The present interpretation is indebted to Stanley Hauerwas, "Jesus: The Story of the Kingdom," *A Community of Character* (Notre Dame: University of Notre Dame Press, 1981).

Whatever the status of the bracketed material, the story in its present form depicts an action in the life of Jesus, although it is composed by Mark. Scholars disagree vigorously about which of the story's elements are attributable to the faith community's remembrance of the risen Lord, which elements go back to an actual encounter, and whether the story hangs together as a whole in spite of its appearing to be a composition. In any event, Mark the evangelist saw it as crucial: it is the hinge on which his whole gospel turns.

Matthew and Luke borrow the story from Mark and tell it in their own ways. Matthew includes a section in which Peter is commended for getting the answer right by a response from Jesus which acclaims Peter as the rock on which the church will be built and as the possessor of the keys of the kingdom (Mt 16:13-23). When people read this version they sometimes neglect the rest of the story in which Peter is horribly rebuked by Jesus (or they treat it as a different story entirely). Luke has no giving of the keys, but also no rebuke of Peter. In each version the focus of the story is much different.

To make sense of Mark's story we must concede that Peter answered correctly at the beginning. Whether Peter answered alone or as representative for all Christians and whether the story is a close reflection of an actual incident are irrelevant here. In this realistic narrative, Peter *is* the person who responds. In the second paragraph, when Jesus spells out the *kind* of Messiah he is, and Peter rebukes him, Jesus lashes out at Peter, "Satan!" An ecumenical group of scholars has commented on these incidents:

> [T]he function of the Son of Man saying introduced by Mark in 8:31 is not a rejection of Peter's confession but a corrective to it by the addition of a note of suffering. Peter's confession is inadequate because he does not see that suffering is part of the career of the Messiah. It is only when Peter rejects this note of suffering that Mark (8:33) has Jesus rebuke him sharply by calling him Satan. The Satanic work of Peter is not in his confession of Jesus as Messiah but in his tempting Jesus toward a notion of

messiahship that does not recognize the divinely
ordained suffering and death of Jesus...[19]

While this interpretation is on the right track, it has not yet
reached the heart of the matter.

The real point is brought out by Stanley Hauerwas:
"Jesus thus rebukes Peter, who had learned *the name*, but
not the story that determines the meaning of the name."[20]
Peter knew the title but not the narrative context which
gives the title meaning. The story of the cross determines the
kind of Messiah Jesus is. A person who calls Jesus the
Messiah or the Christ without understanding that the Messiah gets crucified doesn't understand Jesus' Messiahship. It
is not that Jesus merely "corrects" Peter's confession. He
turns it upside down. The Messiah doesn't win the world by
a display of divine power. He *wins* it in death. Peter expected a Messiah who would beat the powers of the world at
their own game. Jesus upsets Peter's expectations, and the
expectations of anyone who confesses Jesus as Christ and
expects him to overpower the world.

In this story Jesus upsets expectations. He reverses what
Peter expects of a Messiah. His acceptance of the title,
"anointed one," or "messiah," or "christ," reverses the
accepted meaning of the terms by placing them in the context of a story of suffering and death. In short, this story
shows Jesus to be a *parabolic Messiah*.

When we consider the third paragraph of the story, the
reversal becomes more evident. Jesus says that not only did
Peter get the story wrong, but also that Peter's story must fit
his story; "Your story, too, if you would follow me, will be
the same as mine." The story of messiahship and the story of
discipleship are entwined irrevocably. And as the messiah
loses his life, so must the disciple. As messiahship is parabolic, so discipleship must be parabolic.

---

[19]Raymond E. Brown, Karl P. Donfried, and John Reumann, editors, *Peter in
the New Testament: A Collaborative Assessment by Protestant and Roman Catholic Scholars* (Minneapolis: Augsburg, and New York: Paulist, 1963), p. 69.

[20]Hauerwas, "Jesus," p. 48.

What is the force of this story? Scholars differ greatly about this. But it is at least a warning to all the Peters of all generations that the power of the kingdom of God, the power of the Father, the power of the Son, is the power of the cross. To misunderstand the story of the messiah and to misunderstand his power, is to misunderstand the power of discipleship and to get the story of discipleship wrong, too. And those who do will also be addressed, "Satan!"

To enable someone to understand the point of this story, two strategies are possible. A didactic strategy is to consider stories of creative, parabolic discipleship, that is, to show how some Christians have taken up the challenge of making Jesus' story their own story. A practical strategy is to ask a Christian, "Who do *you* say that He is? Whose side are *you* on?" Both strategies are challenging and demanding. Whichever tactic is employed, it should become clear that Jesus' parabolic messiahship invites and demands parabolic discipleship. To follow him is to make room for hope, by abandoning the quest for a powerful victory by a messiah who conforms to the expectations everyone has of him, and by acting so that the link between the parabolic expectation of the reign of God and the liturgies that anticipate and celebrate that reign is manifest for all to see.

Conclusions: A Myth of a Parabolic Messiah?

If parables upset myths, and if Jesus is a parabolic Messiah, can there be a myth of Jesus? If there cannot be, then Christians cannot have a story which directs their religious awe, gives them a sense of their place in the cosmos and society, and provides them with psychological space to grow. If there can be, how can a *myth* preserve that parabolic quality which structures all the stories told of Jesus? There are three guidelines to the ways out of this dilemma.

The many stories of Jesus cannot be reduced to a single coherent master-story. The various attempts to reduce these stories to one story — whether action (as the Diatessaron, see pp. 74-75 above) or myth (as the most popular descent-ascent Christology seems to have done, see pp. 133-136) — are doomed to be upset by the other stories in the New Testament which are incompatible with the proposed overarching myth or "master-story."

Second, although some Christians may have their favorite story, no story can be elevated to the status of THE story about Jesus. When a single story is taken as final and absolute, it becomes an idol. When a single story is taken as *the* key to the canon, the others are degraded to a lower status. The multiplicity of stories of Jesus prevents this idolatry and degradation. When one story is raised above all others, it should be "jostled"[21] out of place by others in the tradition. If Christians could have and tell the final and absolute story about Jesus, they could understand his person and significance. But the presence of many stories in the New Testament warrants the traditional claim that no human story will be fully adequate to tell of him.

Third, the canonicity of the many stories of Jesus implies that there can be no single Christian myth, no final and unalterable story which structures the Christians' world. Even the Christian stories of the acts of God take multiple forms and are told in many ways, as John Shea has shown.[22] If Christians are faithful to their tradition, they claim no ultimate story of God and the world, but rather a set of stories, ultimately inseparable, but irreducibly multiple.

Therefore, the Christian cannot live in a world that is structured by an ultimate myth. The functions of myth so necessary for human existence must be taken up not by one finished story, but by a tradition that is open-ended because it is composed of many parables, many actions, many myths. All of them are in tension with one another and each

---

[21]The notion that stories qualify each other in this way is an adaptation of Ian Ramsey's notion that models qualify each other in this way. For a discussion of Ramsey's work, see T. W. Tilley, *Talking of God* (New York: Paulist, 1978), pp. 79-92, 109-114.

[22]See Shea, *Stories of God: An Unauthorized Biography* (Chicago: Thomas More, 1978), pp. 9-10, 75, and *passim*. Although Shea's stories take a triune form, there is not a single story for each of the "persons" of the Trinity. This is as it should be, especially if *opera trinitatis ad extra indivisa sunt*.

relativizes all others. Rather than directing their religious awe to a god present in one specific time and place, the many stories of Christians direct worship to that One beyond the many gods in the world. Rather than leaving the sense of the cosmos to be directed by the whims of divinities or the forces of historical necessity, the many stories of Christians suggest that the whence and whither of the cosmos is ultimately Mystery. Rather than establishing one social structure as the single and only legitimate social structure, the many stories of Christians suggest that *no* social structure is divinely ordained, but that every social structure needs to be transformed. Rather than providing Christians with psychological support by affirming their claims to have the truth and to know the truth because they know the ultimately true story, the many stories of Christians provide them with room to hope that the ultimate story is better than they can imagine. In short, the movement begun by Jesus is one that must eschew any mythical security short of the reign of God, a reign beyond every myth, a reign that must be told in many stories of Jesus, a reign that cannot be limited to one metaphor nor be ultimately described in one story. A parabolic Messiah saves people from being trapped in one myth or bound to one metaphor.

That no single story is ultimately THE story does not mean that any story can be told. Historians can recover and interpret the old stories. Theologians can criticize the new ones. All must be guided by the ongoing tradition, preserved in Scripture and Sacrament. All must be faithful to the guides of Creeds and Councils if they are to retell and relive the story of Jesus well. Even if no single doctrine is the only key doctrine, nor any single story the whole story, some stories and doctrines are not compatible with those that form Christianity, and those must be excluded.

If a Christian confesses "Jesus is Christ," that confession has a metaphorical form and implicit narrative structure. This chapter has sought to uncover some of those buried narratives and lay out their significance. To the extent that we have understood how narratives variously shape the titles of Jesus, that far we can understand the meaning of confessing faith in a God beyond myth through Jesus, a parabolic Messiah.

> *But there are also many other tales*
> *told of Jesus;*
> *were every one of them to be written,*
> *I suppose that the world itself*
> *could not contain*
> *the books that would be written.*

For Further Reading

New Testament Christology is a highly disputed area. Oscar Cullmann (see n. 18 above) construes the basic New Testament as *Heilsgeschichte* (salvation-history). This concept, which reclaims the New Testament as basically narrative, was quite influential on the Second Vatican Council. Cullmann's critics claim that he is too optimistic about our ability to make historically reliable claims about Jesus' self-consciousness; this may be more a criticism of his style than his substance, however. The standard interpretation in English of the elements of New Testament Christology is Fuller, *Foundations* (see n. 4 above). He takes the various titles in their original and developed contexts to show their meanings in each. Another tightly argued and meticulously researched text is Dunn, *Christology in the Making* (see n. 3 above). Dunn's chief concern is to locate the precise origin of the doctrine of the Incarnation. He scrupulously avoids reading earlier texts in light of later ones. He also refuses to presume that some non-Christian texts antedate the texts of the New Testament. If earlier dating of some of these sources can be established, his work will need revision. C. F. D. Moule, *The Origin of Christology* (Cambridge: Cambridge University Press, 1977) collects lectures which read later texts as developments of earlier ones. J. Ramsey Michaels,

Servant and Son: Jesus in Parable and Gospel (Atlanta: John Knox, 1981) offers a post-critical reconstruction of the religion of Jesus. While it is less suspicious of evolution in the early Christian tradition than most scholars are, it presents a provocative and interesting picture of Jesus' religion.

Investigations into the New Testament do not suffice to answer the questions of who Christians say Jesus is and what he means. Reflective, constructive and speculative Christologies need to go beyond the New Testament studies. Among Protestant theologians, three efforts stand out. D. M. Baillie, *God Was in Christ: An Essay on Incarnation and Atonement* (New York: Scribner's, n.d. [first edition, 1948; revised edition, 1955]) reflects both on the New Testament and on the doctrinal development in the later Christian tradition. The two doctrines of the subtitle focus the text. Wolfhart Pannenberg, *Jesus — God and Man*, trans. L. L. Wilkins and D. A. Priebe (Philadelphia: Westminster, 1968) uses the Chalcedonian formula, "truly God, truly man," to guide his discussion of Jesus' significance, beginning with the New Testament. A more speculative approach is John B. Cobb, Jr., *Christ in a Pluralistic Age* (Philadelphia: Westminster, 1975). Cobb, a theologian influenced deeply by the process philosophies of Alfred North Whitehead and Charles Hartshorne, has written a Christology that focuses on the "logos" theme and speculates more on faith in Christ as logos than on the historical issues which underlie the discussions cited in the previous paragraph.

In 1977 the Church of England was rocked by the publication of the papers that compose *The Myth of God Incarnate*, ed. J. Hick (London: SCM Press and Philadelphia: Westminster, 1977). The papers take a seemingly radical stance (for British-based theologians) on the mythology of the New Testament. Shortly thereafter, *The Truth of God Incarnate*, ed. Michael Green (Sevenoaks, Kent: Hodder and Stoughton, and Grand Rapids: Eerdmans, 1977) trumpeted conservative responses. Further papers and sharp rejoinders from all positions were gathered in *Incarnation and Myth: The Debate Continued* (London: SCM Press and Grand Rapids: Eerdmans, 1979). While scholars will find nothing of earthshaking significance in these collections, the issues are very cleanly drawn and well argued, especially in the last book. Happily, the traditionalists do tend to hold their own rather well in these debates.

However, it must be conceded that the center of contemporary Christological reflection is in Roman Catholic circles. Pride of place belongs to the still unfinished monumental work of Edward Schillebeeckx, *Jesus* (see n. 1 below), *Christ: The Experience of Jesus as Lord*, trans. John Bowden (New York: Seabury Press, 1980), *Interim Report on the Books Jesus and Christ*, trans. John Bowden (New York: Crossroad Publishing Co., 1981) and a promised third major book, *Spirit*. These long and difficult works review and appropriate in a scholarly manner all the research and reflection on Jesus the Christ done in this —and maybe every — century in the service of a critically nuanced and religiously orthodox Christology. The extent of his success is awe-inspiring. A readable and serious review of the Christological work of Walter Kasper, Karl Rahner, Edward Schillebeeckx (*Jesus* only), Hans Küng, Jon Sobrino, Louis Bouyer, and James P. Mackey is Brian McDermott, "Roman Catholic Christology: Two Recurring Themes" *Theological Studies* LXI/2 (June, 1980), pp. 339-367. McDermott's fine article also devotes considerable space to Frans Josef van Beeck, *Christ Proclaimed: Christology as Rhetoric* (New York: Paulist, 1979) which concentrates on the rhetoric of proclaiming faith in Christ rather than the logic of Christo-logy. Van Beeck is thus open to narrative theology as a central proclamation. Those interested in discerning the shape of Roman Catholic Christological reflection should consult McDermott's article.

At a more readable level, two works stand out. An attempt to present in a clear and approachable manner an understanding not only of traditional Christological affirmations but also of recent — and sometimes upsetting —thought about Jesus is Dermot Lane, *The Reality of Jesus: An Essay in Christology* (New York: Paulist Press, 1975). Lane's lucid style shows that solid scholarship can be readable. James P. Mackey, *Jesus: The Man and the Myth*

(New York: Paulist Press, 1979) is a personal reflection on modern Christology by a theologian who is also a gifted stylist. While Mackey could be clearer on the function of myths, those who long for reading both theologically sound and spiritually edifying should find this text rewarding.

Finally, three recent books in Christology represent contemporary trends. Schubert M. Ogden, *The Point of Christology* (San Francisco: Harper and Row, 1982) provides a new liberal Protestant approach that takes cognizance not only of the biblical investigations begun by Bultmann, but also of the philosophical theology of process and liberation theologians in both North and South America. Ogden takes up the mantle of Bultmann and is especially critical of those theologians who talk of the meaning of Christ but neglect the truth-status of those claims. Although there is much of value in Ogden's work, his basic historical stance and his norms for the appropriateness and credibility of christological claims are roundly and rightly criticized by Francis Schüssler Fiorenza, "Reflective Christology," *Cross Currents* XXXII/3 (Fall, 1982). Reginald Fuller and Pheme Perkins, *Who Is This Christ: Gospel Christology and Contemporary Faith* (Philadelphia: Fortress Press, 1983) provides a different view from that of the present chapter on the multiple Christologies of the New Testament and the formation of theological orthodoxy at Nicaea and Chalcedon. This volume provides a superb and readable introduction to New Testament Christologies and their contemporary relevance. Monika K. Hellwig, *Jesus: The Compassion of God* (Wilmington: Michael Glazier, Inc., 1983) retrieves the roots of Christology in soteriology. Hellwig uses both contemporary theological scholarship (especially the works of Piet Schoonenberg, Edward Schillebeeckx and numerous liberation theologians) and historical criticism of the New Testament to structure her reflections. In identifying Jesus as the compassion of God, Hellwig shows what it means to find salvation in Jesus and how that differs from other forms of salvation.

8

THE BODY OF CHRIST

Saints are impregnators of the world,
vivifiers and animaters of
potentialities of goodness
which but for them
would lie forever dormant.
—after William James[1]

Where would you be without your body? What in the
world could you do without your body? These are strange
questions, but ones which can reveal the significance of the
Pauline metaphor for the church as the body of Christ. For
we can ask similar questions: Where would Christ be without his body? What in the world could he do without his
body? If the church is the body of Christ, its members
continue the work of Christ in the world and continue to
make his presence felt in the world. To continue to tell the
story of Christ is to tell the stories of the members of his
body.

This chapter reflects on stories of some who have kept
Christ present in the world and kept alive his mission.

---

[1]Compare William James, *The Varieties of Religious Experience: A Study in*
Human Nature (New York: Collier, 1961 [first published, 1902]), p. 284.

Usually, this part of the story is told as "church history," but distinguishing various aspects of "history" shows a different way to tell the continuing story. Then the heart of the chapter recalls examples from the past and present to demonstrate this way to continue the story. The final section of the chapter will suggest the significance of these stories for understanding the doctrine of the Incarnation.

Inner History and Outer History

The late H. Richard Niebuhr originated the distinction that provides the title for this section. Consider the following two parallel narrations of the same set of events, as he cites them in *The Meaning of Revelation*:

> "Four-score and seven years ago our fathers brought forth on this continent a new nation, conceived in liberty and dedicated to the proposition that all men are created equal."

> "On July 4, 1776, Congress passed the resolution which made the colonies independent communities, issuing at the same time the well-known Declaration of Independence. If we regard the Declaration as the assertion of an abstract political theory, criticism and condemnation are easy. It sets out with a general proposition so vague as to be practically useless. The doctrine of the equality of men, unless it be qualified and conditioned by reference to special circumstance is either a barren truism or a delusion."[2]

The first quotation is from Lincoln's Gettysburg Address. The second is from the *Cambridge Modern History*. Both describe truly the same events while they differ markedly. The former talks of "our history," the latter of "history." The two narratives differ in *perspective*.

---

[2]H. Richard Niebuhr, *The Meaning of Revelation* (New York: Macmillan, 1960 [first published, 1941]), pp. 44, 45.

This difference in perspective can be characterized, according to Niebuhr, in a number of ways. Outer history tends to be impersonal; inner history personal. The data outer history uses focus on what happen*ed*; the data of inner history are the happen*ings*, especially as they affect the people involved. What is valuable for outer history is what is powerful over the many; what is valuable for inner history is what affects the destiny of individuals and communities that tell the story. Outer history seeks to tell the facts from the perspective of the neutral observer, while inner history tells of "events to be celebrated; this history calls for joy and sorrow, for days of rededication and of shriving, for tragic participation and jubilees."[3] Outer history is measured in calendar time; inner history is measured in terms of *our* remembered past, "When I was a boy. . ." "When our family first came to this land. . ." "When our Savior was on earth. . ." Outer history succeeds when it has every actual event, every social force, every actor's role crystallized into a perfect form so that a spectator can see their exquisite geometry. Inner history succeeds when it provides a story in which to live, shatters old notions of what happened, and explodes into a new awareness. In short, inner history is a story told by a participant; outer history a chronicle written by an observer.

Yet because one cannot really separate participation from observation, the relationships between inner and outer history are quite complex. Abstractly, outer history can correct the perspective of inner history when the latter becomes distorted. Sometimes this happens by enlarging the perspective, sometimes by framing a story with other narratives ignored by inner history. Similarly, inner history, often told as a myth, can organize and orient an individual or a community in a way that outer history cannot. Inner history, when proclaimed well as a transforming and exploding story, can change the course of events in a way that forces even those historians doing "outer history" to take notice. Some concrete examples will help illustrate this.

[3]*Ibid.*, p. 50.

First, consider the Exodus of the people of Israel from Egypt under the leadership of Moses. The first leg of the journey is described in the following: "And the people of Israel journeyed from Rameses to Succoth, about six hundred thousand men on foot, besides women and children" (Ex 12:37, RSV). Had such a crowd left Egypt, the Egyptian economy would have been devastated. Yet other sources offer good reason to believe that the Egyptian economy was not destroyed about Moses' time, and report no mass exodus. Additionally, as John L. McKenzie puts it, "Thutmose III of Egypt [had previously] conquered all of Canaan, and a good deal besides, in the fifteenth century B.C., with an army of 18,000 men."[4] To suggest that 600,000 men is an accurate number of men in the Exodus is hardly credible. Although the power of the Exodus story as "inner history" must be recognized, when one tries to fit the story into the geometry of the history of Western Civilization, one realizes the numbers are generally exaggerated. In this way "outer history" can correct some of the claims that "inner history" makes. It cannot show that God did not lead the Jews out of Egypt, but it can show that not so many did leave.

Second, consider that proclamation of the gospel by the early Christians. The gospels are "inner history" stories of what happened to *us*. The people who made the stories of Jesus their own stories embodied a force that reshaped the world. While people writing the history of Western Civilization would not have to participate in the community of Jesus — that is, would not have to try to conform their stories to a story of Jesus — they could not ignore the power these stories have and had on people's lives, nor could they fail to chronicle the actions of people so empowered by believing these stories. Outer history must *account for*, although not necessarily *believe in* or *accept* the stories' power.

In light of these distinctions, what is the best way to write the history of Christianity? The answer to this query

[4]John L. McKenzie, *The Old Testament Without Illusion* (Chicago: Thomas More Press, 1979), p. 90.

changes, of course, with the purposes of the authors and the expectations of the audiences. Most have written "outer histories" of Christianity. They stress what happened, the quantitative expansion of the Church, the social and intellectual movements the Church made or reacted to, the exploits of individuals of great institutional power or authority. Most recent historians of Christianity have attempted to emulate the *Cambridge Modern History* rather than the Gettysburg Address. They have rightly attempted to redress the exaggeration and falsification in many "histories" of the Church by being as scrupulously objective as possible.

However, to complement this work "inner history" is also needed. Changes in the quality of lives in the Church must be recorded. The intellectual and social forces' effect on the institution and their effects on the members of the body of Christ must be narrated. The exploits of those individuals who impregnate the world with actual forms of goodness previously unincarnated must be celebrated. In short, we need a critical "inner history" of the church, one that narrates the personal, qualitative and explosive to balance the "outer histories" of the institutional, quantitative and ordinary forms of Christian life.

The problem is to write an inner history without falling into mindless hagiography and institutional glorification. This historic danger has been noted by Karl Rahner and Herbert Vorgrimler: "Popular piety, it is true, often...yields to unbridled sentimentality and is impressed by religious trash; but such phenomena in Catholicism should not be thought any objection to a sensible veneration of the saints."[5] One way to avoid this danger is to write *critical* hagiography, critically honest and faithfully remembered stories of the saints in their social and religious contexts. To treat the saints as creative individuals within the context of their communities and to tell their stories "warts and all" may avoid the excesses of lugubrious piety.

But the approach raises the problem of how to recognize a

---

[5] Karl Rahner and Herbert Vorgrimler, *Theological Dictionary*, trans. R. Strachas (New York: Herder and Herder, 1965), p. 480.

saint. Not all the officially recognized saints may be worth venerating. Some unrecognized saints may be more worthy of imitation than canonized ones. What must be sought in a saint is a certain *sort* of sanctity, described by Rahner and Vorgrimler as follows:

> This sanctity must be displayed to the world and it has a history: canonized saints are the creative models of sanctity who have set a concrete example, each for his own particular age, of a new way to be Christian, creatively and with new understanding.[6]

In short, an inner history of Christianity could be written by telling the stories of creative saints in their social and religious context.

In fact, two very critical students of history and sanctity follow a path like this. In his Gifford Lectures, *The Varieties of Religious Experience*, William James collected and analyzed autobiographical and hagiographical writings from or about a large number of saints, canonized and uncanonized, in order to show the great variety of ways of being religious. Naturally, James found some of them very *un*edifying. However, William Clebsch's *Christianity in European History* is more useful in providing a critical inner history of Christianity, for it presents an ordered set of stories of saints (in the Rahner and Vorgrimler sense) in their various sociopolitical contexts. The next section will trace Clebsch's history as a way of showing what a Christian inner history can look like.

Stories From the Past

Christianity in European History takes the framework provided by secular cultural history as a context for telling the stories of men and women who initiated new ways of being Christian. All of Clebsch's "saints" sought to follow

[6]*Ibid.*, p. 479.

Christ portrayed in scripture and present in their lives. Each had to develop new forms of Christian life, which became established in the ongoing life of the community.

In the era of the earliest post-biblical expansion of Christianity, the first distinctively Christian lifestyle emerged: *martyr*. Inspired by the stoning and vision of St. Stephen (Acts 7) and persecuted (at least occasionally) by the Roman Empire, Christians celebrated Christ's sacrifice and commemorated the martyrdom of his followers in their liturgies. Polycarp, Perpetua, Cyprian and others accepted martyrdom rather than abandon their Lord or allow the state to usurp his place in their loyalty. They were greeted by the first martyr, Christ, just as Stephen had been when he was killed. They even became other Christs. As he was unjustly tried, so they were. As his body was tortured, so theirs were. As he was raised, so they were. As he was remembered forever, so they would be. As he became the dispenser of graces, so they were. As his place of death became holy, so theirs did. "As his death modeled theirs, their deaths would model those of some of their fellows. And wherever death entered the pattern it signified entry into life" (60).[7]

The pattern the martyrs follow formally endures but materially differs throughout the history of Christianity. Formally, Christians follow Christ; to live loyal to Christ was to live so as to be a person who could die a martyr's death. The martyrs picked out from Christ's life key motifs — metaphors — that they could use to structure their own life and adapt his story for their own. This process characterizes Christians of all ages. Materially, however, the pattern must change. Inside the tradition, narratives powerful for one generation and metaphors central and distinctive for one era lose their power by becoming hackneyed. Outside the tradition, the economic, social and political patterns change. Not only do such changes affect the relations of the Christian tradition to the rest of the society, but also affect the ways Christians structure their lives.

[7]William A. Clebsch, *Christianity in European History* (New York: Oxford University Press, 1979). Parenthetical references in this section are to pages in this book.

Martyrdom became an inspiration from the past, rather than the dominant option for Christians by the end of the third century, as the Roman Empire began to tolerate Christianity. Under the emperor Constantine Christianity was given some official support throughout the Empire. Hence martyrdom could no longer provide a model for those Christians who wanted to follow their Lord heroically. Hence, there appeared another style of Christian life, the "white martyrdom" of the *monks*. While some members of the church generally capitulated to the standards of the Roman state, some still wanted to be rigorous Christians. Since "red martyrdom" was no longer an option, these enthusiastic Christians sought to sacrifice all their passions to become as perfectly passionless as Christ, who died in peace. They could thus become like Christ in a *new* way.

These lifestyles are still viable today. There are martyrs for Christ still, men and women who give their lives for Christ and his people — and who are killed for that gift, as we shall see on pp. 166-174, below. The forms of monasticism continue today, too. Monks can help people learn a spiritual discipline to overcome the passionate vices monks fight and fought: "piggishness, lechery, greed, depression, hatred, inability to care, bragging, and egotism"(76). Monks and martyrs knew that what was good enough to live for was great enough to die for; and that only what was great enough to die for is truly worth living for. Their stories shaped the stories of those who wanted to be real Christians during the early life of the church and can retain their power today.

With the passing of the Roman empire, the political world was thrown into chaos. Two men inspired by the works of St. Augustine, that last Roman Christian, became initiators of ways to be Christian, without being Roman. Civil servant Boethius, while waiting in prison for his execution by his sometime friend and superior Theodoric on a trumped-up charge, composed a book, *The Consolation of Philosophy*. In spite of the chaos into which the known world has fallen, Lady Wisdom teaches that it is wiser to believe that all things are for the good in the long run. This is

a *theodicy*, a justification of God's goodness and the ultimate goodness of things in spite of the chaos, misery, suffering and evil that infects the present age. In his works,
Boethius revivified the image of Christ as Wisdom, the
Logos of things (see pp. 133-136 above) by putting it in a
new story using new metaphors and in so doing showed that
one way to follow Christ faithfully was to wait in hope and
trust — consoled by Wisdom — that in the end all will be
well.

To be consoled by Christ in the face of death was nothing
new. The martyrs met Christ in death. But to imagine Christ
as consoling one in the guise of Lady Philosophy was.
Boethius introduced a new way of coping with suffering,
evil, death, and chaos in life.

In a more active approach to the social chaos of the time,
Gregory the Great as pope from 590 to 604 sought to
reorganize all society as if it were a monastery. The pope
would be as abbot to Europe, leading all, yet conforming to
the rule as an abbot must, and serving all with an abbot's
authority. Gregory sought to emulate the "authority and
charity on earth" of Christ (122). He used the image of
Christ as the Good Shepherd to inaugurate a hierarchy of
service. Each person shepherded the other; each had a place
in the system. Ultimately, Christ was the ruler of humanity,
and the pope was his vicar. Religious rule over the whole
society provided a new story for contextualizing the image
of the Good Shepherd and inaugurated a new style of being
Christian. As Christ bore the burden of ruling all, so a way
to be Christian was to rule well as a *prelate*.

Clebsch comments on the importance of prelacy and
theodicy as ways for Christians to cope with a chaotic social
situation:

> When the Gregorian scheme for ordering chaos was
> successful, Christianity got the credit. When chaos pre-
> vailed and the Boethian theodicy offered the counsel and
> consolation of trusting in providence so as to underscore
> human freedom and responsibility, Christianity was not
> to blame. . .Together they made Christianity a religion of

all seasons, in times of calamity confident and in more
prosperous periods efficient.

It cannot be said that they outlived their usefulness, for
such options enduringly appeal to men and women (130).

As with martyrdom and monasticism, Christian consolation and Christian ruling attract people even today. These
are two ways for Christians to cope with a chaotic society
without rejecting it.

Yet the unity Gregory provided dissolved. His successors
could not sustain his honest and charitable rule. Europe
would not remain a monastery. In a new social and political
era (Clebsch's dates are 962-1555), marked by conflicts
between secular and religious authorities and conflicts
among religious people, new forms of Christian life
emerged. *Theologians* sought to unify all things by coming
to universal knowledge in their theology. *Mystics* sought
true communion with God as ultimate unity beyond all
duality.

The mystics sought to describe a ladder to ascend to reach
unity with the divine:

One made three basic moves in mounting the twelve
steps. Humility began in the awareness of one's carnal
existence, grew as charity checked self-love with concern
for one's neighbor, and rose to purity of heart in desiring
God. Deity entered into partnership at each stage (148).

The end of this ladder was rapture, union with God beyond
words. Christ here appeared as the bridegroom: the mystic
was the bride of Christ, united in rapture. Not all could
mount to the top of the ladder, but even those who scaled
part of it would ascend closer to Christian perfection. The
mystics showed a new way to make sense of the image of
Christ as the bridegroom of the church (2 Cor 11; Eph 5).
They provide a new story to contextualize the image, adapting it for their own age.

Theologians "strove by reason to embody divine reality in
the symbolic form of a unified human history" (168-169).

They became scholars who sorted and classified, compared and synthesized what could be known of the ultimately unknowable. Anselm, Abelard, Aquinas, each made his contribution, grafting newly discovered Greek philosophy into the works of Augustine and Boethius. So did Luther, Calvin, Melanchthon and others. For the theologian Christ was "a son who told everybody about his father" (172). The great teacher was crucified, resurrected and still present through the Eucharist. As Christ taught of the Father, so should those who participate in his life through the Eucharist teach of God. Many varied ways of being a mystic or theologian are still available for those who seek ultimate unity devotionally or intellectually. While the medieval ideal of unifying "culture under the Christendom that Christ founded and headed" (175) may no longer be viable, the forms of life that ideal generated still survive as ways to follow Christ.

With the dissolution of Christendom into territorial monarchies and churches, in which the religion each practiced was the religion of the ruler, a new style of being Christian emerged, *perfectionism*. Christ taught people to be perfect, even as his Father is perfect. So perfectionists sought to train their wills or feelings so that they could be as perfectly moral or as perfectly loving as possible. Seeking to be perfect did not mean withdrawal from the world (as with monks), nor union with God (as with mystics) nor rule over others (as with prelates), but rather perfecting oneself within the community of Christians. For instance *Pilgrim's Progress* could teach one how to follow the moral path to the Celestial City. Count Nicholas von Zinzendorf taught the Moravian Brethren how to perfect their love of the suffering savior by loving him as a bride loves a husband, not by perfecting the rapturous love of the affective mystic, but by modelling one's love of Christ on that of a housewife carrying out the daily duties in her marriage.

In contrast to the mystics' devotion and theologians' intellection, the perfectionists trained themselves by practice. Moralists developed moral perfection by trying as hard as possible to obey the law of Christ and following his example. Pietists increased their passionate love of the suffering Lamb of God by so making real Christ's presence that they could become Christs themselves. John Wesley and Alphonsus Liguori bring this perfectionism to a peak in the era of territorialism (1556-1806). Preaching morality *and* piety "conferred that perfection by which holiness and righteousness became a single skill, the training for and performing of which turned discipline into delight and delight into discipline" (228).

But in the modern nation-states (1806-1945), one no longer received one's religion so much by where one lived as by one's choice. The unity of the church with the state, as begun with Constantine and continued through the territorial religions, was dying. With the emergence of political tolerance of different religions within a single nation, religion became the voluntary choice of autonomous individuals rather than the form of life the culture imposed. New ways of being Christian emerged in this era. *Activists* sought to do whatever they did as Christian individuals; apologists sought to convince the unchurched individuals of the validity, beauty, efficacy or truth of Christianity. Activists carry on the tradition of Christian political and social involvement in a radical way. People like Félicité de Lamennais in the nineteenth century advocated participation in revolution. Lamennais found Christ present in the masses and "reigned divinely as the only master worthy of the masses' allegiance because he had suffered and died humanly for them" (257). To free the masses was true service to Christ. In the twentieth century, Dietrich Bonhoeffer participated in a plot to assassinate Hitler as an expression of Christian activism.

Apologists followed the way of the theodicists and theologians. John Henry Newman, Søren Kierkegaard and Albrecht Ritschl became "ambassadors of Christ to the foreign realm of autonomous humanity, affirming the post-Christian or ex-Christian condition of modernity while showing how to be re-Christian or neo-Christian within that condition" (267-268). They each proclaimed how Christ showed the way to be authentically human even in this era.

Kierkegaard, for instance, presented a Christ who invited people to follow him or "the god-man whose lowliness always shone forth from his illegitimate birth to his ignominious death" (276).

Activists and apologists all provide new models for sanctity. For in an era in which each person is a law unto himself or herself, models drawn from eras in which each must conform to the established paths are not sufficient. This does not imply the uselessness of the older paths. But even those paths must be autonomously chosen, if the new ones are not followed.

Martyrs and monks, theodicists and prelates, mystics and theologians, pietists and moralists, apologists and activists: ten different ways of being Christian, ten different ways to imagine Christ, ten different forms of the presence of Christ in his "mystical Body." While Clebsch ignores other ways, e.g., the emergence of the mendicants in the thirteenth century, this sketch of his approach to the history of Christianity shows it to be a useful way to understand the multiple forms of Christian life, in the varying contexts of Western culture. It thus provides a constructive and critical inner history of Christianity.

Yet there is a side of our "inner history" which Clebsch slides over: the failures. Christian saints have been devout, ascetic, pure, etc. All these qualities have been incarnated in Christianity. But some embodiments of these ideals have been disastrous. William James has diagnosed why this is so. He provides a guide for discerning which saints may be worth emulating:

> Felicity, purity, charity, patience, self-severity — these are splendid excellencies, and the saint of all shows them in the completest possible measure.
>
> But, as we say, all these things together do not make saints infallible. When their intellectual outlook is narrow, they fall into all sorts of holy excesses, fanaticism or theopathic absorption, self-torment, prudery, scrupulosity, gullibility, and morbid inability to meet the world. By the very *intensity* of his fidelity to paltry ideals with which

> an inferior intellect may inspire him, a saint can be even
> more objectionable and damnable than a superficial car-
> nal man would be in the same situation. We must judge
> him not sentimentally only, and not in isolation, but
> using our own intellectual standards, placing him in his
> environment, and estimating his total function.[8]

The key is the combination of intensity with smallness: if a
person is intensely devoted to something trivial, then that
person's story becomes a caricature of what a saint should
be. James uses hagiographical and autobiographical works
on or by Margaret Mary Alacoque, Gertrude, Teresa of
Avila, and Louis Gonzaga to exemplify this distortion. In
short, intensely narrow sanctity does not provide a story
worth reliving.

Yet the one virtue of saintliness that James finds finally
undistortable is charity. James concedes that truly saintly
people who embody virtues of charity and non-resistance
can avoid seduction by the powers of darkness. Such an
excess of charity may even benefit the hardheaded of the
world:

> Momentarily considered, then, the saint may waste his
> tenderness and be the dupe and victim of his charitable
> fever, but the general function of his charity in social
> evolution is vital and essential. If things are ever to move
> upward, some one must be ready to take the first step,
> and assume the risk of it. No one who is not willing to try
> charity, to try non-resistance as the saint is always willing,
> can tell whether these methods will or will not succeed.
> When they do succeed, they are far more powerfully
> successful than force or worldly prudence. *Force destroys
> enemies; and the best that can be said for prudence is that
> it keeps what we already have in safety. But non-
> resistance, when successful, turns enemies into friends;
> and charity regenerates its objects.* These saintly methods

---

[8]James, *Varieties*, 292-293; emphasis added.

are, as I said, creative energies; and genuine saints find in the elevated excitement with which their faith endows them an authority and impressiveness which makes them irresistible in situations where men of shallower nature cannot get on at all without the use of worldly prudence. This practical proof that worldly wisdom may be safely transcended is the saint's magic gift to mankind. Not only does his vision of a better world console us for the generally prevailing prose and barrenness; but even when on the whole we have to consider him ill adapted, he makes some converts, and the environment gets better for his ministry. He is an effective ferment of goodness, a slow transmuter of the earthly into a more heavenly order.[9]

The power of the saint is the ability to transform and convert those to whom s/he bears witness, not the ability to force them into molds. A saint has this power even if accompanied by small ideals and narrow vision.

The saints of the past are those who, through the greatness of their lives and vision, have quickened and enlivened their fellow humans. If there are saints of the present, contemporary "vivifiers and animaters of potentialities of goodness which but for them would lie forever dormant," then our present can be renewed, too. The following section proposes that even in our own time, saints can be found.

Stories in the Present Tense

Who in the present reincarnates atonement? If Christians form the body of Christ, and if the work of Christ is at-one-ment, that is overcoming the sinful separation of each person from the other and of each and all from God through redeeming love, as the stories presented in chapter seven suggest, then who is showing new ways to do that work

[9]*Ibid.*, pp. 284-285; emphasis added.

today? To answer that question is to discover some saints in the present tense, people who demonstrate how to be Christian even in an age when autonomy has degenerated into narcissism. In the work of James W. McClendon, Jr., *Biography as Theology*, four contemporary saints' stories are told.

Dag Hammarskjöld, secretary-general of the United Nations in its most effective era, sought to overcome barriers between nations so that the world of the future could exist. Yet one of his most impressive — even saintly — acts was his 1955 journey to Peking to seek the release of a dozen American pilots who had been captured during the Korean War and sentenced to death as spies by the People's Republic of China. Communist China was the enemy: yet Dag Hammarskjöld entered the enemy's capital without force, without violence, and with patience. Although upon his return early in 1955 he was reviled as a failure by the American press, the pilots were released that summer, in "honor of his fiftieth birthday." Even a diplomat can be a Christian if his seeking to be a civil servant is modelled on the suffering servant.

Martin Luther King, Jr. is often thought of as a leader in the fight for black civil rights. Yet McClendon shows not only that he fought for all people, but also that he was a creative and provocative theologian. The dream that he spoke of so often was never a dream of black rights or black supremacy. The promised land he longed for was not a land of democracy and equality. His images are much more concrete:

> I have a dream that one day on the red hills of Georgia the sons of former slaves and the sons of former slave-owners will be able to sit down together at the table of brotherhood. I have a dream that one day even the state of Mississippi, a state sweltering with the heat of oppression, will be transformed into an oasis of freedom and justice.
>
> I have a dream that my four little children one day will

live in a nation where they will not be judged by the color of their skin, but by the content of their character.[10]

This speech, given in Washington in 1963 in the midst of a *non-violent* campaign for civil rights, highlights not those rights but rather the sort of reconciled society that is the goal King sought, one in which people are judged and treated as people. This view of a Christian society is based in interpreting the present in biblical terms rather than interpreting the Bible for present sensibilities. That is King's basic theological method, so different from that of most contemporary scholars.

Clarence Jordan was once a Baptist preacher who founded Koinonia (the New Testament word for community) Farm as a demonstration plot for what Christian community should be. While the farm in Americus, Georgia, has been through some hard times, especially persecution from its neighbors and an economic boycott by townspeople, the Koinonia Partnership keeps this radical community alive. And Jordan's translation of the New Testament (one sample is on pp. 83-84 above) has kept the New Testament alive and fresh for many who have heard it. This ex-Baptist preacher with a doctorate in Greek used saintly ways to change a small corner of the world.

Charles Ives, the fourth and most unusual of McClendon's "saints," composed music that few listened to, published or played. Beset with ailments and scorned by "professional" musicians for most of his life, Ives kept up composing as long as he could. He would give free copies of his songs to libraries which requested them. Yet few wanted to sing, play or collect music with such dreadful dissonances and scampering signatures. Yet his music could lead people to hear what they hadn't before, if they were willing to listen hard. He received a Pulitzer Prize in 1947 for his work. His

---

[10]James William McClendon, Jr., *Biography as Theology: How Life-Stories Can Remake Today's Theology* (Nashville: Abingdon Press, 1974), p. 77, quoting from Coretta Scott King, *My Life With Martin Luther King, Jr.* (New York: Holt, Rinehart and Winston, 1969), p. 239.

Fourth Symphony, in which heaven, nature, and the human city sing in their authentic diversity and divine unity, complexly conveys in music an image of redemption, of at-one-ment. Even a strange musician can help people to hear of reconciliation.

I have only sketched these stories here for McClendon narrates them splendidly in his book. But this form of biographical theology raises an important question. McClendon attempts to understand the lived doctrine of atonement. This means understanding the doctrine in a narrative, rather than a propositional, theology. Does the narrative understanding of the doctrine of the atonement not *change* the doctrine? James B. Wiggins has suggested that there is "more risk in the religion-story venture" than McClendon seems to acknowledge. Not only does this new narrative form of doing theology "modify content quite markedly, but also the criteria for responding to such a mode of theologizing will no longer be appropriately the same as those employed in defending and responding to other modes."[11] But I would claim that the diversity in the New Testament and in the history of Christianity about what it means to follow Christ and to do his work, shows that Christians must discover new ways to think about, live and evaluate Christian faith. Theologians cannot stagnantly repeat the formulae or forms of life of the past. Theology must be "saintly," too, by providing new ways to "accept Christianity creatively and with new understanding." In sum, the *virtue* of narrative theology is that it is deeply *in touch with* the whole Christian tradition, not just the propositions of the theologians in the tradition.

Yet there is a danger for narrative theology analogous to one for propositional theology. When an individual's or a community's roster of saints, range of metaphors, or compendium of doctrines has been too narrow, the danger of a heresy or apostasy arises. A most impressive case of a one-sided propositional theology is that of Arius (ca. 250-

[11]James B. Wiggins, "Within and Without Stories" in *Religion as Story* (New York: Harper and Row, 1975), p. 21.

336). His obsession with the term "begotten" led him into a position that was to him logical. The church found it so narrow, however, that the church deemed it heretically denying the "truly divine" in Christ. In a narrative theology as well, narrowness of vision can be damning. We need many saints. Mother Teresa of Calcutta is often proposed as a "living saint" to supplement those presented by McClendon and others.[12] None could deny her sublime sanctity and heroic service. Yet she conforms to a long-established tradition. She provides no *new* way to make Christ present. New patterns need to be discerned if narrative theology is not to be excessively narrow.

What those new models for sanctity will be cannot be infallibly predicted before they emerge. Retrospectively, of course, we can discern "white martyrdom" as a fitting response to the changed socio-political context in the Roman Empire. We can recognize that monasticism preserves, yet transforms, the ideal of the rigorous and effective Christian life that the martyrs held. But which of the martyrs could have predicted the shape of the emergence of monasticism as a paradigm for Christian life?

We can, however, seek to discern the shape of the presently emerging patterns of sanctity. These new paradigms must be not only faithful to and preservative of the tradition, but also responsive to the needs of the times. Leonardo Boff, Professor of Systematic Theology at Petropoulis, Brazil, has argued that the saints who have provided models for Christian life have been people who have struggled with their own passions and vices — like those the monks struggled against — in an effort to reach personal purity of heart. Boff argues that a new type of asceticism is needed. Christians must struggle also against the mechanisms of exploitation that warp the community and twist the souls of its members. Purity of heart needs to be understood not as

[12]She is a person whose name comes up when using *Biography as Theology* in a classroom as a model for students to follow, asking them to construct their own biographies as theologies about saints who compel them. McClendon has reported that he has had great success by using the text in this manner.

passionlessness (as the monks understood it), nor as the state of readiness for union with God (as the mystics understood it), nor as willing one thing and willing it passionately and absolutely, the sole condition for the religious life (as Kierkegaard would have it), but as more than any of these. Contemporary Christian asceticism must include new virtues, Boff claims, including:

> [S]olidarity with one's class, participation in community decisions, loyalty to the solutions that are defined, the overcoming of hatred against those who are the agents of the mechanisms of impoverishment, the capacity to see beyond the immediate present and to work for a society that is not yet visible and will perhaps never be enjoyed. This new type of asceticism, if it is to keep the hearts pure and be led by the spirit of the beatitudes has demands and renunciations of its own.[13]

In short, we have need for *political* saints to provide new models for being Christian.

Boff is certainly correct in his call for new political saints and in his listing of socio-political virtues. However, his lamenting the absence of models is incorrect. The "saints" McClendon has discerned are political activists; North Americans also know of Dorothy Day, co-founder of the Catholic Worker movement, a truly political saint.

But there are also saints from other areas. Take, for example, Hector Gallego. He was the oldest of eleven children, the son of a small farmer in the Colombian coffee-growing region of Antioquia. His father earned enough money not only to sustain his family, but even to send his children to high school. As a small boy, Hector wanted to be a priest; but specifically, he dreamed of being a priest of and for the poor.

Hector, like his father, was thin, wiry, strong, stubborn

---

[13]Leonardo Boff, O.F.M., "The Need for Political Saints: From a Spirituality of Liberation to the Practice of Liberation," trans. L. Rivera and L. King, *Cross Currents* XXX/4 (Winter 1980-81), pp. 375-376.

and nearsighted. He was ordained a Roman Catholic priest in 1967. He refused any fancy celebration and opted for a simple family gathering. After his ordination, Hector abandoned the probability of a cushy parish assignment in Colombia for the certainty of difficult and harsh work among indigent people in the rain forests of Panama. This was the only time that he and his father quarreled. Penny Lernoux recounts the situation this way:

> Colombia's conservative, inbred church offered little opportunity for a young man with progressive ideas; whereas Veraguas, which was then under the administration of the forward-looking Archbishop McGrath, was promising ground for new experiments in Church cooperatives and Christian communities. Besides, Hector told his father, there was a greater need of priests in Panama.[14]

In Panama, Hector would be joining a church in which eight out of every ten priests were foreigners.

The area to which Gallego was sent had changed little since the 18th century. There were few roads. No electricity or running water was available outside the principal towns. In the town of Santa Fe, which was to be Gallego's parish base, some 10,000 peasants lived in primitive villages in the hills. Each village was from one to four hours' travel from the next; travel was by mule or by foot. The average peasant was illiterate, never saw a doctor, ate a plate of beans and rice once a day, and earned less than five dollars a month by leaving his family (often irregularly constituted) to work on plantations.

In contrast, the "wealthy" of the area lived in the town of Santa Fe. The typical townsperson owned a small business, could send his children to high school in Panama City or other places, did not go hungry, and could afford to pay a doctor's bills and to buy medicines when ill. The townspeople did not live in the lap of luxury. Although their

[14]Penny Lernoux, *Cry of the People*, (Garden City, NY: Doubleday, 1980), pp. 126-127.

standard of living was far better than the peasants' and their families generally more stable, they were living in conditions most North Americans would find unacceptable.

The peasants occasionally came to town to trade. They brought the produce of their farms to the merchants. The merchants bought the produce at low prices. In turn, the peasants had to buy manufactured goods, such as shoes, at prices far above those in the fanciest shops in Panama City. To enable them to buy manufactured goods, the merchants would lend the peasants money at high rates of interest. Thus the peasants were constantly in debt. Lernoux comments on the political and moral aspects of this economy:

> Totally dependent on the townsmen and their political bosses... the peasants were herded to the polls at election time to vote as directed. The townspeople saw nothing wrong in this, since in their opinion the peasants were ignorant and lazy and spent what little they earned on drink, frequently abandoning their women and children to set up new families in another mountain hamlet where they would hack and burn the jungle to plant a little rice or corn for two or three seasons before the unfertilized, eroded land gave out and forced them to move on.
>
> The storekeepers genuinely believed they were being kind to these peasants when they advanced them a little credit, gave them an old dress or worn-out pair of shoes, or employed one of their children as a servant — for food but no pay. Their fathers and grandfathers had behaved that way and they saw no reason to change.[15]

In sum, the townspeople saw as mercy and charity what might be construed as exploitation. In their context and by their own best lights they would consider themselves truly moral and truly Christian.

Upon his arrival in Veraguas, Father Hector Gallego lived without ostentation. He refused any fees for baptisms, and eked out his subsistence on the dollar a day he received

[15]*Ibid.*, p. 126.

from the diocese. He did not bother with clerical clothes, but dressed like the peasants. His "rectory" was a two-room shack. Lernoux quotes the recollections of a young man who knew him, Yike Fonseca:

> "The peasants said that Hector worked as hard as they did. We university students marveled at him at our volunteer camp at Chilagre, where Hector worked with a machete and a bush hook for seven days. He was always ready to undertake any job, from cooking to felling enormous trees. When we traveled together to the outlying villages, he used to carry almost twice what we students could. He was thin but tough. His pace was rapid, and I understand he covered great distances."[16]

Hector was a faithful, hardworking priest, but one who took his faith in everyday ways to the people. His labor with them became a significant aspect of his ministry.

At the beginning of his ministry, Hector tried to get the townspeople not only to participate in church, but also to work on the social and economic problems that afflicted the area. The problems were not due to poor land: the land was reasonably fertile and could produce coffee, citrus, bananas, potatoes, corn and sugar. The problems resulted from the mismanagement of the land and the difficulty of travel: for half the year the area was accessible only by light plane. An all-weather road was needed to facilitate trade and even bring tourists. A road would allow importation of manufactured goods at a more reasonable cost, benefitting both merchant and peasant. A road would allow export of crops for cash, benefitting land-owner and worker. A good road would help all the members of the community — as the Panamanian National Agency for Community Development had recognized.[17] Gallego pushed for the road.

---

[16] *Ibid.*, p. 128.

[17] Cf. "Report by Panama's National Agency for Community Development," *Latin American Documentation* XXV (Washington, DC: United States Catholic Conference, February 1972), II, 19c, p. 2. (Cited below as LADOC II).

The townspeople rejected the idea of a road as stupid. A further suggestion, that the peasants form co-operatives, was rejected as foolish. The townspeople believed that the peasants couldn't improve their lives because peasants have no initiative. Priests should be preaching and praying in town. Peasants aren't supposed to go to church. In spite of their own real poverty, the townspeople's relative status above the peasants would be threatened if Gallego's plans were to be carried out. Such a revolutionary change in relative social status was intolerable for the townspeople.

Gallego went to work with the peasants. In addition to the usual sacramental ministry, Gallego set up an evangelization program, based on a model inaugurated by Bishop Vasquez Pinto in 1958. The program focused on liturgical life, the state of the world, the message of Christ, and the responsible action that is appropriate in light of Christ's message. Gallego tells the story:

> First we divided the entire parish into 11 areas — allowing for distances and ease of communication, because, as you know, rivers are a serious obstacle in these parts. Then we decentralized the operation of the parish, administering the sacraments and the training program on our regular visits to each local community. The first training program was spread over three months and ended with a common cursillo in May, 1968. That cursillo brought together those who had caught the idea best and were most dedicated. Out of them came those we call the "responsibles" — our local organizers. . . . [18]

These people ("We use the term 'responsibles' for them instead of 'directors' or 'leaders' because we consider these latter terms slightly paternalistic; 'responsible' seems more dynamic and real."[19]) became the focus of the Christian

[18]"An Interview with Father Gallego on His Parish Organization (A tape recording taken down by the editors of *Dialogo Social* (Panama City) five days before Father Gallego was abducted (that is June 4, 1971)" in LADOC II, 19d, p. 1.

[19]*Ibid.*

community that was being built in each area. Another part of their responsibility was to prepare the way for the beginning of agricultural communities/co-operatives. They were assisted by students (sent by Archbishop McGrath) who taught courses in co-operative management.

Eventually a cooperative federation, named after Pope John XXIII, acquired a legal title and set up stores in the towns and the capital. The federation was successful from the start, in spite of the fact that it could not follow the classic cooperative pattern of beginning with savings. The peasants had nothing to save. By the fourth year, the cooperative store in Santiago had become the best store in town. Lazy, uninspirable peasants without initiative were turning into quite responsible cooperators. Archbishop McGrath reflected on the change:

> From humble, passive peasants, with heads bowed and straw hats in hand, they had developed into upright persons, speaking independently and fairly about religion, their families, and their attempts to improve the situation. They spoke with no bitterness or aggressiveness against others, but rather of their own efforts."[20]

The myths about the peasants were being destroyed. With the relieving of chronic malnutrition, the "laziness" disappeared.[21] Improvement in the capacity to earn money brought social and familial stability: children were freed from working the land for going to school, families were regularized, and people became active in church and community affairs. The cooperative also provided loans to the peasants, freeing them from domination by their patrons in the town, and offered technical assistance in farming.

The townspeople resented the changes in the social structure. They decried Gallego and more than once stoned the shack in which he slept. The police — all townspeople — did

---

[20]Lernoux, *Cry of the People*, p. 129.
[21]*Ibid.*, pp. 129-130.

not intervene. The townspeople were losing their power over the peasants. For instance, during the national election in 1968, a local politician tried to bribe the peasants to vote as he directed them by giving the town of Santa Fe an old electrical generator. Not only did the peasants refuse to vote as they were instructed, but also someone allegedly burned some of the generator's wiring as a protest against the bribe — causing $7.50 worth of damage to the generator.[22]

All the while Gallego's program of evangelization progressed. His basic tactic was to contrast the state of the world to the gospel message. This simple constrast was inspiring. Once people could see the difference, a "commitment to change arises spontaneously," Gallego said.[23] But change can be dangerous.

During June of 1970, Gallego was beaten up by a group of townspeople. They were retaliating for his refusal to lead their traditional celebration of their patron saint — literally a drunken brawl. Gallego had wanted a celebration based on prayer and solidarity among all the people. But the townspeople refused to share "their" saint or "their" celebration with peasants or a "communist" priest. They stole the statue of St. Peter and beat Gallego, and carried on the party.

Early in 1971, Gallego was arrested and detained because he was accused of the damage to the generator which had happened some two years earlier. As Lernoux notes,

> The bishop intervened and charges against Gallego were dropped, but Bishop Alejandro Vasquez Pinto then insisted on accompanying the priest back to Santa Fe. They were met by the enraged landowner-politician Alvaro Vernaza, who tried to run Bishop Vasquez down with his Jeep. When he failed, Vernaza beat him with an iron cable.[24]

---

[22]Cf. *ibid.*, p. 131.

[23]"An Interview," *LADOC* II, 19d, p. 2.

[24]Lernoux, *Cry of the People*, p. 132.

On May 23, 1971, Gallego's shack was burned down while he slept in it. He was lucky to emerge alive.

A little before midnight on June 9, 1971, two men in a jeep called Gallego to come out from the peasant hut where he was sleeping. They showed him a document through a half-opened door, told him that he was under arrest, and said that he would have to come to the barracks with them. Gallego refused to go with them. He said that he would present himself in the morning after his eight o'clock appointment with the bishop. As their discussion went on, one of the men suggested that their talking was disturbing the others, and said they should carry on their conversation outside. Hector Gallego agreed, dressed and went out. An eyewitness testified:

> Hector went out slowly, and they accompanied him, one at each side of him. They went over to where the jeep was, parked right behind the pickup truck of the co-operative. Between the two vehicles there was a space of about two yards.
>
> As they passed between the two cars, I lost sight of them in the shadow of the truck. I was watching through the slit in the door of my house. They paused a few seconds. Then I heard two cries, but muffled, so that they weren't cries so much as whimpers. Just as if a hand had been clamped over his mouth, as if he couldn't cry out, and that made him seem to be whimpering.
>
> As soon as I heard those sounds, I went out to see what was going on. I circled all the way around the co-operative truck and saw the jeep clearly: it had a white canvas hood and the chassis was either blue or green, I couldn't be sure which. Its headlights went on and it immediately started off. I called out: "Hey! Why are you carrying off that man that way?" But I couldn't do more than that.[25]

[25] Jacinto Peña, "In the Depth of the Night They Took Him Away," *LADOC* II, 19b, pp. 1-2.

The peasants were roused and chased the jeep with the cooperative's truck, but they failed to find Hector. Bishop Martin Legarra went the next day to the National Guard headquarters where Hector would have been taken if arrested, but they failed to find Hector. Archbishop McGrath asked the late General Omar Torrijos, the Panamanian strongman, about Hector, but Torrijos claimed to know nothing of what went on, and thus they failed to find Hector.

Hector Gallego is Missing In Action and presumed martyred.

Summary: Ways of Incarnating Atonement

No simple pattern can be discerned in the stories of the saints whose lives form the body of Christ in history. Yet the heading for this section is meant to suggest that each has sought, in very different contexts, new ways to Incarnate Atonement. All have given their lives for unity, reconciliation, and some have even died in that quest.

What makes saints interesting is their novelty, the new ways in which they make the presence of Christ real in the world. In the case of Hector Gallego, for instance, the focus is on communal solidarity, a sharing based in human dignity and expressed in worship. The novelty is the way in which leadership is to be exercised in Christian communities: the *responsibles* form a new way of leading and a new focus of leadership. These leaders are first responsible to the community. Their leadership consists in exercising that responsibility. No more is the way to be a Christian seen as keeping to one's place in a pre-established hierarchy. Nor is leadership conceived as authoritarian and rigid ruling, but as flexible responsibility to the "led." In short, a leader's authority emerges from his or her responsibility for reconciling the community rather than from his or her position of power over the rest of the community.

Saints let Christ appear in new ways, in new places, in new times. They make the power of Christ present in the world

— and that power is upsetting. The work of Gallego and others in forming *communidades de base* provides a new image of the work of Christ. And if Christ's work, at-one-ment, happens in these places, then Christ is also present there. If Gallego and others have brought into being a new way of living as Christians, then this notion of a community of people responsible for each other led by those most responsible to the whole, presents a story of sanctity, a new form of life in which all bear each other's burdens, "and thus fulfill the law of Christ." (Gal 6:2).

Yet the price saints have to pay is their lives. They must become *disciples* of Christ. But there are as many ways to be disciples, as many as there are stories to contextualize this metaphor. The variety of the stories of past and present saints shows that. It may be difficult to discern an underlying unity in that variety, but there is a story by which the others can be measured, the story of the anointed one, made clear in the Caesarea Philippi scene (see pp. 136-137 above). To be a disciple of Christ means that one's own story must conform in a new and creative way to the story of Christ. An incident from the life of Clarence Jordan shows the significance of that discipleship:

> As so often, a bit of remembered Jordan dialogue may come nearest to clarifying his notion of discipleship. In the early fifties, it is told, Clarence approached his brother Robert Jordan, later a state senator and justice of the Georgia Supreme Court, asking him to represent Koinonia Farm legally.
>
> "Clarence, I can't do that. You know my political aspirations. Why, if I represented you, I might lose my job, my house, everything I've got."
>
> "*We* might lose everything too, Bob."
>
> "It's different for you."
>
> "Why is it different? I remember, it seems to me, that you and I joined the church the same Sunday, as boys. I expect when we came forward the preacher asked me about the same question he did you. He asked me, 'Do you accept Jesus as your Lord and Savior.' And I said,

'Yes.' What did you say?"

"I follow Jesus, Clarence, up to a point."

"Could that point by any chance be — the cross?"

"That's right. I follow him to the cross, but not *on* the cross. I'm not getting myself crucified."

"Then I don't believe you're a disciple. You're an admirer of Jesus, but not a disciple of his. I think you ought to go back to the church you belong to, and tell them you're an admirer not a disciple."

"Well now, if everyone who felt like I do did that, we wouldn't *have* a church, would we?"

"The question," Clarence said, "is, 'Do you have a church?' "[26]

To be a disciple of Christ is to be a member of his body, to take the stories of the Christian tradition and adapt or adopt them to be one's own story. The stories of Jesus we discussed above in chapters four through seven must be the touch-stone by which all subsequent stories are measured. Insofar as one's own story reincarnates his presence in the world, that far is one a healthy member of his body; insofar as one fails either to tell a story that is adequate to the stories of the tradition or to live a story that retells his story fully, that far one fails to be a healthy member of his body. It is just Jordan's point in the story above that the body of disciples of Christ — the church — must be formed by stories in which the cross, the Christian symbol for suffering and death for the sake of God's kingdom, has a central place.

But why seek to make Christ's story one's own story? Why accept as a model and savior a parabolic messiah? The traditional answer has been that Christianity's doctrines are true and that the way of life in which those doctrines are embedded is truly the way to salvation.

But the contemporary world has made that answer a problem. Today many ways to salvation, healing, wholeness or escape are asserted. Not only do the traditional religions claim to be true and to be truly saving, but various modern

[26]McClendon, *Biography as Theology*, pp. 127-128.

therapies and philosophies make similar claims. When so many ways are said to be true, how can one find which one or ones are really true?

Two resolutions of this problem are proposed. A determinist solution leaves the problem up to God: some are graced by God to see the truth and others aren't. Nothing we can say or do here can affect God's choice of those who see the truth, so "don't worry about it." An egalitarian solution denies the problem: all religions are different ways to the same center, so one should just bloom where one is planted and live as well as one can. The distinctiveness of the various religions is a mere historical accident and it doesn't really matter which one a person believes in just so long as s/he believes with deep conviction — since none is more true than any other.

These resolutions are both attractive and inadequate. The determinist solution is attractive in that it acknowledges that we humans cannot reach ultimate truth. In the end, we are fallible; we *might* be wrong about our most cherished beliefs. The egalitarian solution is attractive in that it recognizes both the intuition that all traditions are in some sense probably the carriers of some truth and the inclination to solve the problem in a practical manner by living as well as one can without needing to scrutinize the inscrutable or solve the insoluble. However, both are inadequate since they simply avoid the problem by denying that Christianity or any other religious tradition can be called true. And why should one believe what one cannot call true — especially if it is about what is ultimate? And why should another person believe what you say if you cannot show the other the truth of what you say? The problem remains: if one believes something, one must also believe that it is true. One cannot consistently say, for instance, "I believe that Jesus is the savior of humanity and I believe that it is false."

Yet both the determinist and the egalitarian are reacting to attempts to show *doctrines* true. But if doctrines are live or dead metaphors (as we claimed in chapter one) extracted from stories, there is good reason for difficulty in showing doctrines to be true. Metaphors are not true — nor are they false. They may be found "good" or "bad," "effective" or "ineffective," "powerful" or "weak," "live" or "dead," but not "true" or "false." Hence, it should be no surprise that it is so difficult to find doctrines true — they may not be the proper items to examine.

In chapter nine, we will examine how we can call stories "true" or "false," thus showing the way to avoid the dead ends of egalitarianism and determinism without giving up on truth. The truth of a religious tradition, I claim, is borne not in its doctrines, but in its stories. To discover that truth, we must learn how to assess those stories.

For Further Reading

The field of Church history has generated an enormous number of handbooks, monographs and short volumes. Among the great handbooks, *History of the Church*, ed. Hubert Jedin and John P. Dolan (New York: Crossroads) has ten volumes that range from the Apostolic Community to the Modern Age. The *Pelican History of the Church* in five paperback volumes (Baltimore: Penguin) is more accessible, but displays its definite Anglican preoccupations, especially in the final volumes. Among single volume histories, Martin Marty, *A Short History of Christianity* (Cleveland: Collins and World, 1959 [now published by Fortress Press]) may be the most readable, although it tends to be impressionistic in places. Paul Johnson, *A History of Christianity* (New York: Athenaeum, 1979) focuses on the reaction of the institutional church and traditionally recognized heroes to social and cultural events. William Clebsch, *Christianity in European History* (see n. 7 above) also does cultural history, but centers, as we have noted above, on creative individuals, whether famous or not, who inaugurated or crystallized new ways of being Christian in the various political and economic contexts. Numerous denominational histories are also available.

The classic reference in English for information on saints is *Butler's Lives of the Saints*, Four Volumes, revised, edited and supplemented by H. Thurston and D. Attwater (New York: P. J. Kenedy, 1956). While better than other works of its sort, this can hardly be called "critical hagiography." I find James' *Varieties of Religious Experience* (see n. 1 above) still one of the finest critical and sympathetic studies undertaken of the significance of saints. While one does not have to agree with all James' evaluations, the very wealth of material correlated is provocative, and the fascination James found in saints never fails to come through. Baron Friedrich von Hügel, *The Mystical Element of Religion as Studied in Saint Catherine of Genoa and Her Friends*, Two Volumes (London: J. M. Dent and Sons and James Clarke and Co., 1961 [first edition, 1908]) is a meticulous study that explores the mystical side of religious life sympathetically and concretely. The whole of the second volume is "critical" and expands the insights into Catherine's life into a reflection on mysticism in Christianity more generally.

More recently, David Burrell, *Exercises in Religious Understanding* (Notre Dame: University of Notre Dame Press, 1974) has attempted to study the story and the theology of five heroes (Augustine, Anselm, Aquinas, Kierkegaard, Jung). Similarly, John Dunne has explored a number of stories both within and without the Christian tradition, especially in *A Search for God in Time and Memory* (New York: Macmillan, 1967) and *The Way of All the Earth* (New York: Macmillan, 1972). He has continued his work with an inward sort of journey, guided by numerous people who have quested inwards and returned to the world in *Reasons of the Heart: A Journey into Solitude and Back Again into the Human Circle* (New York: Macmillan, 1978) and *The Church of the Poor Devil: Reflections on a Riverboat Voyage and a Spiritual Journey* (Notre Dame: University of Notre Dame Press, 1983) wherein he describes a journey deep into the heart of the Amazon — and of Christianity.

The biographical and historical approaches of McClendon and Clebsch highlighted in this chapter can be contrasted with some excellent contemporary typological approaches. Lawrence S. Cunningham, *The Catholic Heritage* (New York: Seabury Press, 1983) takes types of Christians, much like Clebsch, and treats exemplars of these types in various historical epochs. Cunningham is concerned to show the continuities in the Roman Catholic tradition while Clebsch has been concerned to show the diversities in Christianity. Elliot Wright, *Holy Company: Christian Heroes and Heroines* (New York: Macmillan, 1980) groups Christians from every age under each of the Matthean beatitudes. Both texts have excellent bibliographies and are intended to be read by educated lay people and/or college students.

A growing interest in the developmental psychology of Piaget and Erikson has led some thinkers — notably Lawrence Kohlberg and James Fowler — to employ developmental categories to understand moral and religious development and maturity. One good example of this is *Trajectories in Faith* by James W. Fowler, Robin W. Lovin *et al* (Nashville: Abingdon, 1980). A six-phase faith development theory is sketched in the beginning of the book and then a biographical approach to the lives of Malcolm X, Anne Hutchinson, Blaise Pascal, Ludwig Wittgenstein and Dietrich Bonhoeffer is made. The structure of the book shows its weakness: it tends to read its subject in light of the categories rather than to let the categories emerge from the studies. While other work may have "established" these categories, that does not mean that they necessarily apply well to these lives. But most significantly, the authors tend to confuse the descriptive and the normative: because *many* people go through stages (even these stages) of faith does not entail that people *should* go through these stages to have a *full* faith. While they would deny, I suspect, that they are *assessing* (making normative claims about) any person's faith by its progress in the trajectory, the very language they use to describe the stages *is* laden with increasingly positive evaluations the "higher" one goes. While the developmental work of these psychologists of faith may be intrinsically interesting, I find a sort of "psycho-theology" based in their work suspect, at best.

By contrast, many forms of liberation theology seek to develop theological reflections from peoples' liberating and creative *praxis*. Hence, these theologies must have a narrative base, for Crites' claims about experience (see pp. 23-26) apply equally well to *praxis*. Given the concern to do theology from the bottom up and to address primarily people within the Church, I would expect that doing narrative theology would be "a natural" for liberation theologians. However, I have not yet seen any explicitly narrative liberation theology.

Finally, George W. Stroup, *The Promise of Narrative Theology: Recovering the Gospel in the Church* (Atlanta: John Knox, 1981) and Johannes B. Metz, *Followers of Christ: The Religious Life and the Church*, trans. Thomas Linton (New York: Paulist, 1978) reflect on the themes of this chapter. Stroup sees narrative theology as answering a two-fold need in Christianity: the need for Christian identity and the need for a post-critical theology of revelation. He thus concentrates on the theme of life-stories and offers a critical and constructive account of how this type of narrative theology can resolve some vexing classical doctrinal disputes. Metz concentrates on the vocation of vowed religious in the Roman Catholic Church, with special regard to the evangelical counsels (poverty, celibacy and obedience). Like Stroup, he makes a connection between knowing and doing the truth in the context of narratives and shows how reconsideration of the structure of discipleship can help renew the church. Although neither of these books does much narrative theology, both offer valuable insights into understanding the life-stories of Christians and the relevance of those narratives to the rest of theology.

9

MOMENTS OF TRUTH

If you dwell in my word,
in truth are you my disciples
and you will know the truth,
and the truth will free you.
—John 8:31-32

Realistic narratives often center around the "moment of truth," that point at which the key figure (sometimes unrecognized) chooses (sometimes unwittingly) the final shape of the story. The moment of truth often comes near the end of the story. Yet a skillful storyteller can place it at the beginning, so that only the most perceptive will recognize the key actor or the real moment of truth before the *denouement*. The stories of the Son of God (pp. 121-127 above) exemplify the various placements of the moment of truth. Some writers made the crucifixion/resurrection the moment of truth. Others placed it earlier in Jesus' life, at his Baptism, his birth or conception. John's Gospel put the moment of truth out of time. If one is not clear on the main actor or the moment of truth in any one of these stories, then one cannot understand the story.

Yet discovering the moment of truth *in* a story does not necessarily uncover the truth *of* that story. Narrative theology is concerned with both: Previous chapters have shown the moments of truth *in* stories. This chapter will show how to assess the truth *of* stories. This is the moment of truth for a narrative theology: by what standards can we judge whether the stories we hear and tell are true?

The chapter is divided into seven sections. In the first, the notion that "true" is best understood for our purposes as a *grade* is explored. The next five sections develop canons for applying "true" to stories. The final section explores the significance of knowing true stories. The basic thesis of this chapter can be summarized as follows: A story can be assessed "true" (or "false") to the extent that it (1) represents the world (or part of it) revealingly; (2) is coherent by corresponding to the facts (insofar as we recognize them), by referring accurately, and by attributing correctly; (3) shows ways of overcoming self-deception; (4) shows a person how to be faithful (true) to others; and (5) provides a model for constancy in seeking to tell the truth.

"True" As a Grade

Philosophers have been debating the nature of truth for millennia without coming to agreement on how to answer the question, "What is truth?" Rather than attempting to settle those debates, this chapter will use "true" as an appraisal term or grade. The standards for this grade will be developed from our ordinary uses of "true." The standards implicit in our ordinary language can then be made explicit and sharpened by adopting relevant philosophical insights as guides.

Three considerations will show what it means to do so. First, parents and children, enemies and friends, judges and police, spies and diplomats, all have figured out ways to spot the differences between stories that ring true and stories that don't. For the most part, their appraisals have had some success, although they ignore the philosophers' debates over the nature of truth. This success suggests that many professional philosophers may not be worried about the same sort of truth as are ordinary folk. In an analysis of our ordinary uses of "true" and "false," philosopher John L. Austin has noted that these words function much like evaluations:

> There are numerous other adjectives which are in the same class as "true" and "false"... We say, for example, that a certain statement is exaggerated or bald, a description somewhat rough or misleading or not very good, an account rather general or too concise.[1]

In this chapter, this insight is extended to apply to stories. To call a story "true" is to evaluate it, grade it or assess it as "not exaggerated, not too rough, not misleading, not too general," etc. People frequently have to evaluate stories they are told as part of their everyday life. The point of this chapter is to show a way to evaluate stories which structure a religious tradition. People have to evaluate the religious stories they are told as part of their exploring the possibilities of accepting those religious stories as their own.

Second, to assess a story's truth, one must attend to its context, that is, to the kind of story it is, the audience to which it is told, the purposes for which it is told, and the position of the story teller. These vary from situation to situation. Although "the same story was told" in two different contexts, it might be called true in one context but not in another.

The different kinds of stories cannot be reduced to one. If someone labeled the parable of the Good Samaritan false because the Samaritan was not an actual person, that assessment would be wrong. A parable does not claim to represent an actual person or event. If someone labeled a biography of a saint false because that saint had never existed, that assessment would be right. Biographies do claim to represent actual persons. Stories must be evaluated for truth dependent upon their type: the standards for truth will vary by the *type* of story told.

---

[1]John L. Austin, "Truth," *Philosophical Papers*, Second Edition, ed. J. O. Urmson and G. J. Warnock (London: Oxford University Press, 1970), p. 122.

The different forces with which a story is told ("threat," "warning," "prediction," etc.) affect the kind of story it is heard as. For instance, if a child were to ask what would happen to her or him after death, and an adult responded by repeating the eschatological parable of the sheep and the goats, with what force would the child hear the story? Would s/he hear it as a "prediction" or "promise"? If the claims made in chapter four are correct, then in that context the telling of the story would have to be called "false" to the original. If the story is heard as a "warning" or "call to repent," then it could be called "true" to the original. In short, the assessment of the truth of a story is affected by the force of the story and that determines *how the hearer takes it*.

The varying forces of a story also have relevance to the teller of the story and the purposes with which it is told. If the "sheep and goats" story were told with the purpose of predicting the future, then telling it with a different purpose is false to the original telling of the story. If Jesus told that story truly, then it would be hard to tell the story with a different force from his and also consider it true. It might be true — but that is an open question, for the *purposes* to which the story is put are different.

A story that might be called true given one teller might be called false given another narrator. For example, what a child might tell a parent about what happened in the school yard last Tuesday might be reasonably accurate. Yet the child's teacher might tell the parent a very different story about the same events. This latter story might also be accurate. In spite of the fact that the two stories differ markedly, both may properly be called true because the perspectives of the *storytellers* are so different in each case. Moreover, if the teacher told the child's story and the child told the teacher's story, a parent's assessment of the truth of each could easily be rather different.

The task of assessing a story is the task of evaluating the telling of a story by one teller with a given purpose and a given force to a particular audience. A story may be found true in one context. But change the teller, hearer, purpose or force of the story, and the previous assessment no longer necessarily applies. While one can presume that a story found true in one context can be found true in a similar context, as the context changes, so the reliability of that presumption changes. The standards which follow, then, do not apply to a "naked text," but to the telling and hearing or writing and reading of a story in a specific context.

Third, the presupposition of assessing the truth of a story is that it is interesting. To paraphrase Alfred North White-head, it is more important that a story be interesting than that it be true.[2] Uninteresting stories don't raise the question of their truth. Although it may have been different in the past, in the present we call some interesting stories true and others false. We may find many myths interesting, for instance; but that does not mean we find them all true. Those that we don't find interesting we don't bother to grade at all.

Those who know many stories are forced to raise the questions about which are true and which false. Those seriously interested in one myth among the many will want to know whether it portrays truly the way the world is. Those seriously interested by an action story will want to know whether it exhibits truly what ought to be done or how life ought to be lived. Those awakened by a parable will want to know whether it reveals truly the cracks in their myth.

However, it could be objected that the standards set up here are not appropriate standards for *truth*. One might object either that the standards are far too broad to be standards for truth, but are really standards for efficacy and credibility as well, or that some standard is missing. To both sorts of objections, the response is that these five standards cover the basic uses of the word "true" as an appraisal in ordinary English. If any of these standards do not reflect the ordinary uses of "true," or if there are other basic ordinary uses of "true" which they do not reflect, then the standards laid out below would need correction.

[2] Alfred North Whitehead, *Process and Reality* (New York: Macmillan, 1929), pp. 395-396 suggests this point.

The standards proffered may seem to presume extended uses of "true." However, that is because what are being assessed here are not propositions, but narratives. While standards of coherence might be adequate to assess propositions, a narrative is not strings of propositions, but an artistic plotting of events, with a set of purposes dependent on the context. Thus, since narratives are more than the propositions extractable from them, the truth of narratives is not surprisingly to be assessed in terms that go beyond the appraisal of the propositions embedded in them.

Of course, one could argue against the very appeal to ordinary uses of "true" as constituting a satisfactory warrant for this whole approach since our ordinary uses of "true" are embedded in a contemporary myth which needs to be evaluated, and perhaps to be deconstructed. But the strength of the present approach is that it finds room for both deconstruction of stories (as in the first standard below) and for more prosaic approaches to evaluating the truth of stories. Further, if any reconstructions are proposed or developed to replace deconstructed myths, those proposals will also have to meet standards for truth. Thus, I claim that there is no good reason to object to the standards presented as standards for evaluating the truth of stories.

If we need to assess stories, we must know on what bases, by which standards, using which canons and criteria we can judge them. If "true" can be understood as an assessment, and if the assessment of a given narrative varies with the context of that narrative, and if we must discriminate among stories, as this section has argued, we need guides for our judging. The next five sections of the chapter make explicit the standards for finding stories "true" or "false." These guides show the "moments of truth" for a narrative theology.

True Stories as Revealing Stories

We value stories which reveal something that we didn't know or see before. Sometimes we do not *like* these stories. They may upset us, but if they are revealing, we *appreciate* them. Stories which evoke a response like "Oh, my God! It's true!!!" are revealing stories. The first standard to guide assessing stories for their truth is a standard of revelation: *a story is true to the extent that it re-presents our world or part of it in a revealing way.*

There are few stories which have the shock-value to evoke the exclamation quoted above. Some of the best examples of these are the parables of Jesus. In fact, this first standard applies especially to parabolic stories. A parable that did *not* reveal the "cracks" in a myth or the "oversights" in a person's understanding would fail *as a parable.* It would misfire.

Most stories reveal less to their hearers than Jesus' parables. But any story whose purpose is to allow a person to see previously unnoticed connections among the events and people of the world can be evaluated according to this standard. Stories told with other purposes are to be measured by other standards. Ignoring the other purposes of stories and forgetting the other standards by which one can call a story true would lead one to equate the shocking with the true, an unhappy conclusion. That is, revelation provides one standard, but not the only standard, for assessing stories.

One example of a story that can be called true by this standard is the one told by the prophet Nathan to King David, as reported in 2 Samuel. The situation was that David had taken Bathsheba, the wife of Uriah, made love with her, and she was pregnant. David then sent Uriah to the battlefront where Uriah was killed, as David had hoped. David then married Bathsheba. Nathan at this point tells the following story to King David:

> "There were two men in a certain city, the one rich and the other poor. The rich man had very many flocks and herds; but the poor man had nothing but one little ewe lamb, which he had bought. And he brought it up, and it grew up with him and with his children; it used to drink from his cup, and lie in his bosom, and it was like a daughter to him. Now there came a traveler to the rich

man, and he was unwilling to take one of his own flock or herd to prepare for the wayfarer who had come to him, but he took the poor man's lamb, and prepared it for the man who had come to him." Then David's anger was greatly kindled against the man; and he said to Nathan, "As the Lord lives, the man who has done this deserves to die; and he shall restore the lamb fourfold, because he did this thing, and because he had no pity."

Nathan said to David, "You are the man" (2 Sam 12:1-7, RSV).

This story enabled David to see what he had done and to say what he deserved. Nathan forced him to see the significance of his action by telling a story which revealed connections David hadn't acknowledged between his own acts and the moral standards of his world. Thus, by our first standard, this can be appraised as a true story. Its purpose was to reveal and it succeeded.

Revelation is an event in which telling a story uncovers what was hidden. A specific story may be revealing in one context for one audience, but not in another context for another audience. For instance, a committed Christian might tell the story of the passion and death of Jesus of Nazareth to a nominal Christian in order to show her or him the central aspect of the form of Christian life. However, this event of telling and hearing that story might reveal to the hearer that he or she isn't really interested in being a Christian. Or it might show that person that her or his life needs reformation. The teller of the story cannot control a story's power to reveal. As the story of the encounter between Clarence Jordan and his brother Robert suggests (see pp. 175-176 above), the story of the cross can be very revealing to disciples — or admirers — of Jesus. But that doesn't mean that such a story is always revealing. Sometimes the hoped-for revelation simply doesn't happen, or an unexpected disclosure occurs.

Assessing a story's ability to reveal what has been hidden must be done each time that story is told. Some stories become hackneyed and lose their power; others become deformed. Just because a story works at some times and places doesn't mean it won't need to be reformed or retired. One example of the process of reform is the evolution of the stories of Jesus as the Son of God (pp. 121-127 above). New stories need to be told when older ones lose their power to reveal.

That stories reveal does not mean that they cannot conceal as well. A person can tell a story to dazzle and blind people, to manipulate them by evoking invalid insights. For instance, some Christians have told the story of the passion and death of Jesus to other Christians with the purpose of evoking the insight that the Jews are or were "god-killers." However, if the main purpose of telling Jesus' story is to proclaim and manifest faith in him, then an anti-Jewish telling violates the main purpose of the story for its purpose is primarily negative: It becomes a story told to evoke hate, not love or faith. But a hearer could discover that s/he had been manipulated only by evaluating the story s/he was told by the other standards for truth (especially that of coherence) and coming to reject the false conclusion which had been evoked. That a story evokes insight into what had been hidden is not a sufficient measure of the truth of the story or of the insight, although a story told with the purpose of evoking insight must evoke insight to be called true.

Generally, a story told to reveal what has been hidden can be called true if a disclosure occurs. The content of what is revealed and the implications drawn from that disclosure are possibly true, but may require further testing. Specifically, a parable must be evaluated by this standard. For a non-evocative parable (or non-challenging counter-myth) is a failure. In sum, that a story uncovers what had been hidden is a necessary criterion for the truth of some stories in some contexts, but not a sufficient standard of the truth of all stories in all contexts; while it provides good reason to call a story true, people may find better reasons to change that call as they examine the story in light of other standards.

True Stories as Coherent Stories

We value stories which are coherent. If we find a story "incoherent," not only do we imply that we can't believe it, but also that we can't see how anyone could. An incoherent story is one that doesn't "hang together." Naturally, we tend to think that our stories are coherent, that they do hang together. But the way to check this is to measure a story against a standard of coherence: *a story can be called true to the extent that: (1) it is consistent with the other facts we recognize; (2) it refers accurately; (3) it attributes accurately.*

Theories of coherence and correspondence are dear to philosophers as theories of truth. To some minds they provide the most obvious ways to measure stories. In contrast, here we adopt the insights from those theories as standards to be used to assess stories. While the first standard measured a story by its *effectiveness* in getting a hearer to understand, the present one appraises the *content* of a story.

The first way to assess the coherence of a story is to check its *consistency with other facts we recognize.* A story which is self-contradictory (asserting *p* and *not-p*) or which contradicts other facts the hearer or teller comes to recognize will reasonably meet with a response like, "That can't be true!" It may be that this standard is often not met by a person who tells a story which denies facts or precludes procedures which that storyteller implicitly accepts. Someone who hears a story which denies facts or precludes procedures which s/he implicitly *or* explicitly accepts cannot believe the story heard. In both cases a contradiction between the story as told and other facts or procedures recognized implies that the story is incoherent with accepted beliefs or practices. Unless there is a "willing suspension of disbelief" recognized by both teller and hearer (as in the cases of science fiction or historical novels) either the story must be withdrawn or the facts or procedures it contradicts must be forfeited. Either one or the other cannot be true.

One example of such a contradiction is the claim of some

fundamentalist Christians not to *interpret*, but to *believe*, the Bible. They claim that the story of the creation of the world by God as portrayed in the book of Genesis literally pictures what happened over a period of six days (in or about the year 4004 B.C.). Yet this way of telling the creation story is inconsistent with a claim to believe, but not to interpret, the Bible. In fact, they have used their own reason and imagination to interpret this *story* as a *picture* or *history* of events. Hence, someone could not consistently claim both not to interpret the story and to interpret the story in the text as a picture or history. Either the interpretation or the claim not to interpret the text must be sacrificed. For the Bible does not interpret itself. The Bible cannot say what the Bible means. People say what it means. People necessarily interpret the text, whether they are fundamentalist, modernist, or something else. Thus, a different way of retelling the creation story, one that construes the story as a *myth* on the grounds that this is the way the story actually functioned and functions, is to be preferred over one which interprets the story and claims not to do so. A mythical approach is properly assessed as true, for it is more consistent with other procedures accepted and other facts believed true by the hearers or tellers of the story. Of course, a fundamentalist could recognize that s/he interprets the text. But that would mean abandoning a claim not to interpret the text. But then her or his interpretation or reading of the story would have to be assessed and discussed.

A second way to assess the coherence of a story is to check its *accuracy of reference.* The more accurate a story is in pointing to, denoting, an actor, a place or an event, the more reason to call it true.

Consider, for example, the story of the Exodus. Which sea did the Israelites cross in their flight from slavery to the promised land? Apparently it was the "Reed Sea" rather than the Red Sea, and a story which is told including the former denotation rather than the latter may be more accurate in geographical reference, if less spectacular. To tell the story of the Exodus — or any story — more accurately is to tell it more truly according to this standard.

But a main point of the Exodus story is that the central actor in the Exodus was God. Is this an accurate reference to the main actor? That question cannot be answered simply and directly. However, if one concluded that the Israelites *wandered* through the Sea of Reeds, or that the whole story was *nonsense*, or that there were *too few people* in the Exodus to represent or symbolize the people that became Israel, than one would have to conclude that God did not act for the obvious reason that no act of *leading* can be reliably affirmed to have occurred.

But none of those conditions seems to have obtained. Hence, one could not conclude that the story fails to refer accurately. Yet neither could one conclude that the story does refer accurately to the main actor. Typically, a religious story referring to a Transcendent Actor will not be settled by this standard and must be judged on the basis of other tests.[3]

The third measure of the coherence of a story is *accuracy of attribution*. The more accurate a story is in attributing a quality or an action to an agent, the more warranted it is to call it true. This standard differs from the previous one in that the point is not to assess the *naming* of the agent correctly, but the *describing* of the agent accurately and adequately. For example, the stories about Jesus from chapter seven each sought to describe who Jesus was and what he meant as accurately as possible. One of them, reflected in 1 Peter, claimed that "by his wounds you have been healed." This attributes to Jesus — especially through his suffering and death — the power to heal Christians. To evaluate the truth of a Christian's healing story, we need to undertake the complex task of evaluating the accuracy of attribution.

First, one has to know what it means to be ill. As James P. Mackey points out, this is not merely physical illness. It is also the dis-ease of bondage, "the sense of having sold out for small comforts that now seem indispensable, sold into

---

[3]Similar conclusions are reached in James Wm. McClendon, Jr. and James M. Smith, *Understanding Religious Convictions* (Notre Dame: University of Notre Dame Press, 1975), pp. 69-74, and John M. Shea, *Stories of God* (Chicago: Thomas More, 1978), pp. 163-165.

slavery long after the slave-market has disappeared,"[4] and the inability to pay the price for freedom. Yet if we do regain our health, freedom, or wholeness, who paid the price? Christians attribute it to Jesus.

Second, a person must be healed. If someone is still in thrall to small comforts or racked by disease, then there has been no healing to attribute to anyone. But if a person claims to be healed, and still is diseased, that claim is incoherent.

Third, it must be Jesus who heals. Even if the first two conditions are met, the attribution may be inaccurate. For instance, someone may be or feel healed in the context of the interaction of friends who provide a network of acceptance and care as might be found in a Christian community. A critic might then say, "Your *friends* have healed you, not Jesus." A Christian could respond by noting that Jesus lives on in the "body of Christ," the community of his disciples. While it may be true that the power of friendship heals, there is no clear reason to say that a critic's redescription of the source of healing (and consequent re-attribution of the source of health) tells a story somehow "more true" than the story the healed person tells. A Christian can surely recognize that the power of friendship heals and that the community can be an agent of healing; but that does not entail that they are not empowered to do so by Jesus. In some cases, the redescription may be more accurate; but not in all. Especially when a critic considers an attenuated version of a story or attempts to explain a religious dimension in other terms, the critic bears the burden of proof in defending the re-attribution and in accounting for any rebuttal that the original story-teller can make.

In short, to evaluate a story told about an action, we must understand the context for the action, what the action is, and who the actor is said to be. A person assessing the truth of a story will too often err because s/he does not get clear on all the elements in the story.

---

[4]James P. Mackey, *Jesus: The Man and the Myth* (New York: Paulist Press, 1979), p. 80.

A story that we can come to see does attribute accurately meets this third test for coherence. A story that does not attribute accurately fails. In the case of assessing the truth of a modern healing story. an evaluator must assume true (at least for the sake of argument) the master story which provides the background for the present story: the stories of redemption in the suffering of Jesus. Unless one assumes the background story, one will not be in position to assess the particular stories which tell of particular instances of the general, prototypical, story. A person who does not make that general assumption will find a particular story neither true nor false but uninteresting. The question of a particular story's truth will either be prejudged or will not arise at all.

It could be objected that the present criterion is irrelevant to fictional narratives for fictions neither refer nor attribute. Rather, the fact that a narrator does not attempt to refer to a specific set of events, persons, or places, nor to attribute a quality or action to a specific agent shows that the story is told as a fiction. It does not show that the narrative is to be called untrue, but rather that the story refers in an oblique or indirect manner to referents in the author's or hearer's experience. If a narrator attempts to refer or attribute specifically and fails, the story is untrue (but not fictional). If a narrator does not attempt to refer or attribute specifically, then the story is fictional and needs to be explored to discover in what sense, if any, it is to be called true. Thus, the present standard is relevant to fictional stories in that it shows how to distinguish them from "historical" narratives, not whether they are to be called true or false.

As noted in the beginning of this section, people strive to tell coherent stories. Most believe that the stories they make their own are coherent; occasionally that belief is challenged. To respond to that challenge is to show either that the stories told do not contradict any of the other facts recognized, do not mis-refer, and do not mis-attribute qualities or acts to agents; or to recognize that the stories are fictions without specific referents. To the extent that our stories meet a standard of coherence, or can be made to meet that standard, to that extent we have reason to call them true.

True Stories as Stories of Authenticity

We value authenticity in a person. We say, "She's a true human being," or "He's got class," etc. Yet when one of these compliments is given to us, we often realize that we are not as genuine, as authentic, as we could and should be. Lurking behind the false modesty with which most of us receive compliments, there is the true realization that we are not as others perceive us, that their perceptions of our authenticity do not square with ours. So we try to be true to ourselves and to tell ourselves the truth about ourselves. Yet we often fail to realize much truth about ourselves because we conceal so much of the truth from ourselves. This tension between seeking the truth and concealing it is the tension between authenticity and its opposite, self-deception. Thus a third measure of the truth of a story is a criterion for authenticity: *a true story shows us ways to overcome self-deception*, for if a story can contribute to overcoming our tendency to conceal the truth, it will help us to become more authentic human beings.

Yet understanding the phenomenon of self-deception presents a serious problem: How can we account for the fact that people conceal from themselves who they are in spite of their attempts to uncover the truth? How can we explain the woman who searches for a cure for her bronchitis from physician after physician and refuses to quit smoking two packs of cigarettes a day? How can we explain the *primo tenore* who identifies the pain that knocked him out as "indigestion" when a physician shows him abnormal electrocardiograms? How can we explain an army officer who pacifies a village by destroying it? Self-deception apparently consists in the paradoxical inability of a person to see what "anyone" can see, an inability inexplicable if we assume that being aware of — seeing — something is passive looking at it.

However, if we consider awareness and consciousness as active skills rather than passive readinesses, if we understand seeing as a reaching out to the world rather than as a waiting to be impressed by the world, if we allow perception to be not merely "turning on one's receiver" but also "tuning it in," then we may be able to describe self-deception less paradoxically. Assuming consciousness to be an active skill rather than a readiness-state provides a way to begin describing self-deception, as Herbert Fingarette has shown:

> I propose, then, that we do not characterize consciousness as a kind of mental mirror, but as the exercise of the (learned) skill of "spelling-out" some feature of the world as we are engaged in it. Like its model — language skill proper — this skill is ubiquitous among men, though in both cases the subtlety, the range, and the aptness of exercise of the skill varies markedly among individuals...
>
> Colloquially, to spell something out is to make it explicit, to say it in a clearly and fully elaborated way, to make it perfectly apparent. Typical uses which I have in mind are: "He is so stupid you have to spell everything out for him"; "He let me know without actually spelling it out"; and "You know perfectly well what I mean — do I have to spell it out for you?"[5]

Thus, to be conscious is to be able to spell out the connections from where one is to other times and places and to make explicit the connections in what we see. Just as some are better at spelling out connections than others are, so some are more fully conscious than others are.

Assuming that consciousness is this skill, we can describe a self-deceived person as one who "even when [it is] normally appropriate...*persistently* avoids spelling out some feature of his engagement with the world."[6] Yet this description does not explain the reasons people fail to spell things out. One obvious one is that some people simply do not have the skill to do so: they are not fully conscious. They may be too young, psychologically deficient, intellectually de-

---

[5]Herbert Fingarette, *Self-Deception* (London: Routledge and Kegan Paul, 1969), p. 39.

[6]*Ibid.*, p. 47.

prived, socially inept, etc., to be conscious of what they do. In other cases, the root is somewhat different, as Hauerwas and Burrell suggest:

> Each of us needs to establish some sense of identity and unity in order to give coherence to the multifariousness of our history as uniquely ours and as constitutive of the self. Self-deception can accompany this need for unity, as we systematically delude ourselves in order to maintain the story that has hitherto assured our identity. We hesitate to spell out certain engagements when spelling them out would jeopardize the set of avowals we have made about ourselves.[7]

Examples of this can be multiplied almost at will. We all know of people whose lives are entirely invested in athletics or in vocal music. When they retire — or are retired — some have the ability to add a new and different chapter to their stories. They are able to find a metaphor other than "quarterback" or "heldentenor" to organize the stories of their lives. Others are not so graceful. The "old jocks" cannot believe that their athletic careers are truly over. The aging singers cannot believe that the trouble with their voices is not a passing thing. Events force people either to blind themselves more stubbornly to the realities that anyone else can see or to change their lives and reshape their stories — a process that is often painful. In short, fear of change may be one key root for self-deception.

Another root of self-deception is social. In any given society, there are metaphors to be adopted, roles to be played, stories to be lived. These "ready-made" clothes save one the pain and difficulty of tailoring one's own future. Rather, one just slips into the suit. Hauerwas and Burrell comment on this:

---

[7]Stanley Hauerwas and David Burrell, "Self-Deception and Autobiography: Reflections on Speer's Inside the Third Reich," in *Truthfulness and Tragedy: Further Investigations in Christian Ethics* (Notre Dame: University of Notre Dame Press, 1977), p. 87.

> Societal roles provide a ready vehicle for self-deception, since we can easily identify with them without any need to spell out what we are doing. The role is accepted into our identity. . . In the narrow confines of a job and of corporate loyalty, such an individual can easily be caricatured as a "company man," and come under a simple censure of establishment myopia. Where the description is more exalted and vocational, however, the opportunity for deceiving oneself increases. A man may think of himself as a public servant concerned with the public good. Even though he may be party to decisions which compromise the public good, he has a great deal invested in continuing to describe them as contributing to the public good.[8]

If a person *ceases* to describe these decisions as contributing to the public good, and begins to describe them as what they truly are, for example, selfish, power-grabbing, etc., then that person will upset that comfortable story that has been giving unity to the self, be it "company man" story or "civil servant" story. In short, self-deception typically results from filling our need for a unified self by sliding into a ready-made story (a societal role that puts one's self in a specific job or place) and refusing to describe what we do in any way that will upset that story. And a story that supports self-deception cannot be called "true."

Hauerwas and Burrell suggest that the self-deceived person has taken the easy way out by telling the first story that s/he can comfortably live with as his or her story. It is a tendency we all seem to have. Yet how can this tendency be overcome? Hauerwas and Burrell have a solid answer:

> A true story could only be one powerful enough to check the endemic tendency toward self-deception — a tendency which inadequate stories cannot help but foster. Correlatively, if the true God were to provide us with a saving story, it would have to be one that we found

---

[8] *Ibid.*

continually discomforting. For it would be a saving story
only as it empowered us to combat the inertial drift into
self-deception.[9]

By this standard, an upsetting, uncomfortable story can be
called true. For instance, if the parables of Jesus, the stories
about Jesus, and the stories of Jesus' followers are upsetting
and uncomfortable, if these stories check people's tendencies to slide into self-deception by making them aware of
connections they would rather not see, and if these stories
empower people to overcome self-deceptive policies, then
they can be called true by this standard.

It should be noted that many myths will not be found to
be true by this standard. Myths typically provide roles for
people to play and worlds to play them in. They often
provide comfort and prohibit uncomfortable questions
from being raised. Hence, for a myth to be judged true
according to this standard, it would have to be a "parabolic"
myth. It would have to set up a world in which upsetting was
at home. Most importantly, it would have to account for the
most upsetting event of all: death. If a story can show people
something great enough to give their lives to and for, then
that story overcomes the most basic self-deception: the
denial of death. People want to deny that they shall die.
They try to preserve their youth and to postpone their fate.
They deny the power of death by telling stories which fan-
tasize that power into meaninglessness, which ignore that
power by playing in a garden of earthly delights, or which
construct powerful idols who will save them from death. But
a story which shows something worth living for and dying
for without denying the fact that all shall die is one that
discourages self-deception, encourages authenticity, and
thus can be called true by this standard.

However, this standard of truth needs to be balanced by
other ones. Authenticity is not a sufficient measure of the
effective truth of narratives for it does not bring out the

[9]*Ibid.*, p. 95.

necessity of being "true to" people and "true to" ideals. We shall now turn to these standards.

True Stories as Stories of Fidelity

We value fidelity in a person. We say, "He's really true to his friends" or "She is true to her family" or "I've never seen people so true to each other as..." etc. Yet when one of these compliments is referred to us, we often know that we are not as true to our friends, our families, our loves, as we could and should be. We often recognize that along with our quest for fidelity (as with our hope of authenticity) there is a tendency to infidelity (as there is a tendency to self-deception). Thus, a fourth measure of a true story is a criterion of fidelity: *a true story is one that shows a person how to be faithful to others.*

In one way this criterion seems too obvious. The story of Sheppard (see pp. 6-9 above) is the story of a man who does not know how to keep faith with his son. Therefore, the story of Sheppard, if proposed as a model, has rather obvious flaws and would not rank highly by this standard. Yet if it is told as a warning about the sort of hubris to which liberals like Sheppard are prone, then it could be called true by this standard. Indeed, once one understands the force with which the story is told, the verdict about its truth is clear, for the story itself is very obvious.

Yet most stories are not so obvious or clear. Most narratives portray people whose fidelity — or lack thereof — is not so clear as Sheppard's. These stories are much more difficult to evaluate. Presuming that they are proposed as models rather than warnings, whether myths to structure one's own world or actions to be followed in shaping one's own life, I want to suggest that the way to evaluate the truth of such a story is to see how faithful the main character in the story is to those s/he does *not* intend to be faithful. In short, to bring to this standard some clarity and subtlety, we need to use the tactics of the "eschatological judge" of

Matthew 25 (see pp. 60-64 above) to evaluate the stories people offer as models in order to see the extent to which those stories show people how to be faithful to others.

Yet it might be objected that the introduction of the eschatological judge's tactics introduces a Christian bias, and thus prejudices the case in favor of Christian narratives over other stories. This is not the case. First, it must be recognized that the standard has its origins in the central text of the Christian tradition. But that is not the point. The question is whether it is appropriate, which can be shown only as the standard's meaning is unfolded. Second, the point of the tactic is not material but formal. No specific story or set of stories is favored by this standard. As Michael Goldberg has pointed out, both views of life as "gift" or as "trust" can be developed from the biblical texts.[10] Each of these views will be based on different understandings of the biblical narratives or take different biblical narratives as key to understanding others. The present standard does not decide between those views — or any others — in the abstract. Rather, one can concretely apply this standard to evaluate the stories which model those views. The present standard does not prejudge stories, but rather proposes to measure every story for the *range* of fidelity it exemplifies.

Third, as many have noted, there is no such thing as a completely bias-free perspective from which to judge all the earthly stories. In fact, the very standards which I propose as standards for truth must be based in some specific narrative, if the claims made in chapter two are true. Yet the fact that there is a narrative basis for standards does not preclude the possibility for making judgments about the truth of stories. As a number of philosophers have argued,[11] there

[10]Michael Goldberg, *Theology and Narrative: A Critical Introduction* (Nashville: Abingdon, 1982), p. 191.

[11]See the discussions of "soft perspectivism" in Van A. Harvey, *The Historian and the Believer* (New York: Macmillan, 1969 [1966]), pp. 230-242 and McClendon and Smith, *op. cit.*, pp. 7-9, and the imaginative work on the overlapping of our various forms of life and constitutive stories by J. M. Cameron, "The Idea of Christendom," in *The Autonomy of Religious Belief*, edited by Frederick Crosson (Notre Dame: University of Notre Dame Press, 1981), pp. 8-37.

is a way to remedy inevitable biases. Each judge must seek to increase her or his participation in and awareness of other interesting forms of life structured by those other narratives s/he finds worth evaluating. And, indeed, these forms of life overlap in practice. Thus, to be in position to judge the truth of stories is not to abandon one's own master story, but to take in and account for the stories which structure other forms of life and, in some sense, to make those stories a part of one's own "inner history." In short, it is necessarily true that the standards I propose and the judgments I make are based in the narratives I find normative, but the way to overcome the bias thus introduced is not to tell no story (that was the Enlightenment error — see pp. 33-36), but to make my standards formally applicable to the relevant stories and to make my material judgments about content based in a story that understands others' stories as well as it understands my own.

In order to provide standards, I will start with the suggestions of Hauerwas and Burrell. While their list has been criticized and is ambiguous at points, it provides a general guide whose weaknesses can be overcome as we adapt it and unpack the meaning of the standards: Any story proposed *as a model* can be evaluated for fidelity by examining whether: (1) its main character is released from destructive alternatives; (2) its main character is enabled to see through current distortions; (3) its main character avoids resorting to violence; (4) it has a sense of the tragic, showing how meaning transcends brute force.[12]

(1) "Violence is the last refuge of the incompetent." So goes a slogan attributed to fictional hero Hober Mallow, a consummate politician in the *Foundation* series of s.f. nov-

---

[12]Hauerwas and Burrell, "From System to Story: An Alternative Pattern for Rationality in Ethics," in *Truthfulness and Tragedy*, p. 35. Also see Burrell's further discussion of them in "Stories of God: Why We Use Them and How We Judge Them" in *Is God GOD?* edited by J. W. McClendon and Axel Steuer (Nashville: Abingdon, 1981), pp. 213-215, which responds to some of the criticisms raised in J. Wesley Robbins, "Narrative, Morality and Religion," *Journal of Religious Ethics* 8 (Fall, 1980), pp. 161-176, and Gene Outka, "Character, Vision and Narrative," *Religious Studies Review* 6 (April, 1980), pp. 116-118. Goldberg, *Theology and Narrative*, pp. 236-240 is also relevant to this point.

els by Isaac Asimov.[13] Often it seems that nothing a person can do can avoid violence; for instance, a politician will call for a country to go to war as a "last resort." Yet in some instances, at least, a creative politician can avoid war and destruction. One example of this is the response of Dag Hammarskjöld to the dilemma in 1954 of either acquiescing in the illegitimate execution of American pilots as spies by the Peoples' Republic of China or calling for a military expedition to rescue them. In either case, people would die. Rather than sacrificing others, however, Hammarskjöld chose to go to Peking himself. He took the chance of losing his position, and conceivably his life, rather than costing the lives of many others, known or unknown to him. That he was in fact successful (as Hober Mallow was in fiction) suggests that a person whose story shows ways of seeing alternatives where there seem to be none is a person whose story expresses fidelity to others, whether s/ he is aware of it or not. Thus, if this story is proposed as a model in a given situation, then it would have to be ranked high or found true by this standard.[14]

(2) A true story is one in which the main character is able to see through current distortions, those things "everyone knows," but are truly vicious, always unwarranted, and often false. This ability is possessed by Hector Gallego. He could see that the Panamanian peasants were not inevitably shiftless, lazy good-for-nothings who deserved paternalistic charity rather than enabling leadership. Indeed, in fact, new possibilities for all the people of the area were created by his actions. Of course, his acts did not save him from death, but he met death well and avoided having his abductors injure those who shared his cabin when he was arrested. Of course, this story could be disabled (as could all factual narratives) if it failed to meet the standard of coherence. But presuming

[13]Isaac Asimov, *Foundation: Foundation and Empire,* and *Second Foundation* (New York: Avon, 1964-present), *passim.*

[14]The story of the United States' President's commissioning an invasion force to attempt to rescue American hostages in Iran in 1980 could be argued to be an example of a "less powerful" story.

it passes that test, then this story can be called true by the standard of fidelity, too, for Gallego was able to be faithful to those whose lives were distorted by his seeing through those distortions.

(3) A true story shows ways to avoid resorting to violence. James' theories illustrate this, but in practice, the work of Martin Luther King, Jr. shows it. King's story and his nonviolence have been described precisely by McClendon.[15] Now each of us are "unviolent" most of the time. Even those whose lives are shot through with violence aren't always —or even usually — violent. That is not what "nonviolent" means. Nor does nonviolence mean non-resistance. A non-resistant Christian, for instance, will certainly try to avoid violence; but if violence comes his or her way, s/he will not resist the violence done to him or her with more violence, but will have the courage to endure whatever is done without retaliation or violent resistance. Nonviolence has four ingredients. First, the nonviolent person is profoundly committed to not destroying, maiming, or permanently injuring another person. This commitment parallels the non-resistant person's. Second, the nonviolent person wants to *confront* the enemy; the nonviolent person does not think that the enemy should get away with doing what s/he wills without resistance. This confrontation can take the form of sit-ins, marches, sit-down strikes, etc., and is thus not passive, but also avoids the doing of violence. Third, the point of the nonviolent action is to get the enemy to deal with the demonstrators or resisters as persons. Nonviolence requires direct encounter, so that if the enemy chooses violence to beat the demonstrators, s/he must do it personally and see the results immediately. Fourth, the ultimate goal of nonviolent action cannot be victory over the enemy, but must be reconciliation with the enemy, justice for all and peace (not domination). Control and domination of an enemy are intrinsically violent; such an end is contradictory to and thus undermines the strategy and tactics of nonviolence.

[15]This discussion develops the work of James Wm. McClendon, Jr., *Biography as Theology* (Nashville: Abingdon, 1974), pp. 69-70.

The point of this third standard is different from that of the first. On the whole, violence provokes counterviolence. Those to whom we do violence become our enemies. If we do violence to enough people, then we will have more enemies than we know what to do with. If we are violent to most of the people we encounter, then most will become our enemies. The proponent of nonviolence, whether a Gandhi, a King, a Day, or a saint after William James (see pp. 160-161 above), has the possibility not only of avoiding making more enemies, but also of transforming those enemies into friends. Thus, a story that shows how the main character avoids violence and shows how that character could see ways to keep from resorting to violence, may be called true if proposed as a model, for it shows how one can be true to even those seen as enemies, those to whom almost no one primarily intends to be true.

(4) A story must have a sense of the tragic and show how meaning transcends brute force. If a story tells of a person or community which is so overwhelmed by a tragedy or series of tragedies that that person or community is "forced" into being unfaithful to part of that community or to the people they meet, then than story doesn't show how to cope with the tragic situations of life, and should be called false if proposed as a model. Although numerous stories within the Christian tradition could be cited, one told by Elie Wiesel and often-quoted bears retelling to exemplify a story which can be called true by this standard:

> When the great Rabbi Israel Baal Shem Tov saw misfortune threatening the Jews it was his custom to go into a certain part of the forest to meditate. There he would light a fire, say a special prayer, and the miracle would be accomplished and the misfortune averted.
>
> Later, when his disciple, the celebrated Magid of Mezeritch, had occasion, for the same reason, he would go to the same place in the forest and say: "Master of the Universe, listen! I do not know how to light the fire, but I am still able to say the prayer." And again the miracle would be accomplished.
>
> Still later, Rabbi Moshe-Leib of Sassov, in order to

save his people once more, would go into the forest and say: "I do not know how to light the fire, I do not know the prayer, but I know the place and this must be sufficient." It was sufficient and the miracle was accomplished.

Then it fell to Rabbi Israel of Rizhin to overcome misfortune. Sitting in his armchair, his head in his hands, he spoke to God: "I cannot even find the place in the forest. All I can do is to tell the story and this must be sufficient." And it was sufficient.

God made man because he loves stories.[16]

The point I want to make is that the story enabled people to live in spite of misfortune. Insofar as meaning overcomes raw force and a story shows how a people or a person could be faithful to their community and those they met, that far the story can be called true by this standard.[17]

Except for the stories where the assessment is obvious, it is difficult to grade the fidelity of a character in a direct way. Hence, I proposed that when a narrative is presented as a model, we can use the measures above to assess the fidelity of the main character in the stories *not* by seeing how true that character was to those s/he intended to be true to, but how true that character was to those s/he did not intend to be true to, but did encounter. If we do value fidelity, if we do admire people who are true to others, than this standard provides a way to assess model narratives for fidelity; it allows us to discriminate between those who are true only to those who are true to them and those who are true even to those they are not directly concerned about.

True Stories of Constancy

We admire people who are true to their ideals. "She is really true to her ideals" or "I have never met anyone so true

---

[16]John Shea, *Stories of God*, p. 7.

[17]For a powerful criticism of Wiesel's story, see Goldberg, *Theology and Narrative*, pp. 129-145.

to an ideal as he is," etc., are exclamations of admiration. They give reason to think that a final measure of whether a story can be called true is that of constancy: *a story can be called true to the extent that it provides a model for constancy in seeking to tell the truth.* To show what this standard means, I will unearth the idea in which it is rooted and discuss the application of the standard to stories.

The root of this criterion is in the concept of "satyagraha," clinging to truth or being constant in seeking truth. Mohandas K. Gandhi developed the concept as follows:

> Satyagraha is literally holding on to Truth and it means, therefore, Truth-force. Truth is soul or spirit. It is, therefore, known as soul-force. It excludes the use of violence because man is not capable of knowing the absolute truth, and, therefore, not competent to punish. The word was coined in South Africa to distinguish the non-violent resistance of the Indians of South Africa from the contemporary "passive resistance" of the suffragettes and others. It is not conceived as a weapon of the weak.[18]

Gandhi also described satyagraha as a method involving renunciation, hard work, suffering and perhaps death in the service of seeking the truth. He described it as selfless in the sense that self concern is not primary: "In such selfless search for Truth," Gandhi wrote, "nobody can lose his bearings for long. Directly he takes to the wrong path he stumbles and is thus redirected to the right path."[19] In short, if seeking to know and tell the truth is a goal for a person or community, then one can recognize that truth-telling marks those on the path to reaching to truth. A story which provides a model for constancy in reaching this goal, in being true to it, can thus be called true.

Four points will show the relevance of this criterion,

---

[18]Mohandas K. Gandhi, *Non-Violent Resistance* (New York: Schocken Books, 1967), p. 3.

[19]*Ibid.*, p. 39.

which applies primarily to those stories told as models for emulation. First, at a basic level, those stories which portray people who are not faithful to their goals must be called "untrue" by this standard, for these stories cannot be called models for being true to ideals (whatever those ideals may be). However, if a story narrates a single incident, this standard cannot apply, for the story is not about enough events to have a standard of *constancy* apply.

Second, a standard of constancy applies specifically to life-stories. If a biography or autobiography is proposed as a way to re-enact a master story from which the subject's ideals derive (such as Christians telling a life-story to show a way to live out a story of Jesus), and if the subjects of those stories are not constant in modeling their acts after those in the master story, then those subjects fail to show that they are true to the master story. The teller is in no position to claim that a specific master story is so true as to claim the subject's constant allegiance. The infidelity undercuts that claim. Thus, a lack of constancy shows that a subject's story cannot be said to be true to a master story. While such a lack of constancy does not show a master story false, nor does enduring fidelity show a master story true, it does show that in the context of proposing a life story as a model for reenacting a master story, the story-teller cannot be in a position to call the story s/he tells true to the master story (or to call the master story true if the subject's story is autobiographical).

Third, it must be acknowledged that this standard can be misused as a cover. "Fanatics" and "heretics" will often claim that they are being faithful to their own truth. But as noted above (p. 165), heretics are people whose stories are so narrow that they are faithless to many. Their stories will be undercut by the standard for fidelity. Fanatics are those who are blind to inconsistencies in their own stories. Their claims to tell a true story will fail by the standard of authenticity. While both may be constant and propose model stories that may be called true by the present standard, their stories will fail by other standards. More importantly, if we label "heretic" or "fanatic" some whose stories are found true according to all these standards of authenticity, fidelity, and constancy, we will have to revise those labels and learn to appreciate the stories of those we rejected.

Fourth, this standard presumes that no person has shown that s/he *has* the whole truth. This will seem to be begging the very question at issue for it might be objected that it implies that there is no story that we can finally call true, and no Ultimately True Story. That is not the case. The finally true story will be one which has met all the tests for truth relevant to all the contexts in which it is told. Such is an ultimately true story. But notice that the story has to be told and assessed in various times and places. If storytellers continue to propose a story as a model, that story provides the tellers with a model that leads them on in seeking to tell the truth. If they continue telling their story and assessing it, then they continue to meet this standard. If they halt, or seek to impose their stories on others by mental manipulation or physical coercion, then they cannot consistently claim to be *telling* a story whose truth can be shown or learned. Thus they fail to continue to meet this standard of constancy by failing to be constant in seeking to tell the truth. In sum, the absence of constancy in seeking to tell the truth renders a claim for the truth of a model story unwarranted.

If the claims made above are warranted, then a story proposed as a model must avoid both arrogance and violence on the part of its main character(s) if it is to be called true. Those who are portrayed as proclaiming their truth violently cannot trust the power of their claims — or the power behind them — to win the allegiance of others. If they truly believed in that power, why impose their claims with violence rather than persuasion? If they have the truth, they cannot show it to others whom they encounter. If they don't have the truth, they cannot learn it from others they destroy, and cannot seek to tell the truth with the others. This criterion, therefore, implies that a story which advocates violence is one that cannot be called true by a standard of constancy. A story to be called true by this standard is one which shows how strength and fidelity to ideals are possible without violence, and constancy realizable without arrogance. It will advocate conversion and education, not destruction and coercion as the means to come to sharing the truth. It will seek peace or reconciliation rather than conquest or separation. In sum, for a story to be called true by this standard, it will be one that will portray the main characters as constant in seeking to tell the truth by uncovering truth wherever possible and to eliminate the false elements in their own stories. If adopted as a model, such a story empowers the search for more truth, rather than disables it.

Model stories that would be called true by this standard abound, I believe in many religious traditions. Stories of the Buddha, of Jesus the Christ, of Mahat'ma Gandhi, of Charles Ives, of Mother Teresa, of Dorothy Day, to cite only a few, provide examples of people who sought to tell the truth that they had and to seek the truth that they wanted without violent imposition of their views on others or abandoning their views in the face of opposition. Many models are possible for showing ways to seek the truth. But all of those proposed need to be examined using standards such as these to see which stories can be called true.

Moments of Truth, Stories of Truth and the Life of Truth

After all this exploration, can I finally call any specific story simply TRUE? In fact, no; if the claims made in this chapter are warranted, there is no one simply TRUE story. That this is *good news* is what I will show below.

First, there are many kinds of stories told in many contexts, for many purposes, for many audiences. No one story can do the work of all of them. No story can be called true for any and all purposes in any and all contexts. Thus, no single story can be called absolutely true by all standards. Each story must be evaluated in its contexts.

Second, no single story will be likely to meet the unanimous consent of humanity — or possibly even of a culture —to call it true. As Gandhi remarked about absolute truth, so I would remark about an unsurpassable story: it is beyond human capacity to hear or tell. As William James has noted, "Experience has ways of boiling over and making us correct our present formulas."[20] That is to say that not only are our own stories not yet over and thus to be surpassed, but also the Whole Story, whatever its shape, cannot be told yet and any attempt to do so will be surpassed. Hence, no story can yet be found simply TRUE, the Final Story.

But someone might object that this approach then undermines the certainty of religious faith. Yet I would claim that this lack of certainty is indeed *good* news. It gives room for growth and hope. As the experiences of new social conditions allow Christians to experiment with new ways of incarnating the presence of Christ, it becomes clear that the vitality of the Christian tradition, at least, prohibits absolute attachment to any single story of Christ or of Christianity. The lack of a Final Story provides room for growth.

Additionally, we simply cannot say whether our stories fit the contours of the ultimate story or whether the stories which structure our own lives sufficiently reflect that ultimate. But that means that we can *hope* that they do, even if we cannot know it. If we can never *know* whether we have the final truth, then it is possible to go on to *seek* the truth. If we are constant in seeking the truth, that constancy may enable us to tell better stories and to read old stories in a better way. Then we should be able to tell stories more true by revealing what was hidden, showing more authentic, faithful, and constant ways to live, and improving our stories' coherence. This should free people from the bondage of self-deception, loneliness, incoherence, blindness and a certainty without hope. If the present approach undercuts established certainty in holding religious or other stories, it also makes room for hope as it eschews the notion that a story simply has the Truth and suggests that the approach to Truth is rather one of "seeking" than "having," "dwelling in," rather than "possessing."

[20]Compare William James, *Pragmatism* (Cleveland: World Publishing Co., 1964 [1907]), p. 145.

If we dwell in His story,
in truth are we His disciples,
and we will know the Truth,
and the Truth will free us.

For Further Reading

Very little theological work has been done on the assessment of the truth of stories. The most explicit is the work of Hauerwas and Burrell (see notes 7 and 12 above). The essays in part one of Hauerwas, *A Community of Character: Toward a Constructive Christian Social Ethic* (Notre Dame: University of Notre Dame Press, 1981) extend some of these ideas. Hauerwas is especially concerned to differentiate living in truth from living in certainty and security.

Michael Goldberg, *Theology and Narrative* (Nashville: Abingdon, 1982) is concerned with the truth of stories. However, his approach is not to consider stories as the vehicles which one evaluates for truth, but rather the propositional convictions which are embodied in them. Although I have learned much from his work, his willingness to abstract convictions from stories seems to me to beg the question of stories' truth. After all, a false story can include true beliefs and vice versa. Vincent Brümmer, *Theology and Philosophical Analysis* (Philadelphia: Westminster, 1982) also has an appraisal account of truth, but Brümmer appraises specific claims rather than stories. His work is especially valuable for its clear introduction to sympathetic philosophical analysis of theology.

The work of William A. Christian, Sr., *Meaning and Truth in Religion* (Princeton: Princeton University Press, 1964) and *Oppositions of Religious Doctrines* (New York: Herder and Herder, 1972) provides a meticulous analysis of how various religious proposals might be adjudicated. Christian is primarily interested in showing that religious

214 Moments of Truth

believers *do* disagree fundamentally using what we have
here called coherence criteria for truth. The complex work
of David Tracy, *The Analogical Imagination: Christian
Theology and the Culture of Pluralism* (New York: Crossroad Press, 1981) deals with both narratives and truth. Yet
Tracy is not concerned with the truth of narratives, but with
recognizing which narratives are "classics" of a religious (or
a-religious) tradition and with determining the relatively
adequate criteria for judging the truth of theological reflections growing out of narratives. T. W. Tilley, *Talking of
God: An Introduction to Philosophical Analysis of Religious Language* (New York: Paulist Press, 1978), chapter
five, critically reports the theories of truth in religion among
a number of philosophers working in the Anglo-American
philosophical tradition: John Hick, Basil Mitchell, Dewi Z.
Phillips, Ian T. Ramsey, and J. W. McClendon and J. M.
Smith.

The major classic theories of truth are summarized in four
articles in *The Encyclopedia of Philosophy*, ed. Paul
Edwards (New York: Macmillan and Free Press, 1967)
Eight Volumes: "Coherence" "Correspondence" "Perfor-
mative" and "Pragmatic" theories of truth. Each article has
extensive bibliographies including works for and against
each theory.

EPILOGUE

THE LAST ACT

The last act is tragic,
however happy the rest of the play is;
at the last a little earth is thrown upon our head,
and that is the end
for ever.
—Blaise Pascal, Pensées, 210

I have not sought to submerge my own position in a sea of objectivity in *Story Theology*. I have told stories I thought worth telling. I have borrowed shamelessly from others whose work I appreciate. I have criticized many not because they are worthless, but because they are worth learning from. I have not tried to impose my own position on the reader, not because I do not find the stories I tell to be true, but because I recognize that others may tell stories different from mine, yet as true as mine. As I suggested in the last chapter, there is no single key to discovering which stories are true, which actions right. Stories and acts are far too varied to be so easily grouped into true and false, wrong and right, or to be facilely reduced to some hidden essence which implies that the specific style, form and content of each is not really important. Finally, I delight in variety.

Yet not all stories can be called true nor all acts right. That would be a spineless and soft-headed relativism. I am not a relativist, but a pluralist. There is, I believe, finally, an indicator of false stories, myths and actions that can and should be avoided. Those stories that claim that the actor in the story can rewrite the last act are finally deceptive. The last act is either the ultimate tragedy for the actor or must be overcome by something or someone whose power is beyond the story.

There are numerous ways to deny the reality and the power of death, of the ravages of time, of the vicissitudes of fate. One way is to imagine that crossing the river of death is merely changing one horse for another in the waves, and then riding on. Another is the absorption in the therapeutic, in the trivial, or in shopping around for oneself in the supermarkets of self-awareness, idling time away so as to forget reality. Another way of denial was perversely captured in a graffito, "Reality is a crutch for those who can't handle drugs." Any story which encourages one to deny these realities is one that cannot be sustained.

Within the Christian traditions, stories of eternal life have often been told this way. But these are not stories, at their best, which are stories of what *will* happen. These are eschatological stories, stories which express the *hope* that *God* will act. The story of the Resurrection of Jesus expresses that hope. Either the death of that Just Man on a cross was a tragedy or it was transformed into a comedy by a miracle. Either the actor died, or died and was saved by Another. He did not come down. He did not save himself.

One of the great disasters of the Christian tradition has been its frequent telling of stories that deny the tragedy of the "last act." So often the stories of Christian life are told in a way that denies the tragedy of the last act. Death is pictured merely as the door through which we will walk from the cold of this world into the warmth of our eternal home. The trauma of death is denied. The inability of each of us to do anything to avoid death is obliterated. The ability to achieve eternity is attributed to us or to our deserving our just reward. All of these are not only false to the heart of the

Christian tradition by misportraying the tale of the Resurrection of Jesus, but also rooted most deeply in the worst lie
of all, self-deception.

The proper way to understand death in a Christian perspective, I believe, can be seen through Flannery O'Connor's story, "The Lame Shall Enter First." In chapter one,
the story was retold as what happens to a "selfless humanist." Here I want to focus on the suicide of Norton
Sheppard. Either it is a catastrophe, a failure so complete as
to be irredeemable by anything on this earth. Or his flight
into space reached its goal, he is reunited with his mother,
and the incredible joy of reunion has become miraculously
true. If one is a humanist, one will read the story as a
tragedy. If one is a Christian, one will read the story as a
tragedy — and yet have hope that God can overcome such a
disaster in some way beyond our imagination. Even if
human life is no longer solitary, poor, nasty, brutish, and
short, it is still the "only disease with a 100% mortality rate."

A true story is hard to find not because true stories are so
rare, but because they are so true. They are hard to find
because what we often seek is a story that is made for us
ahead of time and into which we can slip like an off-the-rack
suit, or a story that ends "and they lived happily ever after."
When one seeks a story which goes on forever, it is hard to
find a story that tells of the briefness of our moments and the
inevitability of death. When one seeks a story that requires
no thought but mere acceptance of the story, one gives up
seeking the truth, and that makes it difficult if not impossible to find a true story.

Thus, if the reader is looking for the final answer or the
ultimate story, s/he won't find it here. This is the wrong
place to seek. Perhaps the greatest challenge of narrative
theology is that it requires that the hearer *do* some theology.
It doesn't tell the Final Story or provide The Answers;
rather it invites the reader to reflect on the metaphors that
are key to her or his life and the stories which say what they
mean and to evaluate those stories. Thus, a Christian narrative theology attempts not only to retrieve the stories of
Jesus and of his followers, but also to replicate a central

aspect of his method: a challenge to notice what has been hidden, to see things in the light of a kingdom not of this world, and to reshape one's story in hope. The right place to seek is in the reader's own life, the traditions in which that life participates, and the stories which give it meaning. If our venture has been successful here, then you should go out on your own, to evaluate your own story and tell it truthfully. There you may come to find an answer and friends to share that answer with you.

A true story is hard to find *because* it expresses what is true, and truth is sometimes unwelcome or uncomfortable. We *know* we can't perform a miracle so that our story can begin after the curtain has fallen on our last acts. But if the central stories of Christianity are true, we can *hope* for the transformation of tragedy into comedy beyond our wildest dreams.

WORKS CONSULTED

Albright, W. F., and C. S. Mann. *Matthew.* The Anchor Bible 26. Garden City, NY: Doubleday, 1971.

Alonzo-Schökel, Luis. *The Inspired Word: Scripture in the Light of Language and Literature.* New York: Herder and Herder, 1965.

Asimov, Isaac. *Foundation, Foundation and Empire, Second Foundation,* and *Foundation's Edge.* New York: (various publishers), 1952-1982.

Austin, John L. *Philosophical Papers.* Edited by J. O. Urmson and G. J. Warnock. London: Oxford University Press, 1970.

Baillie, Donald M. *God Was in Christ: An Essay on Incarnation and Atonement.* New York: Charles Scribner's Sons, n.d.

Bettenson, Henry. *Documents of the Christian Church.* London and New York: Oxford University Press, 1961.

Boff, Leonardo, O.F.M. "The Need for Political Saints: From a Spirituality of Liberation to the Practice of Liberation," *Cross Currents* XXX/4, Winter 1980-1981.

Bornkamm, Günther. *Jesus of Nazareth.* Translated by I. and F. McLuskey with J. M. Robinson. New York: Harper and Row, 1960.

219

Borsch, Frederick Houk. *Power in Weakness: New Hearing for Gospel Stories of Healing and Discipleship.* Philadelphia: Fortress Press, 1983.

Braithwaite, Richard Bevan. "An Empiricist's View of the Nature of Religious Belief," in *Christian Ethics and Contemporary Philosophy.* Edited by I. T. Ramsey. London: SCM Press, 1966.

Brandon, S. G. F. *Jesus and the Zealots.* New York: Charles Scribner's Sons, 1967.

Brown, Raymond E. *The Birth of the Messiah: A Commentary on the Infancy Narratives of Matthew and Luke.* Garden City, NY: Doubleday, 1977.

_____. *The Critical Meaning of the Bible.* New York: Paulist Press, 1981.

_____. *The Gospel According to John.* The Anchor Bible 29 and 29A. Garden City, NY: Doubleday, 1966 and 1970.

_____. *Jesus: God and Man.* Milwaukee: Bruce, 1967; New York: Macmillan, 1978.

Brown, Raymond, E., K. P. Donfried, and J. Reumann. *Peter in the New Testament: A Collaborative Assessment by Protestant and Roman Catholic Scholars.* Minneapolis: Augsburg, and New York: Paulist, 1963.

Brümmer, Vincent. *Theology and Philosophical Analysis.* Philadelphia: Westminster, 1982.

Buber, Martin. *Tales of the Hasidim.* New York: Schocken Books, 1961.

Bultmann, Rudolf. "The Historical Jesus and the Theology of Paul," in *Faith and Understanding.* Edited by R. W. Funk. Translated by L. P. Smith. New York: Harper and Row, 1969.

_____. *History and Eschatology: The Presence of Eternity.* New York: Harper Torchbooks, 1962.

_____. *The History of the Synoptic Tradition*. Translated by J. Marsh. New York: Harper and Row, 1976.

_____. *Jesus and the Word*. Translated by L. P. Smith and E. H. Lantero. New York: Charles Scribner's Sons, 1958.

_____. *Jesus Christ and Mythology*. New York: Charles Scribner's Sons, 1958.

_____. "The Primitive Christian Kerygma and the Historical Jesus," in *The Historical Jesus and the Kerygmatic Christ*. Edited and translated by Carl E. Braaten and Roy A. Harris. Nashville: Abingdon Press, 1964.

Burrell, David. *Exercises in Religious Understanding*. Notre Dame: University of Notre Dame Press, 1974.

_____. "Stories of God: Why We Use Them and How We Judge Them" in *Is God GOD?* Edited by J. W. McClendon and Axel Steuer. Nashville: Abingdon, 1981.

Cameron, J. M. "The Idea of Christendom," in *The Autonomy of Religious Belief*. Edited by Frederick Crossan. Notre Dame: University of Notre Dame Press, 1981.

Campbell, Joseph. *The Masks of God: Creative Mythology*. New York: Penguin Books, 1976.

Christian, William A., Sr. *Meaning and Truth in Religion*. Princeton: Princeton University Press, 1964.

_____. *Oppositions of Religious Doctrines*. New York: Herder and Herder, 1972.

Clebsch, William. *Christianity in European History*. New York: Oxford University Press, 1979.

Cobb, John B., Jr. *Christ in a Pluralistic Age*. Philadelphia: Westminster Press, 1975.

_____. *God and the World*. Philadelphia: Westminster Press, 1969.

Cohn, Norman. *The Pursuit of the Millennium*. New York: Harper and Row, 1961.

Conzelman, Hans. *Jesus.* Translated by J. R. Lord. Philadelphia: Fortress Press, 1973.

Crites, Stephen. "The Narrative Quality of Experience," *Journal of the American Academy of Religion,* LIX/3, September, 1971.

——————. "Angels We Have Heard," in *Religion as Story.* Edited by J. B. Wiggins. New York: Harper and Row, 1975.

Crossan, John Dominic. *The Dark Interval: Towards a Theology of Story.* Niles, IL: Argus Communications, 1975.

——————. *Finding is the First Act: Trove Folktales and Jesus' Treasure Parable.* Philadelphia: Fortress Press, and Missoula, MT: Scholars Press, 1979.

——————. *In Parables: The Challenge of the Historical Jesus.* New York: Harper and Row, 1973.

Cullmann, Oscar. *The Christology of the New Testament.* Translated by S. C. Guthrie and C. A. M. Hall. Philadelphia: Westminster, 1963.

Cunningham, Lawrence, S. *The Catholic Heritage.* New York: Seabury Press, 1983.

Dodd, C. H. *The Founder of Christianity.* New York: Macmillan, 1963.

——————. *The Parables of the Kingdom.* London: Nisbet, 1935.

Donahue, John R. "Biblical Perspectives on Justice," in *The Faith That Does Justice.* Edited by J. Haughey. New York: Paulist Press, 1977.

Duling, Dennis C. *Jesus Christ Through History.* New York: Harcourt Brace Jovanovich, 1979.

Dunn, James D. G. *Christology in the Making: A New Testament Inquiry into the Origins of the Doctrines of the Incarnation.* Philadelphia: Westminster, 1980.

Dunne, John. *The Church of the Poor Devil: Reflections on a Riverboat Voyage and a Spiritual Journey.* Notre Dame: University of Notre Dame Press, 1983.

_____. *Reasons of the Heart: A Journey into Solitude and Back Again into the Human Circle.* New York: Macmillan, 1978.

_____. *A Search for God in Time and Memory.* New York: Macmillan, 1967.

_____. *The Way of All the Earth.* New York: Macmillan, 1972.

Edwards, Paul, editor. *The Encyclopedia of Philosophy.* New York: Macmillan and Free Press, 1967.

Fingarette, Herbert. *Self-Deception.* London: Routledge and Kegan Paul, 1969.

Fiorenza, Elisabeth Schüssler. *In Memory of Her: A Feminist Theological Reconstruction of Christian Origins.* New York: Crossroad, 1983.

Fiorenza, Francis Schüssler. "Reflective Christology," *Cross Currents* XXXII/3, Fall, 1982.

Fowler, James W. *Stages of Faith.* San Francisco: Harper and Row, 1981.

_____. Robin Lovin, *et al. Trajectories in Faith: The Psychology of Human Development and the Quest for Meaning.* Nashville: Abingdon Press, 1980.

Frankel, Charles. "Progress, The Idea of," in *The Encyclopedia of Philosophy.* Edited by Paul Edwards. New York: Macmillan and Free Press, 1967.

Frei, Hans W. *The Eclipse of the Biblical Narrative: A Study in Eighteenth and Nineteenth Century Hermeneutics.* New Haven: Yale University Press, 1974.

_____. *The Identity of Jesus Christ: The Hermeneutical Bases of Dogmatic Theology.* Philadelphia: Fortress Press, 1975.

Fuller, Reginald H. *The Formation of the Resurrection Narratives.* Second Edition. Philadelphia: Fortress Press, 1980.

_____. *The Foundations of New Testament Christology.* London: Collins, 1976.

_____, editor. *Kerygma and Myth.* New York: Harper and Row, 1961.

_____ and Pheme Perkins. *Who Is This Christ? Gospel Christology and Contemporary Faith.* Philadelphia: Fortress Press, 1983.

Funk, Robert W. "The Good Samaritan as Metaphor," *Semeia* II, 1974.

Gandhi, Mohandas K. *Non-Violent Resistance.* New York: Schocken Books, 1967.

Goldberg, Michael. "Ringing True and Being True." Unpublished Ph.D. dissertation, Graduate Theological Union, Berkeley, 1981.

_____. *Theology and Narrative.* Nashville: Abingdon, 1982.

Grant, Robert C. *The Formation of the New Testament.* London: Hutchinson, 1965.

Green, Michael, editor. *Incarnation and Myth: The Debate Continued.* Grand Rapids: Eerdmans, 1979.

_____, editor. *The Truth of God Incarnate.* Sevenoaks, Kent: Hodder and Stoughton, and Grand Rapids: Eerdmans, 1977.

Harvey, A. E. *Jesus and the Constraints of History.* Philadelphia: Westminster Press, 1982.

Harvey, Van A. *A Handbook of Theological Terms.* New York: Macmillan, 1964.

_____. *The Historian and the Believer.* New York: Macmillan, 1966.

Hauerwas, Stanley. *A Community of Character: Toward a Constructive Christian Social Ethic.* Notre Dame: University of Notre Dame Press, 1981.

_____. *The Peaceable Kingdom.* Notre Dame: University of Notre Dame Press, 1983.

_____. "Self-Deception and Autobiography: Reflections on Speer's *Inside the Third Reich,*" in *Truthfulness and Tragedy.* Notre Dame: University of Notre Dame Press, 1977.

_____ and David Burrell. "From System to Story: An Alternative Pattern for Rationality in Ethics," in *Truthfulness and Tragedy.* Notre Dame: University of Notre Dame Press, 1977.

Hellwig, Monika K. *What Are They Saying About Death and Christian Hope?* New York: Paulist Press, 1978.

_____. *Jesus: The Compassion of God.* Wilmington, DE: Michael Glazier, Inc., 1983.

Hick, John. *Death and Eternal Life.* San Francisco: Harper and Row, 1980.

_____, editor. *The Myth of God Incarnate.* London: SCM, and Philadelphia: Westminster, 1977.

Hollenbach, Paul W. "Jesus, Demoniacs, and Public Authorities: A Socio-Historical Study," *Journal of the American Academy of Religion* XLIX/4, December, 1981.

Holmer, Paul. *The Grammar of Faith.* San Francisco: Harper and Row, 1978.

Hügel, Baron Friedrich von. *The Mystical Element of Religion as Studied in Saint Catherine of Genoa and Her Friends.* London: J. M. Dent and Sons and James Clarke and Co., 1961.

"An Interview with Father Gallego on His Parish Organization" (A tape recording taken down by the editors of

Dialogo Social five days before Father Gallego was abducted) in *Latin American Documentation* XXV. Washington, DC: United States Catholic Conference, February, 1972.

James, William. *Pragmatism.* Cleveland: World, 1964.

——————. *The Varieties of Religious Experience: A Study in Human Nature.* New York: Collier Books, 1961.

Jedin, Hubert, and John P. Dolan, editors. *History of the Church.* Ten Volumes. New York: Crossroad Press, 1980-1981.

Jeremias, Joachim. *The Parables of Jesus* Translated by S. H. Hooke. New York: Charles Scribner's Sons, 1972.

Johnson, Paul. *A History of Christianity.* New York: Atheneum, 1979.

Kazantzakis, Nikos. *Report to Greco.* New York: Bantam, 1966.

——————. *Saint Francis.* New York: Simon and Schuster, 1962.

Kee, Howard C. "The Gospel According to Matthew," in *The Interpreter's One Volume Commentary on the Bible.* Nashville: Abingdon, 1971.

——————. *Jesus in History.* New York: Harcourt Brace Jovanovich, 1977.

Kegley, Charles W., editor. *The Theology of Rudolf Bultmann.* New York: Harper and Row, 1966.

Kennedy, Eugene. "Quiet Mover of the Catholic Church," *The New York Times Magazine,* September 23, 1979.

Kermode, J. Frank. *The Sense of an Ending: Studies in the Theory of Fiction.* New York: Oxford University Press, 1967.

King, Coretta Scott. *My Life With Martin Luther King, Jr.* New York: Holt, Rinehart and Winston, 1969.

Kissinger, Warren S. *The Parables of Jesus: A History of Interpretation and Bibliography.* New York: Scarecrow Press, 1979.

Kittel, G., and G. Friedrich, editors. *Theological Dictionary of the New Testament.* Grand Rapids: Eerdmans, 1971.

Kliever, Lonnie D. *The Shattered Spectrum.* Atlanta: John Knox Press, 1981.

Küng, Hans. *Eternal Life? Life After Death as a Medical, Philosophical and Theological Problem.* Translated by Edward Quinn. Garden City, NY: Doubleday, 1984.

Lane, Dermot. *The Reality of Jesus: An Essay in Christology.* New York: Paulist Press, 1975.

Lasch, Christopher. *The Culture of Narcissism: American Life in an Age of Diminishing Expectations.* New York: Warner Books, 1979.

Lernoux, Penny. *Cry of the People.* Garden City, NY: Doubleday, 1980.

Linnemann, Eta. *The Parables of Jesus: Introduction and Exposition.* Translated by John Sturdy. London: S.P.C.K., 1966.

Livingston, James C. *Modern Christian Thought: From The Enlightenment to Vatican II.* New York: Macmillan, 1971.

MacIntyre, Alasdair. *After Virtue: A Study in Moral Theory.* Notre Dame: University of Notre Dame Press, 1981.

Mackey, James P. *Jesus: The Man and the Myth.* New York: Paulist Press, 1979.

MacQuarrie, John. *The Faith of the People of God: A Lay Theology.* New York: Charles Scribner's Sons, 1972.

_____. *The Scope of Demythologizing.* New York: Harper and Row, 1960.

Manson, T. W. *The Sayings of Jesus*. Cambridge: Cambridge University Press, 1931.

Marty, Martin. *A Short History of Christianity*. Cleveland: Collins and World, 1959.

Marxsen, Willi. *The New Testament as the Church's Book*. Philadelphia: Fortress, 1972.

McBrien, Richard P. *Catholicism*. Minneapolis: Winston Press, 1980.

McClendon, James W., Jr. *Biography as Theology: How Life Stories Can Remake Today's Theology*. Nashville: Abingdon, 1974.

_____ and James M. Smith. *Understanding Religious Convictions*. Notre Dame: University of Notre Dame Press, 1975.

McDermott, Brian. "Roman Catholic Christology: Two Recurring Themes," *Theological Studies* XLI/2, June, 1980.

McGill, Arthur C. *Suffering: A Test of Theological Method*. Philadelphia: Westminster, 1982.

McKenzie, John L. "The Gospel According to Matthew," in *The Jerome Biblical Commentary*. Englewood Cliffs, NJ: Prentice Hall, 1968.

_____. *The New Testament Without Illusion*. Chicago: Thomas More Press, 1980.

_____. *The Old Testament Without Illusion*. Chicago: Thomas More Press, 1979.

Metz, J. B. *Faith in History and Society: Toward a Practical Fundamental Theology*. Translated by David Smith. New York: Seabury Press, 1980.

_____. *Followers of Christ: The Religious Life and the Church*. Translated by Thomas Linton. New York: Paulist Press, 1978.

Michaels, J. Ramsey. *Servant and Son: Jesus in Parable and Gospel.* Atlanta: John Knox Press, 1981.

Miller, William, editor. *The New Christianity.* New York: Dell Books, 1967.

Miranda, José Porfirio. *Communism in the Bible.* Translated by R. R. Barr. Maryknoll: Orbis Books, 1982.

Mitchell, Basil, editor. *The Philosophy of Religion.* London: Oxford University Press, 1971.

Moule, C. F. D. *The Birth of the New Testament.* New York: Harper and Row, 1962.

_____. *The Origin of Christology.* Cambridge: Cambridge University Press, 1977.

Navone, John, S.J. *The Jesus Story: Our Life as Story in Jesus.* Collegeville, MN: The Liturgical Press, 1979.

_____ and Thomas Cooper. *Tellers of the Word.* New York: Le Jacq Publishing, 1981.

Nicholls, William. *Systematic and Philosophical Theology.* Baltimore: Penguin Books, 1971.

Niebuhr, H. Richard. *The Meaning of Revelation.* New York: Macmillan, 1960.

Nisbet, Robert. *History of the Idea of Progress.* New York: Basic Books, 1979.

O'Connor, Flannery. *The Complete Stories.* New York: Farrar, Straus, and Giroux, 1981.

_____. *The Habit of Being: Letters.* New York: Vintage Books, 1980.

Ogden, Schubert M. *Christ Without Myth.* New York: Harper and Row, 1961.

_____. *The Point of Christology.* San Francisco: Harper and Row, 1982.

O'Meara, T. and D. Weisser, editors. *Rudolf Bultmann in Catholic Thought*. New York: Herder and Herder, 1968.

Outka, Gene. "Character, Vision and Narrative," *Religious Studies Review* 6/2, April, 1980.

Pennenberg, Wolfhart. *Jesus — God and Man*. Translated by L. L. Wilkins, and D. A. Priebe. Philadelphia: Westminster, 1968.

Perrin, Norman. *Jesus and the Language of the Kingdom*. Philadelphia: Fortress Press, 1976.

_____. *The Kingdom of God in the Teaching of Jesus*. Philadelphia: Westminster Press, 1963.

_____. *The New Testament: An Introduction*. New York: Harcourt Brace Jovanovich, 1974.

_____. *The Promise of Bultmann*. Philadelphia: Fortress, 1978.

_____. *Rediscovering the Teaching of Jesus*. New York: Harper and Row, 1967.

_____ and Dennis Duling. *The New Testament: An Introduction*, Second Edition. New York: Harcourt Brace Jovanovich, 1982.

Rahner, Karl. *Foundations of Christian Faith: An Introduction to the Idea of Christianity*. Translated by William V. Dych. New York: Seabury Press, 1978.

_____. "The Hermeneutics of Eschatological Assertions," in *Theological Investigations* IV . Baltimore: Helicon Press, 1966.

_____ and Herbert Vorgrimler, editors. *Theological Dictionary*. New York: Herder and Herder, 1965.

Ramsey, Ian T. *Christian Discourse: Some Logical Explorations*. London: Oxford University Press, 1965.

_____. *On Being Sure in Religion*. London: Athlone Press, 1963.

Rawls, John. *A Theory of Justice.* Cambridge, MA: Harvard University Press, 1971.

"Report by Panama's National Agency for Community Development," *Latin American Documentation XXV.* Washington, DC: United States Catholic Conference, February, 1972.

Rivkin, Ellis. *What Crucified Jesus? The Political Execution of a Charismatic.* Nashville: Abingdon, 1984.

Robbins, J. Wesley. "Narrative, Morality and Religion," *Journal of Religious Ethics* 8, Fall, 1980.

Robinson, James M. *A New Quest of the Historical Jesus.* Naperville, IL: Allenson, and London: SCM Press, 1959.

Rorty, Richard. *Philosophy and the Mirror of Nature.* Princeton: Princeton University Press, 1979.

Ruether, Rosemary. *The Radical Kingdom: The Western Experience of Messianic Hope.* New York: Harper and Row, 1970.

Russell, Bertrand. "A Free Man's Worship," in *Mysticism and Logic.* Garden City, NY: Doubleday, n.d.

Sacks, Sheldon. *Fiction and the Shape of Belief: A Study of Henry Fielding with Glances at Swift, Johnson, and Richardson.* Chicago: University of Chicago Press, 1964.

Schillebeeckx, Edward. *Christ: The Experience of Jesus as Lord.* Translated by J. Bowden. New York: Crossroad Press, 1981.

_____. *Interim Report on the Books Jesus and Christ.* Translated by J. Bowden. New York: Crossroad Press, 1981.

_____. *Jesus: An Experiment in Christology.* Translated by H. Hoskins. New York: Seabury Press, 1979.

Shea, John. *Stories of Faith.* Chicago: Thomas More Press, 1980.

_____. *Stories of God: An Unauthorized Biography.* Chicago: Thomas More Press, 1978.

Stroup, George W. *The Promise of Narrative Theology: Recovering the Gospel in the Church.* Atlanta: John Knox, 1981.

Tambasco, Anthony. *In the Days of Jesus.* New York: Paulist Press, 1983.

Thompson, William H. "The Hope for Humanity: Rahner's Eschatology," in *A World of Grace: An Introduction to the Themes and Foundations of Karl Rahner's Theology.* Edited by Leo O'Donovan. New York: Seabury Press, 1980.

Thurston, H. and Attwater, D., editors. *Butler's Lives of the Saints.* New York: P. J. Kenedy, 1956.

Tilley, T. W. *Talking of God: An Introduction to Philosophical Analysis of Religious Language.* New York: Paulist, 1978.

Tracy, David. *The Analogical Imagination: Christian Theology and the Culture of Pluralism.* New York: Crossroad Press, 1981.

Tyrrell, George. *Christianity at the Crossroads.* London: Allen and Unwin, 1963.

van Beeck, Franz Joseph. *Christ Proclaimed: Christology as Rhetoric.* New York: Paulist, 1979.

Via, Dan Otto. *Kerygma and Comedy in the New Testament.* Philadelphia: Fortress, 1975.

_____. *The Parables: Their Literary and Existential Dimension.* Philadelphia: Fortress Press, 1967.

Whitehead, Alfred North. *Process and Reality.* New York: Macmillan, 1929.

Wiesel, Elie. *The Gates of the Forest.* New York: Holt, Rinehart, and Winston, 1966.

_____. *Messengers of God.* New York: Random House, 1976.

_____. *Souls on Fire.* New York: Random House, 1972.

Wiggins, James B. "Within and Without Stories," in *Religion as Story.* Edited by J. B. Wiggins. New York: Harper and Row, 1975.

Wilde, Oscar. "The Master," in *Religion From Tolstoy to Camus.* Edited by W. Kaufmann. New York: Harper and Row, 1964.

Wilder, Amos Niven. *Early Christian Rhetoric: The Language of the Gospel.* Cambridge, MA: Harvard University Press, 1971.

_____. *Theopoetic: Theology and Religious Imagination.* Philadelphia: Fortress Press, 1976.

Wiles, Maurice. *The Christian Fathers.* London: SCM Press, 1977.

_____. *The Making of Christian Doctrine: A Study in the Principles of Early Doctrinal Development.* Cambridge: Cambridge University Press, 1975.

Wright, Elliot. *Holy Company: Christian Heroes and Heroines.* New York: Macmillan, 1980.

Yoder, John Howard. *The Politics of Jesus.* Grand Rapids: Eerdmans, 1972.

BIBLICAL INDEX

GENERAL INDEX

Abelard, Peter, 151
Abortion, 21
Abraham, 16, 20, 125
Act of God, 15, 77, 107, 192-193
Action (genre), 39, 50-52, 101-115
Activists, 158
Adam, see New Adam
Adventist, 57
Alonzo-Schökel, Luis, 38
Anselm of Canterbury, 157, 179
Apocalyptic, 57, 119, 121; also see
  Eschatology
Apologists, 158
Aquinas, Thomas, 19, 157, 179
Arius, 13, 165
Armageddon, 57
Arnold, Matthew, 23, 29
Art and science, 34
Ascension, 135
Asceticism, 165
Asimov, Isaac, 72, 204
Atman, 68
Atonement, 12, 31, 67-68, 110-111, 124,
  126, 128-131, 161-178; also see
  reconciliation, redemption
Augustine of Hippo, 154, 157, 179
Austin, John L., 184
Autonomy, 30, 31, 158

Baal Shem Tov, Israel, 206
Babylon, 45
Baillie, D. M., 144
Banquet, 88, 104, 110

Baptism, 124, 129, 182
Barr, Robert R., 113
Barth, Karl, 19
Bartsch, Hans W., 98
Bathsheba, 188
Beatitudes, 86-87
Bettenson, Henry, 127
Bias, remedy for, 203
Biblical criticism, 26-30, 73-78, 97, 101
Biography of Jesus, 104
Blasphemy, 105
Boethius, 154-155, 157
Boff, Leonardo, 165-166
Bonhoeffer, Dietrich, 158, 180
Bornkamm, Günther, 115
Borsch, Frederick Houk, 116
Bouyer, Louis, 145
Bowser, 20-21
Braaten, C. E., 99
Braithwaite, R. B., 22-23, 39
Brandon, S. G. F., 113, 115
Bride and bridegroom, 156
Brown, R. E., 115, 125, 126, 133, 139
Brümmer, Vincent, 213
Buber, Martin, 53, 54
Buddha, 68, 211
Bultmann, Rudolf, 19, 40, 70, 77, 78, 98,
  99, 105, 109, 137, 146
Burrell, David, 35-37, 179, 198-199, 203

Caesarea Philipi, 136-140
Calvin, John, 157
Cameron, J. M., 202

237